SECOND CUTTING

Also by Richard M. Ketchum

AUTHOR

The World of George Washington

Will Rogers: His Life and Times

The Winter Soldiers

The Secret Life of the Forest

Faces from the Past

The American Heritage Book of Great Historic Places

What Is Communism?

Male Husbandry

The Battle of Bunker Hill

Decisive Day

EDITOR

American Testament: Fifty Great Documents of American History

The Original Water Color Paintings by John James Audubon for the Birds of America

Four Days

The Horizon Book of the Renaissance

The American Heritage Picture History of the Civil War

The American Heritage Book of the Pioneer Spirit

The American Heritage Book of the Revolution

What Is Democracy?

SECOND CUTTING

Letters from the Country

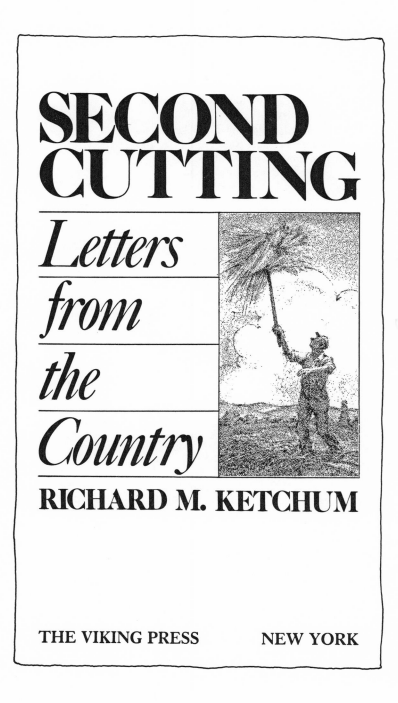

RICHARD M. KETCHUM

THE VIKING PRESS   NEW YORK

Portions of this book originally appeared in *Country Journal*
in slightly different form.

LIBRARY OF CONGRESS CATALOGING IN PUBLICATION DATA
Ketchum, Richard M., 1922–
Second cutting.
1. Country life—New England.   2. Ketchum,
Richard M., 1922– .   I. Title.
S521.5.N35K47   974'.009'734   81-50516
ISBN 0-670-42588-5   AACR5

Printed in the United States of America

Set in CRT Caslon
Illustrations by Elayne Sears

For my partners in the adventure,
B B K and W S B

Contents

Introduction

For the past seven years I have been a sometime farmer, while my main business has been editing a monthly magazine called *Blair & Ketchum's Country Journal.* For the maiden issue of that publication I wrote a short editorial comment, which appeared under the heading "Letter from the Country," and—habit being a pesky and persistent bedfellow—I continued the practice in each subsequent issue.

What follows is a collection of most of those essays, which I have titled *Second Cutting.* The term refers to the second round of making hay—since this is the second time around for these pieces, it seems apt. More than that, I like the sound of the phrase and I enjoy immensely the activity it describes. In our part of New England you can't count on more than two cuttings of hay. If you're lucky—which means that the weather has been unusually obliging—you get in the first cut in early June; but the longer the grass grows, the coarser and tougher the stems and the less the livestock like it.

Second cutting is another matter. You're in the meadow during those long, hot July days when the air is still, when the unforgettable scents of new-mown timothy and alfalfa hang in the fields, when the whole lush, green world is taking advantage of every moment of sunlight to prepare for the long, cold time ahead. You can't expect the same quantity the second time around, but you have a shot at putting up hay that is more tender and nutritious, with a high protein content and quality that won't deteriorate during the winter.

Like the farmer, the essayist grows fidgety thinking about the protein level in his product, but except for minor revisions, almost all these pieces appear in the form in which they were first published. Some of the individuals and circumstances described are no longer in the news, some of the statistics have been superseded, but neither human nature nor the ways of the world change much, and the principles that concerned me in the first place concern me still.

Although they did not see the light of day until 1974 and later, the essays and the magazine in which they appeared began their long gestation period a decade earlier, when my wife, Bobs, and I acquired a farm that lies at the edge of a small town in southwestern Vermont. Since 1970 this has been our year-round home, which explains why so much of the content of this book has to do with Saddleback Farm and the sometimes erratic life of which it is the center. Like so many newcomers to country places, we came by our experience and knowledge the hard way, learning as we went, barking our shins and knuckles until we absorbed the lessons. Not that what I have written about the farm pretends to be a guide to how things should be done; what you see is merely an account of what occurred or what was observed, and as often as not points the way to how *not* to do something or other. A good many of the events described are small, mundane matters, but often small, mundane matters are at the core of country living.

If the farm has been central to our lives, the next concentric ring is the community of which it, and we, are a part. Physically, our town has changed very little in the three and a half decades we have known it. When we first came here to live for five years at the end of World War II, there were only 171 more residents in the village than there had been in 1790, the year of the first census, and in the past forty years the population has increased by only 690 souls. In other words, it is a small country town, where the cycle of the seasons sets the rhythm of our lives, where it remains possible to see a pig on the loose by day or to hear a bear hoot at night, where one shares a meal with friends in the same room where the food is cooked, and where—as the two hundredth anniversary of that 1790 census approaches—we and our neighbors move ever closer to the fire. The woodsman's axe is heard in the clearing once more, but to my surprise, I am the woodsman.

Another group of essays deals with the circle of life outside the farm and the village—the rest of the world, which occasionally clamors at our gates, demanding to be noticed or even let in. My wife and I had lived in or near urban centers before we came here, and as is often the case with transplants from city to country, there are metropolitan amenities for which we yearn now and then—concerts, the theater, dance, museums and galleries, a choice of more than one movie, the sheer excitement of a great city, and most of all, old friends. There are times when we want more companionship or cultural rewards than our community affords, so we leave it to sop up what we have missed, to renew old friendships, and then return. And return we do, for our roots here run deep.

Finally, I want to explain that the use of the first-person plural in these essays is not an editorial conceit. From the outset, my wife and I were partners in this rural enterprise, as we have been in many ventures for a long time, and when I began writing about the farm it was natural to think of what was going on in terms of how *we*—not I—perceived it. The other side of that coin is that Bobs—or B. as she appears here—has been intimately involved with the editorial course of *Country Journal* since it was launched, though not in any official capacity. On the one hand she has been the full-time farmer, minding the operation that has provided so much inspiration for the magazine; on the other she has suggested countless ideas for articles, read manuscripts, and served as an incisive critic of these essays—doing it all with the perception, patience, and quiet understanding which are her particular gifts. So this is her book as well as mine, although I cannot hold her responsible for whatever faults may be perceived in it.

R. M. K.

The Farm

There is a strange ambivalence to the season. The time of plenty just past, with its profligate, American-style outpouring of gifts, is succeeded by nature's leanest, cruelest hours. And what bounties nature does bestow are snatched away so quickly as to make the heart despair. One morning when we least expect it we will be treated to one of those magically beautiful days without a cloud in sight, mountaintops outlined with incredible clarity against a cerulean sky, the whole snow-blanketed world agleam in a flood of sunlight. But not for nothing are these sirenlike days known as weather-breeders: in their wake the clouds will pile up, bringing a cold, driving wind that stings the face with sleet, turning our thoughts to spring.

Inside we go, to throw another log on the fire and settle down with our January opiate, the seed catalogues. They are magic carpet and genie's lamp and Norman Vincent Peale rolled into one, these marvelous books, transporting the suggestible into a world where it is always summer—a landscape lush with dark, red, juicy tomatoes, raspberry bushes groaning with berries, succulent melons, and ordered rows of beans, peas, carrots, and lettuce stretching as far as the mind's eye can see.

The curse of seed-catalogue time, however, is that it turns us into wild, devil-may-care shoppers. There are never enough lines on the order blank to contain the desires of the flesh. Naturally, we write in the tried and the true—Black Seeded Simpson and Boston, Butter Crunch and Bibb. But what's this? Oak Leaf, an improved strain that will yield in only forty days? Better have some of that too, hadn't we?

By January we have unhappily forgotten the August nightmare of the squash—how, after eating it twice a day for weeks and giving it away to every chance passerby (we have even considered taking it after dark and leaving it, like a foundling, on the neighbor's doorstep), we still haul yards of the gigantic things to the compost heap, where they stack up in a lumpy green-and-yellow mountain. We forget how those fecund hills of squash filled us with terror, reminding us of the old George Price cartoon in which a man is being chased around the house by a wildly growing vine. "Watch out, Fred!" his wife shouts from a window. "Here it comes again!"

But by January we have forgotten. Oh, how we have forgotten. And instead of ordering enough seed for two hills, as we took a blood oath to do, we recall that we didn't have any White Patty Pan last year, and we decide to get just one packet to add variety to the Zucchini, the Early Golden Summer Crookneck, and the Cocozelle Bush.

The trouble with turning over these seasonal contrasts in the mind is that they set us to thinking about the paradoxes in human affairs. We recall a statement by Paul Moore, Jr., the Episcopal Bishop of New York. Speaking of the starving and desperate poor in the famine-stricken nations of Central Africa and Southern Asia, the bishop called on his flock to observe meatless Wednesdays as one way of helping others to eat. While half a billion people are enduring some degree of famine, he said, America's pets alone consume the equivalent of a year's supply of grain for 35 million people. The Biafrans, in company with the people of Chad, Upper Volta, northeastern Brazil, and many other lands, have no need of seed catalogues to make them dream of abundance; what is before them is a starving child dying in their arms, his eyes wide and frightened, his emaciated body covered with flies.

For some years the U.S. government regarded the small farmer with something resembling contempt. Someone down there in Washington concluded that there was no longer a place in the scheme of things for a unit so uneconomic as the family farm, and the small farmer was set adrift like a cast-away, to shift for himself if he could or to sell out if he could not, while everything was geared to the support and mainte-nance of "agribusiness."

New Englanders have never been comfortable with catch phrases, and agribusiness, which is so out of place here, is no exception. This is, after all, the traditional home of the small farmer—the fellow who scratched out a living from the rocky soil, usually growing more stones than crops. Independent, tough, hardworking, he made a livelihood and not much else; but in so doing he managed to produce a little more than his family required, and this surplus went to the village store in the form of fresh produce or meat or eggs or milk, thereby sustaining a few others in the community. The small farmer and his fellows also helped support a variety of local indus-tries—creameries, grain mills, tanneries, food lockers, farm-supply stores, sawmills, and the like. So when the government and the truckers and the milk companies and the land devel-opers and a host of related economic factors combined to put this man out of business, a good many other local enterprises went along with him. And in recent times, the surviving farm-ers' only friend seemed to be the environmentalist, crying in the dark to keep the land open.

It is no longer a matter of aesthetics or conservation, this business of keeping land open. When there are Americans who go to bed hungry every night, it becomes more and more a question of survival. Connecticut, Massachusetts, and other states made studies of the food situation and concluded—as anyone might have told them—that their farms were dwin-dling and that they were almost wholly dependent upon food-stuffs shipped in from outside New England.

In this country, we have begun to see the dilemma of the farms in terms of ever-mounting food prices; abroad, the hor-ror of famine has been loosed. Connecticut and Massachusetts are attempting to preserve the farms that remain; so are New York, New Jersey, Maryland, Michigan, and California, which have devised special programs to assist farmers and make it possible for them to continue doing what only they can do.

The people of New York City, to whom Bishop Moore's eloquent appeal was addressed, can do little more than give up meat one day a week. But in many areas of New England, there is an opportunity to achieve something far more positive and lasting, beginning with the proposition that existing farms must continue to exist. What is essential, of course, is that efforts be taken on a community as well as a state level to encourage the farmer to keep going; and perhaps, as a result, the small farmer will be accorded the respect he once enjoyed. This requires a change in attitude: we have to stop thinking of his land as prime acreage for development; we have to think of the subsistence farmer as an invaluable member of society, a man who feeds his own family reasonably well while adding to the produce available in his community.

Along with this, we can foresee a marked change in the habits of those nonfarmers fortunate enough to own a plot of land. We suspect that the wartime victory gardens are on their way back, and that victory in this present cause is no less essential than it was during World War II. If every able-bodied landowner had a vegetable garden, several animals for meat, a few chickens, a cow or a milking goat, and a fruit tree or two, we can discern all sorts of side benefits. The vegetables would be fresh and nutritious; no one would have to wonder if the tomato on the bottom of the plastic-wrapped package was rotten; thousands of people would get in touch with the soil and discover the marvels of nature; they would be outdoors, exercising, and saving the electricity now used for television-viewing because they would fall into bed exhausted after a day in the garden. It would be beneficial for the land, for the pocketbook, and for the soul. And imagine the look of gratitude on the neighbor's face when he receives the first offering of squash!

If country living has taught us anything, it is that nothing is predictable on a farm. *Que será, será.* If something happens, it happens; and "it" is most likely what you least expect.

Take the afternoon, awhile back, when Meg came in heat. We had two or three things we *had* to do and something else we *wanted* to do, but when a milking goat shows heat, not a moment is to be lost, and you and your wife (mostly the latter, since she is the patient, capable one) catch the nervous, twitching nanny in order to bundle her into the pickup truck and head up the road to the nearest billy. That buck may be fifty miles distant, but once you've loaded your trembling virgin, off you go in any kind of weather. Or so the scenario reads. Reality is never so simple.

For starters, Meg doesn't want to go. Anywhere. It seems, also, that she has never had a halter on before and that a calf halter doesn't properly fit a goat. But you truss her up as best you can and then try to lead her through the barn toward the truck, soothing her with promises of the romance that awaits at the end of the ride. What you find is that goats are not easily led—at least not the first time—even to an amorous rendezvous. In fact, goats do the leading, and it turns out that a big strong girl like Meg is capable of dragging a worried, middle-aged man through a barn at something approaching the speed of Ben Hur's chariot. Fortunately, goats change their minds frequently and quickly, and after careening around the machinery for a while, Meg suddenly elects to hide under the plow. She is obviously the only one who thinks she is hiding, since you and all the cats and the other goats can see her, and there is a great deal of bleating and meowing about who does she think she's fooling, but at least her maneuver gives you time to pick yourself up off the barn floor and catch your breath, after which both sides regroup and head uneasily for the truck.

Surprisingly, getting Meg into the back of the pickup is less difficult than you anticipated. In a trice, she is tied with ropes on the right and left sides to two stakes and you stand there patting her, telling her quietly about the flights of joy that will be hers when she meets Mr. Right. You half close your eyes, conjuring up this scene for Meg, and when you open them you notice that the halter is still tied securely to the two stakes but that Meg isn't in it. She is heading down the road.

There is no need to dwell here on the ensuing chase, the angry recriminations, the renewed struggle to wrestle Meg into the truck and tie her again (this time with a stout collar and stout ropes), the final departure with your wife at the wheel, gamely listening to Meg's tearful bleats, or—at the last—the pitiful baa-baa-*baa*-a-a-ing trailing off into the gathering dusk. No, the point is that this sort of episode is the rule, not the exception, on a farm, and for someone who was not brought up in the country it takes getting used to. Probably it accounts for the fact that farmers are among the very select group known to the Census Bureau as "self-employed." (It turns out that only 1.5 percent of our work force today is in that category; all the rest—98.5 percent of American workers—are hired by organizations. Less than seventy-five years ago, exactly the opposite ratio prevailed.) We know that self-employment has saved our bacon on many an occasion. We cringe to think what the reaction might be if we were to arrive late one morning at the shoe-button factory and face the foreman with the excuse, "The goat was in heat."

This whole business of being self-employed and attending to the unexpected suits our mood in February, when the household and the farm seem to draw in upon themselves, cocoonlike, and the world beyond is so much more remote than at any other season. Somehow the power of Nature to hold man in thrall is never so evident as when the big blizzards of winter come, when it is not unusual for the snow to fall all day and all night and on into the next day, building up quietly, slowly re-shaping the landscape, making the familiar all but unrecog-nizable. February is no time for major projects on the farm; there is always more snow to be shoveled, more to be plowed. It is when the business of living can become a full-time occu-pation.

When the shoveling is done and we drive to the office on one of these still, frosty mornings, we are treated to the sight of Manchester Center off in the distance, still half asleep, plumes of white smoke rising straight into the air and steam coming off the Battenkill in enormous billowing clouds. The low morning sun slants in from the east, illuminating thin wisps of smoke against the dark mountain backdrop, glisten-ing on rooftops and the church steeples, and we feel like the English clergyman who used to open his bedroom window on such a morning, put his head outside, look toward the heavens and say, briskly, "Good morning, God!"

The February days—perceptibly longer and a little warmer than those of January—occasionally give the illusion that win-ter's back is broken. But nightfall brings an altogether differ-ent tale. There are nights when we doubt if spring will ever come—the nights of no winds, when the temperature starts to fall with the waning sun, until the snow squeaks underfoot and the air freezes in your nostrils. And there are the nights that follow a metallic, greenish glow in the late-afternoon sky, when the winds howl again with unearthly cruelty and vio-lence. We sit by the fire reading or thumbing through seed catalogues, but our thoughts are out there in the swirling snow with Loren and Joe and the others who drive the plows all night so we can drive to the village for the newspaper in the morning. We wonder if they become half-hypnotized, as we do, by the snowflakes shooting straight into the headlights hour after hour. We wonder if they ever become frightened on those empty highways in the terrible winter storm. We wonder what they think about as they roll through the blizzard, pushing that great curling wave of snow off the road. And we wonder if anyone ever thanks them for what they do.

Mud Season is a notation of Nature, not of the calendar, and describes an interval of indeterminate duration between winter and spring. It has none of spring's fripperies or fall's harlot colors, none of winter's white mantle or summer's lushness. The going is sloppy and slow, the ground underfoot soggy and treacherous. Patches of water lie in low spots in the meadow, riffled by the wind; the road to the house is a rutted slough; and back of the barn the cows stand in mud halfway to their bellies, hesitant to move lest another step take them in deeper.

We enjoy our companionship with this plain, no-nonsense time. It reminds us, among other things, that the countryman's life is not an escape—that it is, in fact, the reverse. One morning recently we were astonished to discover a new calf in the pasture, born during the night. The cow was not due to freshen for another six weeks, but here was this unexpected arrival, shivering in the cold wind, unable to stand, not yet ready for life in the world. So we carried our foundling into the barn, laid it on some hay and a blanket under a heat lamp, rubbed its back and gave it some warm milk from a bottle, and now we wait and watch—wondering if one creature's care for another will provide the strength it needs to stand up and nurse from its mother in a day or two.

Living on the land seems to us a condition in which people are closer to reality than they are in the city, thrown more on their own resources. It is good to have one's life punctuated by seasons, to know that all things change, and perhaps this is the principal difference between the city person and the countryman. The former, having all but lost his seasonal sense, tends to follow a routine that bears little relationship to the elements; in the city, Mud Season has been done away with by means of concrete. The countryman learns to live with the weather and accept it. No two days are ever the same, no man can be certain what the next morning will bring. He may have planned to fix fence in the forenoon, but in the early hour of dawn he hears the beat of rain on the roof. Well, the following day, then. And he turns to another job until the time is right for fence-mending.

Country living is a succession of hard-learned lessons, not all of which we are eager to learn. Just when you think you are beginning to get the hang of something—the proper management of a vegetable garden, let's say—along comes a totally new and unwanted experience, a disaster never before encountered, and there you are, back at Square One. You might suppose some bright fellow could apply a computer to this problem in order to spare us the woes suffered by those who have passed this way before. But no, since nothing ever happens the same way twice in the country, the computer has insufficient data on which to base its predictions. And so do we.

Not even those talented folk known as county agents seem to appreciate this dilemma. Along about March, the county agents determine that the rest of us had better get ready for the arrival of spring, and the next thing we know, in come mimeographed reminders from our friends John Page and Dave Newton. These helpful, immensely knowledgeable fellows do their best to keep the farmer one jump ahead of the Furies nipping at his heels, and the only fault we have to pick with their advice is that we are always on the receiving end of it. One of these days we want a job in which *we* make out lists of things to be done by someone else. Anyway, it isn't that their checklists don't make sense; it's that they don't seem to take into consideration all the things that might go awry.

Our farm operates on the basis of Murphy's Law, which says that anything that can go wrong will go wrong, and neither John nor Dave seems to realize this. They don't know, for instance, that the bucket loader is almost certain to quit operating on the first good morning we have for cleaning up manure. They don't seem to be aware that we will break a couple of plow points on the second swing around the cornfield. And they lose sight altogether of the fact that these calamities—or others of a similar nature—will necessitate a trip across the mountain to Salem for a part that will be out of stock and will have to be ordered. It will arrive eventually, but not until we are about three weeks behind the timetable outlined on the checklist.

Not all advice comes from county agents, of course. Take what happened on a Sunday in early April. The *New York Times* Garden Section was abristle with helpful suggestions for the week. "Catch up with grounds cleanup, planting of hardy vegetables, and grounds preparation for later planting," Joan Lee Faust admonished us. "Start fruit tree spraying."

All well and good, you might think. Nothing like tidying things up in the garden and persuading those first hardy vegetables to stick their toes into the frozen ground. What better on an April morning than to sweep away the dregs of winter, get out the spray equipment, and start life anew? Ordinarily the blood would have coursed through our veins at this prospect. As any member of the family can tell you, we are by nature the most pliant chap imaginable—tractable, obliging, quick to fall in with suggestions, a soft touch for the breezy, won't-take-no-for-an-answer instructions of the shelter magazines and the garden pages of large city newspapers.

But this was no ordinary April morning. As a matter of fact, on this particular Sunday it had been snowing since the previous Thursday night, and by the time we got to the village for the paper and Ms. Faust's advice, the snow was coming down harder than ever, driven on the teeth of a stiff wind (the radio station in Schenectady was reporting gusts up to a hundred miles an hour). More than two feet of snow had fallen already, and on the lee slopes drifts four and five feet deep had accumulated.

To the denizens of our pasture, the world must have seemed a bleak place indeed. Icicles hung from the cows' ears and nostrils and the animals wore expressions of total disgust. April is calving time, their accusing looks reminded us, and calving time is no time to have two feet of snow. Six calves had already arrived, and because of the snow were crowded into the small barn with their mothers. Three more were due any day now, and suddenly it was of the utmost importance that we keep constant tabs on those expectant cows.

For the next few days we hauled hay through waist-deep snow to the herd, watched by the first arrivals from the south—red-wing blackbirds who had come chattering into town a day or two before the storm broke and who huddled now in the trees, filled with self-pity, all the bluster knocked out of them. We decided we had better feed them, too.

For all our efforts, three calves were born unseen at night, and two of them didn't make it. One was dying when our wife arrived in the pasture at daybreak; although she gave it artificial respiration, wrapped it in a blanket, and rubbed it for an hour or more, there was no saving it. Much the same thing happened the following morning. A beautiful big heifer calf was down in the snow and seemed ready to die—no fight in her. The two of us rubbed and patted her and got her to suck a bit of warm milk, but it was no good; finally we picked her up, laid her across the seat of the truck, and raced off to the veterinarian in hopes he could save her. Just as we lifted her onto the operating table she let out a sob and died. April, we concluded as soon as we could be philosophical about it, is too fickle a time to march to the *New York Times*'s drum.

After giving us so much snow that month, the heavens grew weary and there was, instead, no moisture at all. By early May the garden was dry and lifeless. Digging a new bed for herbs, we raised only powdery dirt; harrowing the old alfalfa piece, we were trailed by a huge cloud of dust that swirled around the tractor before settling at last on the neighbor's field. We begrudged him that topsoil.

Then something happened. Suddenly the cowslips, those bright-yellow watchmen of the swamp, were in bloom. The first rain in weeks fell and the shadbush blossomed hesitantly, not quite daring to remain with us for fear that a sudden change in the weather would damage its dainty white frock. Beautiful white clusters appeared on the black cherry trees—each laden with tiny, incredibly delicate, five-petaled flowers. Stubbornly, the apple blossoms held back—tight little nubs of red waiting patiently for their moment in the sun. So with the lilacs, biding their time until Memorial Day, to have the whole show to themselves. Frothy catkins hung from willows and birches but the maple leaves were still shriveled, wrinkled like fingers that have been too long under water. The evergreens set out their new, pale-green candles with instructions to reach and stretch and strain, to see how tall they could grow this year. Suddenly the fields were dotted, then covered, with dandelion blossoms and the air was soft and seductive. The calves were frolicking, the snows of April forgotten, and a neighbor stopped by to talk of buying piglets.

It was spring.

During April a pair of mallard ducks arrived, inspected the neighborhood, and decided to take up housekeeping. For a week they cruised the perimeter of the pond, scouting for a nesting site. We would see them rounding the woods, wheeling past the big spruce like a couple of hot Navy pilots, then they would splash down and paddle ashore. The female went first on each of these inland forays, moving purposefully and unhesitatingly into the tall grass while her mate hove to offshore like a small gunboat, trying to look unconcerned yet alert. When he saw that the coast was clear and his lady friend unscathed, he headed boldly toward the bank and followed her into the weeds. For days this house-hunting continued, and it became increasingly clear that she would be a tough client for any realtor to please. Nothing suited her. After each inspection tour she stomped back to the pond, flung herself into the water, and swam off with a cross little shake of the scapulars and never a glance behind.

Toward month's end the duo was augmented by the arrival of an unattached male—an event that produced a splashing and churning of water not seen since the Battle of Jutland. As far as could be told, no blood was drawn during these violent onslaughts, but for days the pond was a bedlam of flapping wings, quacking, scolding, and name-calling between the two males, while the female, now turned demure and fluttery, spent hours primping and preening, oblivious to the suitors flailing away at each other.

Suddenly they wearied of this and all three ducks flew off, we knew not where, were gone for days, and as suddenly returned. Only this time, bless buttons, the triangle consisted of one male and two females and all was blissfully quiet. Happiness, it seemed, was a pond with one male and two female mallards on it. Then one day a dark shadow flashed across the water, the ducks looked up uneasily, and continued to watch as a single, unattached male flew over on a scouting mission, sizing up the situation below. Back and forth he went, putting on a spectacular aerial display and quacking noisily, circling the pond four or five times before taxiing in for a landing with his flaps down. As soon as he hit the water he raised himself up to stand on his tail, flapped his wings as if crowing (looking for all the world like a show-off at Muscle Beach), and immediately one of the females—certain that this was destiny calling—paddled over to join him.

For a week the two pairs of honeymooners pottered about on love's errands and then they were gone. We had almost given them up for good when, one morning in June, there emerged from the tall grass near the outlet two female mallards and ten tiny yellow balls of fluff—so light they could literally run across the water—all quacking happily. All that day the two mothers convoyed their brood around the pond, giving them swimming and diving lessons. The next morning we looked out the window expectantly and were struck with deep foreboding. Now there was only one mother and eight little ones. Three days later, all the ducks had vanished. A month passed and one of the adult females returned to the pond for a day or so, but there was no further sign of the ducklings. In the meantime, we had caught sight one evening of a gray fox, heading into the swamp near the pond's outlet. We thought we knew what had happened.

Then there were the swallows. They are here every summer, darting about the pond and the barn, a constant source of amazement, amusement, and delight. We don't know if it's the same family that comes every year to the mud nest over the milkhouse door, but come they do, as regularly as clockwork, and before long we hear the tiny chirps from inside the nest and behold with awe the frantic, unceasing trips for food for those hungry mouths. Out over the pond, there is a continuous flash of dark wings and cinnamon-colored breasts pursuing insects, and if you watch closely you see that each bird follows its own peculiar flight pattern, making a run across the length of the pond, soaring up toward the trees as it finishes, then wheeling back in a parabola to repeat the run. They're incredibly courageous or foolhardy, these birds, for they hit the water repeatedly on each attack, bouncing off the surface and making little splashes as though someone had skipped a stone across the water. Once we saw a little fellow hit at what was obviously the wrong angle and sink out of sight immediately.

This summer a pair of swallows decided to build a nest inside the garage, up near the peak of the roof, and before we suspected anything there was a nearly finished edifice of mud pats. As the construction work continued we saw what was happening to our new car beneath the nest and decided the swallows would have to go. We began shutting the garage doors during the day to keep them out. But it's easy to forget to close a door and each time we neglected it the swallows would swoop in, plunk themselves down in the nest, and refuse to leave. We banged on the rafters with the rake, but that only made them fly about nervously, causing further surface damage to the car.

Our determination mounted. We shut the garage doors without fail. But we noticed that the swallows were becoming increasingly belligerent. They took to dive-bombing us each time we walked between the house and the garage, making a nervous wreck of the dog, who finally refused to go outside. Fortunately, the swallows gave up at last, but we'd bet they'll come back next year. Isn't that what swallows always do?

Tragedy—major or minor—seems a concomitant of farm life, and one warm day in June we sensed that something terrible had happened when the killdeer took to shrieking louder and more persistently than ever, flying round and round the meadow above the house, calling "Kill*deer*! Kill*deer*! Kill*deer*!" long after darkness had fallen. At last it dawned on us: of course, the meadow had been mowed that morning—later than usual because of the weather—and the birds' nest must have been destroyed. Next day they were out early, flying what proved to be a special search pattern—one adult about twenty-five feet above ground, calling, calling; the other not more than three or four feet above the meadow but directly under its mate, silent, looking, listening for a response. As it turned out, we found what they were seeking before they did; that afternoon we were tedding the hay and saw the crumpled little ball of feathers under the hay swath, barely recognizable as a baby killdeer.

While these small dramas were being played out by the wildlings, our unwanted domesticated bird stalked the barnyard, supremely self-centered, crowing shrill and clear at twenty-five-second intervals from three-thirty in the morning until eight at night. Charley is a rooster that came uninvited to the farm, the sole survivor of a neighboring flock of chickens. One morning several years ago he watched from a roost in a tree while his harem was rounded up one by one, clucking and flapping furiously, and dispatched to the locker. Charley decided he wanted no part of what was going on and remained prudently in the tree until the executioner tired of his work and disappeared. Ever since that day, Charley has made his home with our cows, which means that—unlike most roosters—he is exposed to the rigorous Vermont winters. But Charley, considering his options, chose the outdoor life. From November until April he stays with the cows for company and warmth, sharing their steaming corn silage and the calves' grain, coming through the ordeal as well as a rooster can— except for the loss of what was once his crowning glory. On a bitter cold night Charley's comb froze and dropped off, giving him the look of a reprobate survivor of Verdun. Happily, Charley doesn't seem aware of what happened and we don't intend to tell him, so he goes on crowing merrily, telling the world about himself and his happiness to be alive, a disreputable pensioner strutting about the barnyard in search of the hens that aren't there.

Each April finds us pondering once more the arcane tongue spoken at Internal Revenue Service headquarters. The opening line of Instructions for Schedule F (Form 1040), Farm Income and Expenses, suggests what all those who farm are up against. It reads:

> **Note:** You may be entitled to claim the new jobs credit if you hired additional employees this year. However, you may not take a deduction for that portion of the wages or salaries paid or incurred which is equal to the amount of the new jobs credit allowable before application of the tax liability limitation. Please see **Form 5884, New Jobs Credit,** for additional information.

We read on. Past Cash Receipts and Disbursements Method of Reporting, through discussions of the accrual method, cooperative allocations, commodities futures, deductions for farming syndicates (with a long pause over a mysterious note that states: *To determine whether you participated materially in the farm management or production, do not consider the activities of any agent who acted for you*), and finally to Retirement Plans. On Line 48, it was explained, you should "enter the amount you claim as a deduction for contributions to a pension, profit-sharing or annuity plan . . . for the benefit of your employees." It was the only instruction that seemed to fit Charley's situation. We entered $2.10 on Line 48.

As a rooster, Charley is not actually an employee. But we don't know how to describe his present state unless it is retirement, and it's difficult to see where we should enter the $2.10—what we paid for twenty-five pounds of laying mash—unless it's as part of Charley's retirement program.

We have never known what type of rooster he is—only that when he first came to the farm he was a splendid specimen, a real cock o' the walk, in his prime and proud of it, constantly preening his black and yellow-white feathers, the fiery red comb, and the dark-green plumes that arched like a fountain when he strutted around the corner of the barn. Every now and then he would cross the road to survey the scene from Edith's big pine, but most of the time he stayed around our barn, content to be with the cows, which he seemed to regard as large brown-and-white chickens.

After he lost his comb, Charley's personality underwent a change. Before then, he was a popinjay, vain, concerned only with appearances; now he was transformed into an old reprobate, a roué with a rolling gait and a wandering eye, and we heard later that he had made several forays to neighboring henhouses, only to be driven off by younger, bigger roosters.

Time passed, and Charley looked tackier than ever—no comb, tail feathers all askew, a rake gone to seed. Meantime, the cattle were sold, except for two young bulls that roamed the small pasture at the east end of the barn, and Charley moved over to roam with them. Then the bulls were sold and Charley was alone, still crowing before break of day, wandering in and out of the empty bullpens, occasionally strutting around to the other side of the barn to visit the goats (which ranked far below cows in Charley's caste system).

One day Charley vanished, and for a week there was neither sight nor sound of him. Maybe, we thought, he's moved to the Butlers' henhouse, beyond the swamp, and has found companionship at last. But no, he was not at the Butlers; we heard him crowing in the middle of the swamp, on the far side of the pond, where he must have been living off what seeds he could scrounge. Then silence. No Charley. Perhaps a hawk or a fox had surprised the old boy, we worried.

In December we had an early snow—an unusually big one—snow that kept falling softly day after day until the woods were full and even the pond vanished beneath the blanket of white. It turned cold—down to minus fifteen degrees one night—and still no news from Charley. The next morning we went in search of him, expecting to find nothing but a bundle of feathers on the snow, but as we emerged from the kitchen door we heard his *cock-a-doodle-doo* for the first time in a week—he was somewhere in the vicinity of the biggest pine tree in the swamp and we headed through knee-deep snow for it, carrying a little can of seed to see if we might tempt him. We caught sight of him roosting on a limb halfway up the pine tree, but try as we might there was no luring Charley down. He gave us a baleful stare, crowed once or twice, and then looked the other way. We left the seed on a small hummock, thinking he might come down to eat if we went away. Not until later did it dawn on us why Charley hadn't left his perch. He'd be helpless in the deep snow. Charley was marooned.

Next afternoon the two of us set out for the swamp. It was bitter cold, and when we looked up into the pine's branches we saw that Charley was gone. Back and forth through the swamp we tramped, peering into every tree and bush, finally spotting him huddled on a low branch at the edge of the back pasture, where he could catch the last rays of a dying sun. He looked like a goner. We walked up, making comforting noises, but just as we reached out to grab him he squawked raucously and flapped off, landing in a pile of snow by the springhouse, where he flailed about. Back to the house we went for a bushel basket, back once more through the drifting snow to the springhouse, and after a couple of tries we managed to get the basket over Charley. He began to scream— the piercing, unearthly shrieks of a nightmare—and all the way back to the barn we wondered what the neighbors thought we had tucked beneath our arm.

We brought Charley into the bullpen, emptied him out of the basket, and he lay on the hay too exhausted to move. Only when we gave him a bit of grain and some warm water did we begin to think he might make it. For a few days he remained in a catatonic state and then began to perk up noticeably, as though he had made a decision to live. Several mornings later when we walked into the milkhouse and heard him crowing, we knew he was going to be all right.

That was when we bought the laying mash—$2.10 worth, knowing we would have to provide for the old boy's retirement. Through the winter Charley roosted on a metal stanchion, looking like a disreputable remittance man, disdaining the nest we created for him. Each time we fed him he fixed us with a malevolent eye, as if to say that life wasn't a patch on those days when he had the company of the cows. And when the wind was out of the east you had the feeling Charley was getting the wanderlust again and might strike out to seek his fortune if only the snow would melt.

Soon it will be spring and we'll have to get Charley some hens—a couple of maiden ladies that will cluck solicitously over him and look after the old vagabond in his declining years.

Probably we shouldn't set such store by May, but we do. The month is full of promises too good to keep, and we are always taken in by them. Yet we bear no grudge. The moment the May sun ducks behind a cloud we feel the chill, but the instant it returns we sense the makings of July.

Once again we will experience the garden's propensity to produce an entire new crop of rocks, but that seems a small price to pay for the privilege of being outdoors with the sun on our back, stirring the receptive soil while thoughts of vegetables in orderly rows dance round in our head.

Because it is May we can even be somewhat philosophical about the skunks. Presently we will learn whether or not the *Mephitis mephitis* family will take up residence with us again, now that it is warm. (We assume it was a family that visited last fall—we didn't catch their names, but there were four of them and they certainly looked enough alike to be closely related.) For most of November they shared the cats' dish in the barn, arriving just after the warm goat's milk was set out for supper. It was a sight not given to many to see: nine cats and four skunks crowding around a bowl, taking turns eating, each of them on his best behavior, mannerly and polite—the skunks all fluffy in black and white, looking a bit gauche and unaccustomed to formal dining, the cats wearing an air of pained superiority, sleek in their yellow and tortoiseshell coats. We couldn't tell who acted as hostess at these integrated dinner parties, but the nightly affairs came off beautifully, as though the guest list had been carefully planned. Very little, if anything, was said during the meal, which may explain why the evenings were so successful; in fact, the whole thing reminded us of a small child's tea party, with each guest concentrating intently on his plate, afraid to look to left or right for fear of what he might see.

At the moment we are awaiting developments—not with real enthusiasm. It has occurred to us that we have no idea how to get rid of one skunk, let alone four. Our only hope is that they may have forgotten the directions to our barn.

May is a month we always associate with fencing—probably because it's when most work of this kind got done on our farm. By May the frost is out of the ground, snow is gone except for the occasional freak storm, it's too early to start haying, and you can count on some decent weather before the essential tasks of summer begin crowding in on you. In years past a more important reason was that mid-May was the time our fencing crew became available, in the weeks just after college let out. They arrived in a snarl of duffel bags, hockey sticks, tennis racquets, and the accumulation of weeks of unlaundered clothes, tumbled out of a friend's father's car, and before half their gear was in the house had found the brownies, the beer, and the leftover chicken in the refrigerator.

What made it possible to run cattle on the farm was that our son, with his friends, would exchange several weeks' time fencing the pastures for pocket money to finance whatever adventure they were bound on during July and August. For three or four years the boys kept coming back, each season handling the work with greater skill, taking increasing pride in doing the job right, and by the time they left us they were as good as any professional crew. By then they had also had enough of fencing to last a lifetime. For fencing, in case you haven't tried it, is the hardest job on the farm—backbreaking, tedious work that leaves you with aching muscles, wrists lacerated by barbed wire and thorns, hands blistered from hours with a post maul, the back of your neck crawling with insect bites.

The first year, Tom brought Greg and Peter with him. Neither of the latter two had spent any time on a farm before

and knew nothing of fence building. (If they had, they probably wouldn't have come.) Not that Tom knew a great deal
more—but somehow, after a few days' trial and error and
much profanity, they began to get the hang of it and had
profited sufficiently from their mistakes that the job began to
go more smoothly. As smoothly, that is, as is possible on a
steep New England hill farm where every fence line goes up
or down or across a slope. On the first day they unloaded several hundred-pound rolls of barbed wire from the truck, but
someone neglected to lay one roll flat, and the next they knew
it was rumbling down a steep pitch like a cannonball, a mass of
barbed steel gathering momentum and chunks of grass and
dirt as it plummeted down into a ravine, lodging at last against
a tree a quarter-mile below the starting point, from where it
had to be lugged uphill by two unhappy but wiser young men.
Several times a roll of woven wire got loose on a hillside and
unrolled as it ran downhill with the boys in hot pursuit, trying
to stop it before the whole thing unraveled.

Years later, certain sites remain engraved in the minds of
the fence builders and their former employers. There is a
sharp downhill stretch across from the Roberts place where
Tom and Greg spent an entire day trying to get a single post
to stay in the ground. The problem was that the fence ran
downhill on either side to the stream, and each time they
would get the posts driven and the woven wire stretched and
stapled to the posts, the tension from the two sides would lift
the bottom post out of the ground. There is a fifty-foot section
by the upper barn where one summer's crew forgot to string
barbed wire along the top of the woven wire. The next thing
we knew, our Number 36 cow—who was tall and strong and
adventuresome—had her head and neck over it, knocked
down a post, and she and the rest of the herd stepped over the
fence and into the lush grass on the other side. Another crew
repaired this section the following summer, but they didn't put
the posts in straight the first time and had to reset them. A
week later a hurricane hit, washing out the road and the fence

along with it. When we put up that fifty feet of fence again, it was for the fourth time in two years.

"Good fences make good neighbors," Robert Frost once wrote, and indeed they may. But good fences make demands that nobody who has never built one can comprehend.

One year Tom, Greg, and Bob built a corral—a project for which we were forever grateful to them each time we had a sick animal or had to load a bull or give shots to the cattle or separate the calves from the cows. For the corral, we had decided to go all out—pressure-treated posts, hemlock planks, special spikes that wouldn't pull out of the wood—and it was laid out with infinite care so that the two sides of the loading chute would be exactly twenty-one inches apart, and a complicated system of gates would swing just so. For most of a day all went well. A neighbor came by and drilled holes for the posts and everything fell into place precisely. Then the boys began digging the hole for the post where the squeeze was to join the chute. A foot down, they struck rock. Not just the small-, medium-, and large-size assortment of stones you find in every hole you dig in Vermont, but a truly enormous rock. A rock that filled a hole five feet in diameter. A rock that occupied four strong males and a tractor for nearly two days before it was out of the ground. All in order to set a single fencepost. Which is what fencing can be.

Inevitably, our fencing crews had to fight blackflies, deerflies, sweat bees, mosquitoes, chiggers, and ticks—always worse in May and early June than at any other time—and for days at a stretch these pests made their life miserable in hot, humid weather. We would drive up to see how things were going and find Mark or Cam soaked with perspiration, hats pulled down to their eyes, shirts buttoned tight at the neck, swatting at the merciless insects between blows with the hammer.

We never paid the boys much—their hourly rate, on the face of it, seemed paltry reward for so much sweat and tears—but we were reminded each summer, when we paid the grocery bills, what the true cost was. Under ordinary circumstances, husky, eighteen-year-old males put away prodigious quantities of food and drink; but when they are compensating for the energy expended in fencing, their consumption—and the food bills—are staggering.

For Tom's mother, who provided the food and drink, the onset of fencing also generated an array of logistical problems that might have defied a quartermaster. Even to calculate the amount of Page wire, barbed wire, staples, nails, electric-fence wire, insulators, cedar posts, creosote, gates and gateposts, and gas and oil for the chainsaw was difficult enough; what was dismaying was to assemble all these articles from half a dozen different sources, since no one place ever had enough of any single item, and to get it all here before the boys arrived.

In the winter a dead limb falls across a section of fence and breaks that painstakingly stretched barbed wire, so that even after it is fixed, it is never quite as tight again. The deep snows or deer snap a span of wire or push over a post. You expect that. What you never quite expect or forgive are the snowmobilers who cut the barbed wire because it's in their way, or the hunters who climb over the fences and break them down, never thinking or caring about the cost in time and effort—thinking only of taking the shortest route instead of walking a little farther and using a gate. And anytime you see a section of woven wire that sags and bows where someone has pushed it down in order to cross, you grow angry, remembering how proud the boys were when they stretched that fence so tight it hummed like the strings of a musical instrument.

Once again the swallows have returned to Saddleback Farm, winging in on a soft breeze from the south to announce that spring is here and all's right with the world. We have not seen fit to capitalize on this annual reappearance as the Chamber of Commerce has done at Junípero Serra's ruined mission of San Juan Capistrano, but our birds have been staging a lively festival of their own, filling the air with the blue flash of wings, dazzling somersaults and turns, and what the *Audubon Society Field Guide to North American Birds* aptly terms "constant liquid twittering and chattering." It occurs to us that these daring stunt pilots have shared the big cow barn with us and our animals ever since we took title to the place, but "shared" is probably too generous a word for the relationship. We know that there is more to the commotion they make than "liquid twittering and chattering": it is scolding, pure and simple, and its frequency and volume tell us that they barely tolerate us, suffering our presence in the manner of old residents who see the neighborhood going to hell and complain to anyone who will listen.

We did not see the swallows depart last fall. We only knew, one day, that they were no longer here and that they had headed south for the season, having received their orders from an inner calendar that told them it was time to be moving. How far south, it came as a considerable surprise to discover; indeed, the very birds that nest and raise their young in our barn probably spent the winter in Argentina—a good five thousand miles, as the swallow flies, from our milkhouse door. So they are not only acrobats, these birds, but exceptionally strong, heroic fliers, as we learned in reading Robin Baker's

The Mystery of Migration. In fact, their British cousins migrate each autumn to the extreme south of Africa, making the hazardous crossing of the Sahara desert on both their southward and northward journeys.

The first recorded effort to explain migration appears in Aristotle's *Historia Animalium,* and while many of Aristotle's conclusions were quite sound, he seems to have gone astray on swallows, believing that they hibernated. It was a theory that survived unchallenged for twenty-one centuries, but the reason Aristotle saw no swallows during the winter months, and thus surmised that they went underground, was that the birds are total migrants: that is, the entire population leaves its summer breeding and nesting grounds in the north for a locale, far to the south, that provides conditions suitable for survival. Members of the swallow family feed exclusively on flying insects, and as any fool could have told Aristotle, no mosquito or gnat is aloft during a New England winter.

Unlike certain songbirds which migrate according to seasonal changes, swallows are calendar-watchers, and their internal engagement book drives them to make their traditional appearance at the San Juan Capistrano Mission each year on March 19 and to depart on October 23. Now and then, the ornithologist Alan Pistorius tells us, their calendar does them dirt: about eight years ago, the swallow population returning to New England was decimated during a week of unseasonable, drenching rain, when there were no insects to eat; but in a normal year the birds fly north on a schedule that keeps their food supply within reach.

Although individual swallows in North America have been known to reach five to eight years of age, it is probably fair to assume that the average life expectancy of these birds is from one to three years. If their allotted span is so brief, we wondered, how is it that the same individuals seem to return to the same nest in our barn each year? The answer is that adult barn swallows nest in the immediate area of their previous nest; in fact, the location of their first nesting place is imprinted indelibly in their consciousness. With their young, it is a different story. What is imprinted is the last area visited before the young birds migrated the previous autumn—a system that expands the gene pool, so to speak, spreading out the population so that inbreeding becomes less likely.

Last fall Dan O'Leary painted the cow barn, and one casualty of the cosmetic work was the nest just under the roof overhang to one side of the milkhouse door—a nest that has been home to at least ten generations of swallows. This spring we waited to see what would happen. Just as we had supposed, the returnees swooped in one morning in April after the long flight from the pampas, took one horrified look at the nest site, and without pausing long enough to unpack their flight bags went to work on the reconstruction project, tamping little pellets of mud into position, shaping a new nest while they nattered at us for allowing the place to be vandalized. Meanwhile, inside the grain barn the old mud nests that perch on the metal shades of overhead lights are being patched and redecorated by two pairs of swallows, and within the main barn, above the anxious eyes of the ewes and their lambs, another swallow family is setting up housekeeping.

Before long, eggs will hatch, the insides of those nests will come alive with rustling movement and piteous cries of hunger, and the unceasing ritual of bringing food to the babies will begin. Overhead, above the garden and the pasture, the aerial acrobatics of the parents will go on all day, and on warm summer evenings the air space over the pond will teem with swallows, wheeling and darting, hovering, splashing off the surface of the water, hauling God only knows how many insects back to the nest to those insatiable mouths inside. It is estimated that a mature swallow covers as much as six hundred miles each day in search of food for its young, and one wonders, watching these incredibly swift and tireless forays, if the estimate is not low.

One day last August we looked from a second-story window at a line of young swallows perched on the telephone wire, clinging uncertainly to it, teetering precariously now and then, waiting for one parent or the other to deposit a beakful of insects into their throats. Occasionally one of the fledglings would take to the air for a trial spin, to try out its wings, after which it would return to the wire to await the next meal. There was so little time, it occurred to us, before those young ones would have to be on their own, ready to fly south—ready for what birders call the Great Gathering of the Swallows, when thousands, hundreds of thousands, of these small creatures assemble, drawn by an unfathomable urge no human can possibly comprehend, and suddenly take off in the direction of the midday sun, bound on their ancient, unbelievable journey toward the vast skies of the Southern Cross. Now that we know where they are going, we will worry even more about them. It is such a long trip.

Just mention June and we think of haying. In this part of New England, June is the earliest you can count on cutting, and even though there's no 100 percent certainty about that, it's the month we associate with putting the first crop in the barn.

There's a sense of anticipation about haying that's rather special, like a holiday coming, and for a week or more ahead of time we turn over in our mind all the remembered sights and sounds and smells, the things we like best about it. We picture one of those perfect early-summer days, the kind Winslow Homer often painted—hot sun, the air cool and fresh, with just enough breeze to rustle the tops of the timothy and alfalfa. A good drying day it is, with puffy white cumulus clouds scudding across the sky, and down at our level, the soft, purposeful buzzing of insects in the grass. Chet mows, Barbara usually does the tedding, and we rake whenever we have the chance. That's the job we like best. There's something immensely satisfying about making order out of chaos in a big meadow—putting the tangle of tumbled hay left by the tedder into long neat rows to be gobbled up by the baler. The challenge is to see if you can roll up windrows that are evenly sized, perfectly parallel, row after row so that when the field is finished and you get off a ways to look at it, you see something resembling a picture-postcard view of the English countryside, everything tidy, the windrows dark stripes of green against the lighter green swaths of stubble.

Whether you're mowing or tedding or raking, you're aware constantly of the swallows and other birds, usually sparrows or killdeer, swooping and darting in the wake of the machinery for the insects that have been turned out of their lodgings and stirred into flight. We love the sound of the rake, mostly because it's one of the few farm implements that doesn't demand a lot of power and therefore make a lot of noise. You can run the tractor in fourth gear, pulling a rake that turns over with a methodical *clickety-click, clickety-click*—a sound of efficiency at a decibel level that just suits the kind of unfocused woolgathering we like to do.

We recall the day, late in June a few years ago, when we caught sight of a deer at the far end of the meadow. We were putt-putting along on the tractor, raking up the endless windrows, and we thought surely the animal would bound off in fright when we rounded the bend at its end of the field. Not at all. It stood its ground, browsing contentedly, and although we passed within thirty feet of it, the only movement it made was to look at us a bit more closely, taking our measure as we drove by. Perhaps it knew we were a friend; perhaps it realized we had work to do. But we wouldn't be surprised if the soothing, unthreatening *clickety-click* of the rake lulled it into a sense of security. In any case, we made two or three more circuits of the meadow before the deer ambled off, unconcerned, to greener grazing.

You can see the kind of idyllic picture we have in mind before haying begins, and oh, how we wish it always worked out that way. Like most activities on a farm, there are so many opportunities for things to go wrong that it's a wonder any hay ever gets in the barn. We were running over the list the other night and the array of potential problems is positively numbing.

It should be mentioned at the outset that for one who has never understood machines nor had the least talent for fixing them when they run amok, the complexities of modern farming are often frightening to contemplate. The machines know this, of course, and do everything they can to make life miserable. They deliberately lose nuts, bolts, and other important parts; they break; they run out of oil or grease or gasoline; they refuse to start; they refuse to stop. Or, let's say there are two separate parts that are supposed to connect (supposed to connect, hell—*did* once connect): just let us come within wrench's range and they immediately stiffen up or shrink, freezing into position so there's no possibility of joining them. We know there are people with a knack for dealing with machines, who use persuasion or cajolery, deftly sliding pieces together, whereas we go at them with an expletive and a large hammer. But for us the machine remains an enigma and a potential adversary, and this is never more apparent than in haying season.

To begin with, there's a seemingly endless list of chores to be done before haying can commence. If luck is with you, the cows have calved, you've fixed the fences, and the herd has been turned out to summer pasture. If the manure has also been spread, the plowing done, the corn planted, and the machinery greased and tested and ready to go, then all you need is a good weather report, calling for at least three fine, clear days. That's a lot of ifs.

We long ago concluded that the likelihood of finishing all these prehaying tasks *and* getting a run of good weather is slim. Maybe impossible. What usually happens is that we're not quite ready when the weather is right, so we go to haying anyway—this on the theory that you can generally find someone to patch up a piece of machinery, but you can't find anyone to do anything about the weather. However, it means that there is a better than even chance that something will go awry. We can be almost certain, for instance, that a knife on the haybine will break and that Chet will come into the barn with that disgusted "It's broken" look and start rummaging around, hoping to find a spare. We may or may not have remembered to order extras; if not, it's a two-hour trip to Crosby's or Salem Farm Supply, depending on which of them has knives in stock.

If things go the way they often do, not until it's time to start tedding will someone recall that Barbara sideswiped a fencepost the last time out last summer; the tedder, now that it's missing a few tines, is operating at less than peak efficiency. Then there's that little clip for the wheel of the rake; did we remember to get a new one? If not, it means that we'll lumber down the road like a tank, since we can't take the rake out of gear. The baler, perverse as ever, will probably shear a couple of pins the first few times around the meadow. And a tire on the hay wagon is bound to develop a slow leak.

When we get back to the barn with the first load (after pumping up the tire out in the field), we expect to find that the hay elevator isn't working as well as it did last year. In fact, it isn't working at all. About this time, our neighbor Fred usually stops by to see if he can help, and he putters with the motor for a while—sometimes successfully, sometimes not, in which case we call Pete, the electrician, to ask if he'll swing by the barn and see what he can do. And now, if everything goes according to pattern, there's a rumbling off to the west. We look toward Rupert Mountain and see that a lot of dark clouds have begun to form. Funny, the weather report didn't mention anything about rain. Looks as if we might have a shower, someone says. And sure enough, we do.

Each June reminds us how astonishing the countryside is on the edge of summer. Busting out all over, as the song has it: every growing thing determined to make the most of its brief season in the sun, to outdo its rivals in a display of vitality and color. Like any other season, this has its anticipatory pleasures, so it came as a jolt to learn that some of our favorite creatures may be missing from view this year. Certain types of butterflies—among them the Bog Elfin, Hessel's Hairstreak, and the Karner Blue—are making their final futile stand against the encroachment of man. (What genius the naturalists reveal in the names they give the fauna of this world! We would have thought that something called Hessel's Hairstreak was a Bavarian troll with frosted hair, but it turns out to be an unassuming little green-colored fellow with rust and white markings, that feeds at the tips of branches.)

Just as we were preparing to enjoy again the butterflies' outrageously brilliant aerial ballet, the Department of the Interior annnounced that forty-one of the seven hundred kinds of butterflies in the United States may have to be added to the list of threatened or endangered species, joining the Eastern cougar, the whooping crane, the grizzly bear, and others on that somber roster.

It appears that the chief villain in the butterfly tragedy is the continuing spread of concrete across the land, the gobbling of countryside by city and suburb, so that the larva that went to sleep last fall awakes to find that its favorite playground is now a Pizza Hut. One of the problems of being a butterfly is that you have to have a favorable habitat in which to be one, and the way favorable habitats are going these days, we suspect that the endangered species list will provide little comfort for these lovely creatures. About the only good thing to be said for inclusion in this select group is that protection of a sort sometimes comes of it, and the Interior Department's solicitude may have a salutary effect in restricting the collection and sale of butterfly specimens. We have never understood the urge some people have to destroy a living creature for the sake of seeing it under glass or mounted on a wall—a thought that must have crossed the mind of the missionary who stumbled onto a party of Jivaro headhunters. Whether the trophy is a butterfly impaled on a pin, a stuffed gnu, or a shrunken human head, our sympathies lie with the victim.

If these people have to collect their jujus, we wish they would concentrate on something whose elimination would benefit the human race—blackflies, for instance, or Japanese beetles, or those killer bees from Africa, whose deadly northward progress through South America we have been following so nervously on the map.

To come back to the butterflies: these wondrous insects have always been associated in our mind with the aimless, carefree summers of childhood, when life was one discovery after another, a new joy revealed, a path that led nowhere in particular and was of no importance to anyone but the seeker. What characterizes the butterfly is a seemingly footloose meandering from one flower to the next, pottering about, if you will, without apparent purpose. Like other lovely things whose chief delight is to show off a pretty frock to a crowd of admirers, the butterfly is probably a bit of a bore and difficult to engage in serious conversation, but the plants on which it pays its giddy social calls gladly put up with the visits for the sake of sending it away laden with pollen.

We believe there is a moral here if we could put a finger on it. On the one hand, the butterfly: bearing no ill will to anyone, content to flutter about from flower to leaf, enjoying to the full its heartbreakingly brief time with us, doing double duty as a vision of gossamer beauty and artificial inseminator. On the other hand, those damned bees: swarming northward like a Mongol horde, leaving a trail of pain and death in their wake, serving no purpose so far as we can tell but to remind the world once again that nice guys finish last.

You get the best view of The Saddle from southwest of town, but not many people know there's a big meadow up there. It's an unmistakable landmark—a pronounced dip, or saddle, between two prominent hills. From one side of it, on a clear day, you can see the Adirondacks, fifty miles to the northwest, and from the other side you look south down the valley that leads to Bennington. The view from The Saddle is something special.

What interests us more than the view is the nature of the place. New England once had a lot of these high meadows, but with the decreasing number of farms, the tendency to feed livestock in the barn all year instead of turning them out to pasture, and an understandable reluctance to haul a lot of expensive hay machinery up and down a narrow mountain road, the mountain meadows and pastures have fallen into disuse and most of them are growing up to brush and trees. This is a pity, because they're one of the features that make the region's landscape, giving it beauty and character. It's easy enough to think of the valley we live in as an unspoiled, natural environment, but in fact it is no such thing. It is the product of two centuries of unremitting toil, and it reminds us of how man is sometimes capable of improving upon nature. Speaking of the way certain wilderness areas have been preserved, René Dubos argues that it is equally important to preserve areas "where the partnership between humankind and Earth has generated values that transcend those created by natural forces working alone. A village green, a pasture, or a wheat field created by clearing the land has social, aesthetic, and emotional values of its own different from those of the surrounding wilderness."

And so The Saddle has always seemed to us. Its particular allure is its size—some forty acres—and the gentleness of its slope, which is surprising, since it lies at the top of the ridge. One gets to it by means of an old road that slants up the side of the mountain. You walk in shade all the way because the trees are so thick, and when you suddenly emerge into the sun-drenched meadow and marvel at the sight of all that brilliant openness, you recall Brigham Young's words to the brethren when they arrived near the Great Salt Lake: "This is the place." In fact, because you come upon it so abruptly you have a better than average chance of seeing the wild creatures that love it here—deer, black bear, a variety of hawks, possibly even a golden eagle.

With second-growth forest crowding in on all sides there is something remarkable about the continuing existence of the high meadow. "Humanized environments," Dr. Dubos writes, "give us confidence because nature has been reduced to the human scale, but the wilderness in whatever form almost compels us to measure ourselves against the cosmos." He's right, of course. Staring into the Grand Canyon or the Muir Woods makes us feel insignificant, while the sight of The Saddle gives us confidence in the human race. These forty acres, some twelve hundred feet above the valley floor, were once upon a time cleared of trees and the rocky detritus of the glaciers to become a productive meadow where sheep and cattle grazed and men and horses cut hay for the winter.

Old-timers tell us that the hay they made on The Saddle was the best around, but it's impossible to know whether these are the tales of old men who savor the recollection of difficulties they once encountered, or whether there was indeed something special in the soil that produced an unusual crop. In those days all the work was done with horses, and after the grass was cut and raked they got it to the barn by a technique known as roping. A team of horses, dragging a rope—or more often a chain—along the ground between them, walked down either side of a windrow. As they moved, the hay gradually accumulated on the chain, building up like a snowball, and was carried to the barn where it was pitched inside by hand while the team returned to the next row to repeat the process. It's curious, but it was possible to accomplish a lot more work on these steep hill farms with horses than you can with a tractor. (Tractors aren't so sure-footed; there are places on our farm where we wouldn't dare take a tractor, where the land was once worked regularly with animals.)

The Saddle lies along the western ridge of a mountain that curves in a great arc to form a half-circle, enclosing a bowl of land known as Kirby Hollow. Local tradition is that this constricted valley, which is one of the town's principal watersheds, was named for Joseph Kirby, a veteran of the Revolutionary War, who settled here when Vermont was still an independent republic. But whether Kirby himself or members of his family cleared the land on The Saddle, no one knows. Nor can anyone say who built the stone walls that rim the high meadow. The likeliest candidate appears to be Chet Baldwin's great-grandfather Sherman Nichols, who brought his bride, Harriet, there about 1840 to "set up housekeeping." On the north side of the road that leads across The Saddle you can still see a pile of stones—all that remains of the cellar hole of their house. A spring is nearby, and on the other side of the road a few more stones mark the site of their barn. From here to the village it's a good five miles by road and a twelve-hundred-foot drop in altitude, so the young couple probably didn't make any unnecessary trips to the store—even in the autumn, when they had to haul barrels of flour and salt and other supplies up the mountain to last through the winter.

Sometimes on an August evening we take a picnic to The Saddle, and as we lie there in the tall grass looking at the heavens and watching the spectacular display of shooting stars, our thoughts turn occasionally to Sherman Nichols and his bride.

Already in August the night air is chilly, with a hint of what is to come, and it occurs to us that their winters must have been unimaginably long.

How many winters they endured up there on The Saddle we don't know. There was a lot more to Sherman's life than clearing meadows and building walls; he served in numerous town and county offices, including two terms as county judge, and after 1884, when Harriet died, he survived for another thirty-six years, residing first with a son and then, when the son died, with a granddaughter, outliving all but one of his seven children. "The air up on The Saddle must be pretty good," Chet Baldwin says with a grin, thinking of his great-grandfather. "He lived to be one hundred years, one month, and one week old."

The air up there *is* good, so is the view—and so, we are bound to admit, are the haunting reminders of Sherman and Harriet Nichols and all the others who worked the land after they were gone. What troubles us now is the difficulty of using this land. It's impractical to buy cattle or sheep to graze there for four or five months of the year, not to mention what it would cost to fence the field or to feed the animals through the winter. Unless you have a shepherd (or are one) you can't risk pasturing sheep on the mountain because of dogs, coyotes, and bear. And you can't bring a loaded wagon down the steep road behind a tractor, so no one is willing to cut the hay. Yet our county extension agent keeps telling us what we instinctively long to do: "Keep it open. Keep it open. We're going to need land like that twenty years from now."

Unless we mow The Saddle before long, brush and trees will take over and it will be impossible to reclaim the land. Wooded, it will be less attractive to the wild animals and birds that are drawn to it now. Which brings us to our dilemma.

Do we mow the high meadow for the same reason they climb Everest—because it's there? That pleases us aesthetically.

Do we give primary consideration to the gasoline we'll have

to burn to cut forty acres of grass? That brings out the con-servationist in us.

Or should we think how forty acres of good open land might benefit the community a generation hence? That speaks to the conscience.

By August, the vegetable garden is going critical. What began, back in April and May, as an orderly succession of compliant rows is out of hand, a runaway situation. For one thing, the weeds are now beyond us; it has been a trial of wills, ours versus theirs, and as usual they have triumphed. Until late July we managed to keep more or less abreast of the pigweed and wild geranium, but this is a race that belongs to the swift, the vigorous, and the determined. Indeed, it is a contest that reminds us of the marathon we sometimes run in our dreams, a fantasy in which we are always late getting off the starting line; the other runners surge ahead, and as the race continues its agonizing pace we see them becoming ever more distant, finally crossing a finish line that seems utterly unattainable. We hear the crowd roar; we watch the spectators file out of the stadium. Night falls and we are still running, alone and cheerless. And that's the way we think of our struggle with the weeds. The only difference is that we have the wit to quit the uneven battle in the garden when there is no longer a chance of keeping up—much less of winning.

So by August the weeds are rampant, challenged only by the squash, of which we unfailingly plant too much of too many varieties. We first become aware of the squash problem when B. says, "Have you seen what the squash is doing." It isn't a question. It is a Red Alert.

Every August it's the same: the acorn and butternut squash run amok. On the south side of the garden enormous vines and leaves are crawling up the bullpen fence; on the north end they are moving ominously close to the road, preparing, no doubt, to stop traffic and smother passing motorists. There have been occasions when we watched ever so closely and actually thought we could *see* squash growing, sliding tentacles outward like a great green octopus, and we are always careful not to get too close to one for fear of what it will do to us. For explosive vine and leaf growth, nothing can touch the winter squashes; all you have to do is drop a few of those innocent-looking flat seeds into the most barren hill and you have taken the first step toward creating a jungle. But zucchini, as we have often remarked, holds the record for vegetable growth. Each evening we peer anxiously beneath the leaves of our two zucchini plants and pick all but the tiniest squashes. Twenty-four hours later without fail, a minimum of seven dark-green objects the size of Goodyear blimps will be found in the undergrowth—enormous bloated things that have to be hauled off by wheelbarrow. And of course no one wants them. Last year our friends Nardi and Tom reported that they could no longer leave their car windows open when they parked on the streets of Hanover; if they did, someone was sure to dump surplus zucchini in their automobile. By August nearly *all* zucchini is surplus zucchini.

Probably we should spend most of the month patrolling the garden, armed with a hatchet for the squash and a hoe for the weeds; that way we might stand a chance of bridling the fecundity that is so rife here. But barn chores and other tasks engage us, and we awake too late to the condition of our plot. Not until we catch sight of Rima the woods-girl flitting silently through the verdant foliage do we notice how much it resembles the rain forest of *Green Mansions.*

In the August garden we reap the follies of our spring enthusiasms—in particular, of too-large plantings of squash, tomatoes, and beans. We never learn. Each year we follow the same tiresome scenario with tomatoes. It is May and we have once again neglected to start our own plants for lack of time, so we buy half a dozen from a local nursery. Six is all we're going to have. Determined not to make the same mistake this year as last, we have taken a blood oath not to set out sixteen of them, which bore roughly a ton and a half of tomatoes. We take our six plants home and put them in the cold frame to await transplanting. A week later, one of us visits another nursery in search of red onions and spies tomato plants that are twice as vigorous as the ones we bought originally. On the theory that some of those first spindly plants are sure to die, six more come home as insurance against loss. And then a friend appears with a cardboard box choked with greenery. (Beware of friends bearing cardboard boxes, we have learned.) He planted too many tomatoes this year, he says, and wants us to have eight or ten of them. They *are* beautiful plants.

So it is that when Memorial Day weekend comes and we set out the tomato plants, twenty of them go in the ground. (None of them will die.) And so it is that when August rolls around we have enough tomatoes to give Heinz a run for its money. We have to take the pickup truck to the garden just to haul them to the house. Our problem, being children of the Depression, is that we can't stand to waste anything or throw anything away; and in the same way that we clean our plates even though we are stuffed, we bring every last tomato into the house to be eaten or canned or fried or pickled, and the following spring find dozens of unconsumed jars of tomatoes glinting reproachfully from the canning cupboard.

August. Sere brown peavines cling to the wire, a few undetected pods—giant now—rattling in the wind, silent rebukes to our failure to pick them, and we glance toward the pole beans and notice that the leaves resemble Brussels lace. The Japanese beetles are out in force. *Popillia japonica* Newman, having arrived in the United States accidentally and unbeckoned in 1916, took nearly sixty years to reach our garden. Recognizing a good thing when they saw one, they decided to stay, and we remember thinking, Well, there goes the neighborhood. Although they are considerably more destructive than Genghis Khan's Mongol hordes, Japanese beetles are not noted for intelligence. Or flying ability. They zip around the garden like spent bronze bullets, caroming off cornstalks and beanpoles, and when not engaged in this aimless bouncing they are busy procreating or devouring bean leaves, or both.

So intent are they upon these sensual gratifications that it is a simple matter to pick them off the plants and drop them into a can of kerosene. It is equally easy to trap them, following a technique first explained to us by our naturalist brother-in-law. After cutting holes three or four inches in diameter in the sides of a one-gallon plastic jug, you hang some bait (geranium blossoms seem to be peculiarly seductive) in the neck of the jug, put an inch or more of water in the bottom of it, and suspend the thing from a pole in the garden. Since Japanese beetles react to geraniums the way violinists respond to a whiff of Tabu, they head immediately for one of the openings in the jug, hit the inside, and—being rotten fliers—fall into the water below. And Japanese beetles are rotten swimmers.

It is relatively easy to dispatch dozens, even hundreds, of these metallic–green–and–brown insects, but anyone who supposes that he will put an end to them has not reckoned with the supply. As with weeds, so with Japanese beetles: they are numerous beyond all counting.

Before the month is out we will be looking nervously over one shoulder for signs of the first frost, but in the meantime it would be unseemly and ungrateful not to remark upon the benisons of the August garden. Surely nothing can compare with a meal made largely of freshly picked corn on the cob, homegrown lettuce, sliced ripe tomatoes, and tender young cucumbers. And we comfort ourself with the thought of how the fruits of our labors—frozen, canned, or stored in the root cellar—will sustain us throughout the winter. Until time, in fact, to set out a few tomato plants.

Now and then, when we are poised to leave home for a few days and must negotiate kennel space for the dog and arrange for someone to milk and feed the goats and tend the sheep, we think how different life would be without animals. And different it would surely be, but ah, how much less enjoyable and interesting. The animals amuse, they entertain, they earn their keep by cropping the pastures, adding motion and life to the landscape, and they manage, without being pedantic about it, to remind us of lessons we so often forget. Asking nothing in return, they offer companionship and affection without conditions. They understand that each day marks a new beginning and that the way to make the most of it is to savor the moment, to rest when weary, to eat when hungry, to take advantage of the sun's warmth or the shade of a maple tree.

The rhythm of the farm animals' lives becomes the rhythm that governs our days, and to a somewhat lesser extent the same is true of dogs. We have a dog named Sandwich, whose daily routine is only slightly less ritualistic than that of an Aztec priest. Now Sandwich is not your run-of-the-mill name for a dog, but that is what she was called when she arrived at our house, and as she showed no disposition to answer to anything else, we left it at that. The name and the dog—a medium-size black animal of multiple ancestry—came from our son, who went away to seek his fortune in the city, leaving behind a horse and Sandwich. At the time, we were not especially eager to have either legacy, but we reasoned that you can always sell a horse, and that we were not the first parents to take on a departing child's dog, in particular a dog that could smile and wag her tail in a circle. (With a strange dog, when the upper lip curls back on one side to expose the teeth, we back away, but with Sandwich the expression occurs when she greets you or is being praised, and is accompanied by a furious circular wagging of the tail. It is definitely a smile.)

She has been with us for seven years now, and we realized this winter that she has reached middle age. There are flecks of gray under her chin and she no longer wants to stay outdoors all day when it's cold, as she once did. Like many dogs we have known, she is a creature of fixed habits. When she goes out to greet the morning, it is a certainty that she will head for the back pasture, travel up the fenceline to the ridge, and—silhouetted against the sky—trot along the path she has worn there with her worried pacing, industriously checking for the scent of intrusions into her territory. When she reaches the line of spruce trees she turns back, heading for another clump of trees on a knoll—a knoll pockmarked with small craters she has dug and the unmarked graves of woodchuck remains. Once she has decided that everything is in order, she comes to the kitchen door, gives us that ingratiating smile, and announces her readiness for breakfast. For the remainder of the day, except when she is sleeping or out on patrol, she takes up a post on the hill overlooking the pond, her nose in the air sniffing the breeze, her motto Eternal Vigilance Is the Price of Liberty.

Sandwich is a country dog, whose world is restricted only by limits she has set herself. Her predecessor, a farm shepherd named Shelley, divided her time traveling back and forth, as we did then, between two vastly different places—a suburb of New York City and a Vermont farm—somehow managing to deal with both. We acquired her after a long search (working dogs having gone out of style, like work) from a farmer in New York State. At the age of six months she was already bringing in the cows every evening and we took to each other on sight. Not long after she joined our household we discovered that she had been chewing on a log in the woodpile and, it turned out, had damaged her esophagus—leaving some scar tissue that prevented her, ever afterward, from eating a normal meal. From that day on, a Waring Blendor accompanied her wherever she went, for she could only swallow food that had been beaten to the consistency of gruel. That was all right as long as she stayed home, but Shelley had been bred and trained to be a herder, and as we were then living in a community where no livestock had been seen for half a century, she kept her hand in by herding schoolchildren. She would follow one or more of them home and, since it was teatime and she was the friendliest and gentlest of dogs, she would inevitably be invited in for a snack. At which point the mother of the child who wanted to adopt her would discover Shelley's weakness: what went down immediately came back up. And before long we would get a call from the local police, who had been through this before with Shelley.

As far as we could determine, her only real enemies were squirrels, and in a neighborhood filled with oak trees her foes were everywhere in evidence. The children delighted in calling her attention to a squirrel lurking under a tree, and it got so that all it took to throw Shelley into a frenzy was to pronounce the first two letters of the hated word—"s-q-"—and she would fly to the nearest window to see where it was. For hours on end she sat in the living room peering through the picture window, and when a squirrel came in view, bent upon some fool's errand, her muscles tensed, she began to quiver, and at last—unable to stand the suspense—she leaped straight at the glass, never learning that an attack on a squirrel from inside the house produced headache and humiliation.

With people, on the other hand, she was all love and trust: she would sit up, put her front paws in your hand, and while you scratched her white ruff, look soulfully into your eyes and deliver a simple, heart-melting gesture. She would lick your wrist—just once, slowly, and ever so gently—in a manner that revealed all there was to know about love between two creatures.

Shelley came close to mastering the art of communication. She had a brown beach towel for a bed, and on evenings when we entertained guests too late, she would suddenly prance into the living room, dragging the towel behind her, to let everyone know it was bedtime. When she had done something of which she was ashamed she confessed her sin by appearing with an abashed, downcast look that was a dead giveaway before you even suspected trouble. Her barks were informative: there was a muffled woof that said the noise outside was not worth worrying about; a fierce, deep-throated barking that heralded an approaching visitor; a single, sharp yelp that caused us to leap from bed in the middle of the night because it meant she had to go out, desperately, that very minute; and occasionally a near-hysterical barking that indicated a situation completely out of hand, as it was one morning when we found her in the kitchen, leaping at a bat that was swooping back and forth just beyond reach.

Shelley lived to the age of fourteen and ironically it was not the damaged esophagus that did her in but tired kidneys. We had her put to sleep, wrapped her in the brown towel she loved, and buried her in a high pasture that looks out over the valley. We knew she would prefer that to a resting place in suburbia: in our mind's eye she walks with us there still, prancing ahead, stepping high like a circus pony, head up, her tail like a plume in the wind, certain that she will spy a squirrel.

Like Shelley, Sandwich is a partial cripple. Before she came to live with us she had been run over by a car and for a time was paralyzed and blind. Thanks to the unwillingness of our son and Dr. Bob, the veterinarian, to give up on her, she survived, but she has imperfect vision. That, and another accident, cured her of ever leaving the place. Once, when we were away, she was riding in the box of a friend's pickup truck and fell out when it hit a bump. She picked herself up, trotted purposefully back to our house, and has never again left, on the assumption that if you go a-roaming there's no telling what may happen to you. She is content to occupy her days with the familiar, with what she can smell or dimly see, dedicated to the proposition that if you keep your house in order, remain cheerful, and patrol the boundaries vigilantly, all will be right with the world.

It was a soft summer night, moonless and velvety black, with the air balmy and still. About two o'clock a muffled scream came from the other side of the bed.

"What's the matter?"

"Something just brushed across my face!" B. announced.

"Nonsense. You were just dreaming. Go back to sleep."

Upon which we sensed, rather than saw, a sinister black shape swoop past, clearing the bedclothes by about six inches. We held a brief conference under the sheet to determine which of us should deal with the problem. The decision was that it was a man's job.

By now the intruder had flapped into the upstairs sitting room. We crept out of bed, turned on a light, flattened ourself against the doorframe like the heavy in a Grade B movie, peered down the narrow hall to make sure nothing was coming, and in three giant lunges made it to the sitting room and slammed the door shut. We stood there for a minute, breathing hard, then opened the door a crack, reached in, and turned on the light in case the flying object was afraid of the dark, and went in search of something with which to catch it.

Now there are various methods of capturing or dispatching bats—the technique used being in direct ratio to the courage of the pursuer. We once watched our old friend Sted Aldrich pick a bat off the window screen and, with the thumb and forefinger of each hand, hold its wings outstretched while the bat made nasty clicking sounds. "Don't know why you'd want to get rid of him," Sted said. "He'll catch a few flies." And Bill Barrows caught a bat for us by stealing up on it ever so quietly from behind while it was resting. He had a towel twisted around one hand and, reaching out slowly, picked the bat off the ceiling, wrapped it up, carried it downstairs, and released it outside.

When we think of bats we remember how B., when the children were small, went with a group of mothers and their youngsters to visit Bat Cave, up on the mountain. Entering the cave, it seemed a lark; but coming out she could see, silhouetted against the sky, bats beyond all counting, passing simultaneously through the same small opening.

The only occasion on which we personally attempted to catch, rather than dispose of, a bat was that August night we were discussing, when we could find no suitable weapon and had to settle for the mosquito netting from our daughter's bassinet. With a wire coat hanger we fashioned a net of sorts and, so armed, returned cautiously to the sitting room, where the bat was still flying. As one who finds it extremely unnerving to enter a room where a bat is winging about, we opened the door ever so slowly—just a bit—and, seeing nothing, opened it wider and . . . *Watch out! That bat's making a power dive at us!* We slammed the door and, breathing hard again, went into the bedroom to tell B. that the bat had just made a power dive at us and to ask if she knew any other way of getting into the room. She did not. Back we went to try again. This time we entered the room just as the bat was making its turn at the other end.

We have no desire to resurrect the controversy between short and tall people that consumed so many Americans not long ago, but we can state unequivocally that short people are in far less danger from flying bats than tall people. Consider. It was an old house. The ceiling in the room was six feet five inches off the floor—maybe a fraction less. We stand six feet three inches—maybe a hair more. And what occupied our thoughts that night, as it has on similar occasions since, was that only the most exceptional bat, a skillful veteran with an uncanny sense of timing and accuracy, could possibly negotiate the two-inch clearance between the top of our head and the ceiling of the room. Oh, we know about bat radar. But we are skeptical of technology in general and of bat technology in particular. What if the radar isn't properly tuned? What if the bat has forgotten to get new batteries, or whatever operates the system? No, our watchword when it comes to bats is never to rely on *their* sensory mechanism to avoid a collision. So, for what seemed an eternity we stood there in the half-crouch of a sumo wrestler, clad in a ski hat and pajama pants, swinging this homemade bat-net each time it flew by, and all to no avail. For as suddenly as it had appeared, it vanished. It simply flew out of sight behind the big wing chair and was no more. Perhaps it's fainted or had a heart attack, we thought as we waited for it to reemerge. After an appropriate delay we tiptoed over to the wing chair, looked behind it, under it, and saw nothing. Search as we might, we could find no trace of any bat. A month later, when someone was cleaning the room, the bat crawled from behind a radiator and flew out an open window.

That old house was bat-prone. On one memorable night a bat showed up and sent B.'s mother screaming from the room. She slammed the door behind her and held it closed so the bat couldn't get out. Neither could her sister, of course, who was trying frantically to open the door and escape while B.'s mother held it shut in a grip of steel. She had her eyes closed, and thought the bat was trying to open the door.

The worst time ever was the summer we had at least one bat in our bedroom every night for a week. It reached the point where we slept (if you can call lying in the dark with your eyes and ears open sleeping) with a tennis racquet at our side, and whenever we heard the unmistakable flutter of wings we would reach for the racquet, roll out of bed, and in the same motion hit the bat with an overhead backhand smash. It took a while to discover that they were coming into the house through a hole in the screening in an attic louver and working their way into the bedroom through the ceiling, alongside the beams. After we repaired the screen and stuffed every nook and cranny with steel wool, the nightly visitations ended.

In fact, we hadn't thought about bats for some time until this spring. One evening the two of us were sitting at the kitchen table after dinner, talking, when suddenly—out of nowhere—a bat flew over our heads. There was too much china and glassware around to permit the use of a tennis racquet, so we resorted to our Preferred Method—also known as the Coward's Way Out, or Lead Kindly Light. Over the years it has proved to be about 75 percent effective and on that April night it worked. The trick is to isolate the bat in a room adjacent to an outside door; then, after turning out all the lights in the house, to turn on an outside light or flashlight, open the door, and hope that it will fly to the light. (We generally try to get another member of the family to go through the house, turning off lights, while we stand guard outside to make sure the bat comes through the door.)

So if you should come upon us some summer evening, standing outside a darkened house, aiming an expectant look and a flashlight at the kitchen door, speak kindly, stranger. Don't jump to the conclusion that we're ready for the funny farm. We're fighting bats, that's all, and this happens to be the way we like to do it.

It must have been ten years ago when Tony announced that he and two partners were buying a farm in Vermont, somewhere near Randolph. One look at Tony tells you he's spent his entire life in New York City, and the thought of him emerging from the rented Thunderbird and walking through the barnyard in a bright-yellow sweater, gray flannels, and loafers was too much.

"What will you do with it?" we asked. "Spend the summers there? And who's going to farm it for you?"

A look of disbelief came over his face.

"Farm it? Are you kidding? I've never even seen the place. We're just going to hold on till the interstate's finished. Then it should be worth a bundle."

By now it probably is.

For Tony and his partners, it was just another investment, but for Vermont, it meant one less farm. Land is where a lot of the smart money has been going for a decade or two, and in recent years enough smart foreign money—attracted by our stable government and cheap dollars—has gone that way to buy an estimated 3 to 5 million acres of the U.S.A. After all, the price of farmland has been increasing at two and a half times the rate of inflation, and how can you beat that?

The gap that separates country and city is reflected in many ways, but particularly in the city folks' lack of concern for the dwindling number of farms and the disappearance of open space. All too many of them regard food as something you get at the supermarket—frozen, canned, or wrapped in plastic—and open space as somewhere else.

We see food in terms of the family and farm that produced

it; we see the nurturing and toil and occasional heartbreak that went into its growth. We see open land as something to elevate the human spirit; we see it also as the farm being auctioned to become something it was never intended to be, and we wonder how many mouths will go unfed a few years or a generation hence because that farm and many like it have vanished.

Unless you happen to be a farmer and appreciate what the loss of even a hundred acres of rich bottomland means, chances are you haven't paid much attention to what's been going on. Most of us are so mesmerized by the possibilities for doom threatening the nation that almost no one talks about what may be the most fateful problem of all. This is our failure to protect and preserve the greatest, most productive farmland possessed by any nation on the face of the earth— a failure compounded by our unwillingness as a society to recognize the farmer's needs and his worth.

The main reason for our own concern about husbandry is an uneasy feeling that we will awake on some future morning to find that there is not enough food to go around. While we Americans continue to pave over our land, selling off the best and most productive to developers and builders, we do little to encourage the farmer to keep going. We are ignoring him out of existence. Farming, as Gene Logsdon reminded us recently, is a lot more than a business—it's "a calling, a sort of art demanding a certain discipline and constancy all its own." Discipline and constancy—we like that. Not many people are up to the hours and the work demanded of farmers. Yet we read that the reason farm income was higher in 1978 was that *for the fourth year in a row farmers earned more from nonfarm jobs than from farm work.* What a terrible indictment of our society this is! Can you imagine lawyers or civil servants or any group, for that matter, being forced to earn a majority of their income elsewhere in order to support their chosen profession? And what other group of workers is so essential to our well-being, our survival?

Off there in the distance, coming closer all the time, we

hear the tramp of feet. The population bomb, agent of man's undoing, keeps ticking as he continues to reproduce himself beyond what the resources of this planet can sustain. Loren Eiseley once portrayed *Homo sapiens,* the most aggressive carnivore the world has ever known, appearing with his flint ax and his flaming torch at the edge of the grasslands below the last ice sheet, and seeing meadows alive with seemingly inexhaustible herds of game. Soon man appropriated the animal kingdom's vast stores of protein for his own until the great herds were at last destroyed. And then, at some remote moment in time, some equally remote ancestor of ours plucked a fistful of grass seed, held it contemplatively, and in that instant, Eiseley writes, "the golden towers of man, his swarming millions, his turning wheels, the vast learning of his packed libraries . . . glimmer[ed] dimly there in the ancestor of wheat, a few seeds held in a muddy hand." So, from hunting, *Homo sapiens* turned to agriculture, which would fuel his metabolism and support the growing human population and the civilization that accompanied it.

Today more than 4 billion people depend for life on the earth's cropland, grassland, fisheries, and forests, but we are consuming all of them faster than they can be replenished. And the bomb keeps ticking, ticking. Twenty years hence there will be 6 billion mouths to feed from the same, but diminished, resources.

Vermont affords a classic example of what is occurring all over rural America. Most farmers simply aren't in the same economic ball game as the rest of the nation. As William Darrow, Vermont's commissioner of agriculture, puts it, farming "is sort of forgotten . . . like a runt pig. A farmer with forty cows is making an average of $7800 a year. He probably works a minimum of ten hours a day, seven days a week—it comes out to 3500 hours a year at about $2.25 an hour. When you see a $30,000-a-year supermarket manager complain to a $10,000-a-year sales clerk about the cost of food, when the food was produced by a $7800-a-year farmer, it makes you wonder why there are any farmers left at all."

Look at it another way—through the eyes of an elderly farmer who has no pension plan, no retirement benefits, no sons who are willing to take over the farm. When he can get $2000 or $3000 an acre for his land, who can blame him for selling out after a lifetime of hard work? The tragedy is that speculation in land has pushed its price beyond the reach of young would-be farmers. Today it takes a minimum of $300,000 to purchase the land, the machinery, and the livestock to set up that forty-cow herd Darrow is talking about. And even if a prospective farmer has the $300,000, why should he work a ten-hour day, seven days a week, for $7800 when he could put the money into Treasury bonds that will yield $35,000 a year without his having to lift a finger?

In Vermont, really good farmland has always been in short supply, but in thirty years' time we've seen the acreage devoted to agriculture drop from almost 6 million to 1.4 million, from 19,000 farms covering 60 percent of the state to 3500 farms occupying 25 percent of the state. And now, having watched all that land disappear from productive use, we suddenly have to face up to the possibility of feeding ourselves. If we don't, we're in for big trouble. The problem, you see, is that we have tended over the years to depend more and more upon states like California for our food, with the result that Vermont now imports 85 percent of what it eats. But a few people here—among them, William Darrow—have been asking how much longer we dare count on someone else to feed us. It has been reported that by the year 2000, California will have so many people it won't be able to export any food. But the biggest story coming out of the richest and most populous state in the Union concerns water. Irrigated land in the West produces one-fourth of all agricultural products in the United States, but every year they have to go deeper to find water and pay more to bring it to the surface. So how the Sunbelt copes with its declining water table in the months and years ahead is going to affect how well the rest of us eat—unless we are prepared to do something about our own situation.

———

There are two ways to increase food production. One is to increase your yield per acre. The other is to increase the amount of acreage you have in production. And here we hit the horns of the dilemma. Since World War II we have been counting on an agricultural revolution to provide us with cheap food and to save the world from hunger. We've gotten our cheap food, all right, and we've kept millions of people from starving, but at a price. In the process we have eliminated hundreds of thousands of America's family farms and pushed many of those farm families into the city and onto welfare rolls. And the revolution isn't running as smoothly as it once was: capital- and energy-intensive, it relies heavily on chemical fertilizers, pesticides, herbicides, and monocultural systems that eventually deplete the soil. Since 1972, after nearly three decades of rising productivity, crop yields in America have been steadily declining.

At the same time, we have been losing farmland just as steadily—3 million acres a year, nationwide, between 1967 and 1975—losing it to Tony and other investors, to housing, to industry, to shopping malls, to highways, to dams. And when it's gone, it's gone.

Not until we stop thinking of land as a commodity will we be on our way to solving this problem. Indeed, the only way to save what is left of our farmland, our most precious communal heritage, is for society to care enough about it to do something. James Clark, a Maryland senator and dairy farmer, observed not long ago: "I have a theory which I have developed over the years . . . about getting things done in a representative democracy. By the time 80 percent of the people realize something has to be done, it is generally too late to do it. I think that is exactly where we stand with saving farmland." Clark urges action at the local level, since the federal government won't recognize the problem in time to do anything about it.

Recently we flew across the continental United States and saw once again the awesome sight of those endless fields out in the heartland, stretching bountifully to the horizon and beyond. By comparison, the small piece of land that most Vermonters have seems inconsequential and insignificant, and you wonder what difference it would make if most of the farmland that is left in New England were to be abandoned to the developers.

Then we saw, on a side street in Berkeley, California, what the people at the Farallones Institute have done with a small, one-family house on an average-size city lot. Not an inch of soil is wasted on lawn. Alfalfa—which is fed to the rabbits and chickens—grows in front of the house, right to the curb. Strawberries, rhubarb, onions, and half a dozen other plants are everywhere you look in one of the side yards. The entire backyard is filled with a vegetable garden, fruit trees, a small pond where fish are raised, and beehives. In the other side yard, rabbits are grown for meat and chickens for their eggs. An attached greenhouse provides fresh produce year-round and helps to heat the house.

This doesn't begin to do justice to the imaginative, energy-saving experiments that are also going on there, but it suggested to us what can be done—indeed, what may soon *have* to be done—with a tiny piece of land on a city street. If we have learned nothing else from our own modest experience with farming, it is to care about and for the land, for neither our crops nor our animals nor our children's children will be any better than the soil that nurtures them.

In Europe, where they had far less land to begin with, they have never been so prodigal with it. The impression one gets in England and Wales, for example, is of endless farmland, covered with cattle and sheep, the hills a wondrous checkerboard of hedgerows, pasture, and meadows. And in fact, some 73 percent of the countryside there *is* farmland—is, because the British have been determined to keep it that way. If someone wants to develop a piece of agricultural land in Great Britain, he must first go to the local planning authority, which can approve or deny the request. If approval is granted, and if the development involves more than ten acres, the Ministry of Agriculture may speak for the land, as it were, by lodging an objection to the development. If this occurs, the matter is re-solved by the Secretary of State for the Environment, who has final jurisdiction. If the developer's request is turned down on environmental grounds, that's the end of it—the land remains in agriculture.

No such problems would have occurred to the Americans who were here before us, of course. Their attitude toward the land, which Tony and his partners would never understand, was expressed by a Blackfoot chief at a treaty council. "As long as the sun shines and the waters flow," the Indian stated, "this land will be here to give life to man and animals. We cannot sell the lives of men or animals; therefore we cannot sell this land. It was put here for us by the Great Spirit and we cannot sell it because it does not belong to us."

If you see us glancing apprehensively over our shoulder these days, lay it to the hurricane that came our way some years ago. The storm was unusual in that it struck early in August, before the traditional hurricane season of September, but it was no less cruel for the premature appearance. Through no wish of our own, we have had intimate relations with an astonishingly large number of hurricanes—one at sea in a small ship, another on a Revolutionary War battlefield, several in cities and suburbs, others in the open country—and we can testify that while each storm differed in character from the others, each was terrifying in its own way. Which is the reason we always view the coming of September with heightened awareness of the skies.

Weather must have made it very easy to believe in God and the Devil in those simpler times when mankind's preoccupation was almost solely with the land or the sea. Nothing, on the one hand, could bring such bounty and rejoicing; nothing, on the other, could produce such devastation and suffering. And even today, for all our confidence that we have somehow triumphed over nature, we are as helpless as babes when the gods are wrathful. In the country, weather is a constant companion, the one item not on the balance sheet that can make or break a farmer, no matter how skilled or hard working he is. It is the great unpredictable. On our farm, for instance, in a decade's time we have lost cows to lightning on three separate occasions, and we seldom hear the rumble of approaching thunder in the night without wondering how soon the storm will be upon us, or if it will pass us by.

In August 1976, when we heard of Hurricane Belle's approach, our concern was for other members of the family. Mother had rented a cottage on Martha's Vineyard and the Graysons were with her; the night the storm was supposed to hit there we called, worried, to ask what preparations had been made, and were relieved to learn that they had spent the day battening down, nailing shutters closed, stocking up on food and bottled water. Fortunately for them, the storm never hit the Vineyard; unhappily for us, it changed course during the night and headed north and west into Vermont, awakening us in the hour before dawn with a roar like that of an angry bull. We could hear the wind thundering toward us from miles off, the noise building into a deafening crescendo before it hit the house like a giant wave, shaking it until the rain came—rain in unimaginable quantities, torrents of water that beat on the roof and the windows in sheets, flooding the eaves troughs in less than a minute.

By morning the gale had passed and the sun reached through the clouds, but when we went outside we heard a different roar—a strange, unaccustomed sound that came from the direction of the upper farm. For a moment we couldn't identify it; then it came to us. It was the stream that flows down the valley from Kirby Hollow—normally, in August, an anemic little creek that potters lazily down the mountainside. In the span of perhaps three hours, the anemic little creek had become a raging torrent that could not be contained by a six-foot culvert, had burst from its bed to destroy half a mile of our farm road and four bridges, and plummeted downhill to surge over the town road, gouging out canyons six or eight feet deep before subsiding into its course again. By the time we saw it, it was still an angry, swollen river, but by then the worst of the damage had been done. Up at the other end of the Hollow, enormous landslides had ripped the skin right off the mountainside, taking huge trees and every shred of growth off the hill, stripping it down to bedrock. From miles around came horror stories of people nearly killed, roads demolished, livestock stranded, barns and houses and automobiles swept away by dirty, boiling streams that left in their wake mountains of debris—tangled masses of trees and mud and rock.

What occupied our thoughts during the next few weeks was the half mile of farm road and the bridges that had been wiped out—our only access to the upper farm and the woods beyond. Then we heard that the president had declared our county a disaster area, and that a Disaster Assistance Center was open in Rutland to help those who had been affected by the storm. Off we drove to Rutland.

That tale is quickly told. A coordinator greeted us, handed us a Disaster Assistance Registration Form to fill out, and said that representatives from several agencies were there in the building. We should talk with them, he went on, and see what sort of help we qualified for.

We began with the Farmers Home Administration (FHA) and asked if we could obtain a loan. With a look of surprise, the FHA man said, "We have no disaster program. I don't know why they sent you here."

We reported this comment to the coordinator, who said, "What do they mean they don't have a program? The President declares this a disaster area and these guys aren't going to go along with him?"

Our next stop was the Small Business Administration (SBA), where a man gave us Forms 739, 5C, 394, 1018, 601, and 1123 to fill out. One of these documents assured us that no creditor could discriminate against us on the basis of our sex or marital status. Another repeated this assurance and, for good measure, added race, color, and national origin. Another form threatened us with prison or a $5000 fine or both if we made a false statement. Another said we could obtain the assistance of an attorney, accountant, appraiser, or engineer when applying for a loan. Another required us to swear that no one in the family had been arrested in connection with a riot or civil disorder. And finally, there was a form for describing the property damage. Just as we were about to complete it, the SBA man told us we did not qualify for assistance.

"Why?" we asked.

"Because," he replied, "this is a business loan, and a farm is not a business."

We went on to the next office. There, a man from the Disaster Grant Program told us we did not qualify for a grant.

"Why?" we asked.

"Because," he replied, "grants are only for individuals, and you operate a business."

"What business?"

"A farm," he said.

At the IRS office a man gave us a copy of the rules governing casualty losses and told us how to report them on Form 1040.

A Red Cross lady who was sitting in the hall volunteered the information that she didn't live in Rutland. "I just travel around," she said, "wherever there's a disaster."

At the last, the assistance we got came not from any of these agencies, but through local farmers who are elected to work with Agriculture Department officials in our county—men who know, and care, what happens in the community. Our experience with the others persuaded us that it's all very well for the President to declare a region a disaster area, but the victims had better not count on much relief from the Washington bureaucrats. The only disaster they'd recognize would be the loss of those forms.

Since Charles Darwin's day the human race has made some headway in its understanding of man and the animal kingdom. But progress did not begin immediately. Shortly after publication of *On the Origin of Species,* the wife of the Bishop of Worcester learned what the book was about and exclaimed: "Descended from the apes! Let us hope it is not true, but if it is, let us pray that it will not become generally known."

Humans, scientists now realize, have no monopoly on communicating with one another. In recent years, biologists have discovered that whales apparently converse across miles of deep ocean. (No one has figured out what they are saying, but we suppose that these gregarious creatures, being mammals, are simply telling their friends to have a nice day.) Wolves in a pack, who often hunt singly over a large area at night, howl to keep in touch when they are separated; and because they need all their strength for survival and cannot afford to waste it on fighting other packs, also howl to warn rivals to keep a proper distance. Most songbirds sing for practical reasons, too—to drive away competitors and to woo their mates (although certain varieties, it is reassuring to note, just happen to like music, and are diligent about practicing their scales).

For what the ethologists may make of it, we observe that our farm animals are continually expressing ideas and emotions. As the neighbors will tell you, chore time at our place sounds like a German band that is badly out of tune; all it takes to set off the caterwauling and braying is for one of us to appear at the barn door. Mamie, the cat, whose voice is even more unfortunate than her looks, greets us with a raspy accu-

sation of tardiness. From inside the barn comes the testy blat-
ting of goats. Three male sheep peer through the fence with
an expression that blends criticism and hope, two young bari-
tones singing counterpoint to the *basso profundo* of the old
ram. From behind the barn one hears the baa-ing of the ewes,
from the far pasture the bellow of a cow. Each wants to be
fed—first. Each is impatient. Each has a melancholy tale of
privation and special need to report.

Goats, we have found, express themselves in various
ways—almost none of them compatible with the wishes of the
goatkeeper. We have a goat named Dill, who has the bland,
expressionless face of a Madison Avenue bus driver, but it is
an appearance of fake respectability. With the amiable fraudu-
lence of a conjurer who can make things seem what they are
not, she will look you straight in the eye while plotting some
outrageous piece of deviltry. You know there is mischief
afoot. She knows it. But she is capable of such guile there is no
telling what form the mischief will take—only that it will
occur, and when you least expect it.

We doubt if any serious psychological studies of goats have
been undertaken, but we would like to put our little flock up
for observation. Dill, for example, has an abnormal fear of
strangers (xenophobia). She regards every outsider as a security risk, a fifth columnist intent on overthrowing the small
republic of which she is president, and we have watched her
sail effortlessly over a four-foot-high gate, from a standing
start, because she didn't care to have Dr. Bob, our veterinarian, join her in the pen. Our billy goat, Phoenix, can't stand to
be left alone (autophobia). His manner of expressing this is an
ear-shattering wail that sounds like "Wow–oh-wow-wow-
oh-wow!" repeated incessantly until someone—man or beast
—joins him. Popover, the other doe in the barn, is a hypochon-
driac with an acute fear of pain (algophobia). Now the fact is
that she has never suffered any pain whatever but from the
way she glances apprehensively over one shoulder and blats
pitifully, you know she expects the worst.

———

If the coats are anxiety-ridden, Mamie the cat positively exudes confidence. Despite evidence to the contrary, she has complete faith that things will turn out right. Someone cut off her tail before we acquired her as a kitten, yet she is affectionate and utterly trusting, and wears the stub without shame, realizing that she is an ugly daughter who didn't get her mother's good looks. Her brindled coat would give any other cat an inferiority complex, but Mamie has adopted an insouciant air, lets her tongue hang out about a quarter of an inch, and you will see her trotting by, bent upon some feline errand, the small pink lozenge of a tongue protruding ever so slightly.

Mamie has had the worst luck with kittens of any cat we know. Three years ago she and her mother, Goldie, had litters at the same time. As it happened, we had a surplus of barn cats then, and were delighted to give away two of Goldie's offspring. The trouble was that Goldie was not only top cat in the barn, and Mamie's mother to boot, but she operated on the assumption that anything she wanted, she should have. So she abducted two of Mamie's kittens to replace the ones she had lost. It was the first time we knew Goldie could count: she had had four to start with, and, by George, she meant to have four. Mamie, who lived in awe of her parent, adjusted to the realities of the situation, but she never again let her remaining kitten leave her side. Whenever we saw the two of them, they were curled up together; Mamie had obviously told the kitten about the ogre that would carry her off if she strayed. Before long Mamie and Goldie arrived at a *modus vivendi:* they began taking turns nursing their combined families. Whether there was a system to the rotation, we never discovered, but there was no doubt that they had worked out an accommodation of some sort so that one could take an occasional day off while the other fed the kittens.

That was the beginning of a long losing streak for Mamie. She had two kittens the next year and, being wary of what might happen to them, led them into a long storm drain and hid them. The difficulty was that the kittens tried to find their way out at the wrong end of the pipe and got stuck in an elbow eight feet below the barn floor, from which predicament it was impossible to extricate them. It was one of the darkest moments in the history of the barn—not unlike having a pair of miners hopelessly trapped in an inaccessible shaft—and finally we took the only step possible and sealed the pipe, knowing it was kinder to kill them quickly than to let them starve.

The following year we were certain that Mamie had had kittens, but we couldn't find them. They were located at last in the hay overhead, both of them dead. The yellow tomcat known as Evil Knievel had killed them. Now this particular cat was one of Goldie's offspring, and because no one had ever managed to get close to him, he was feral—wily, mean, blessed with at least nine lives. He had eluded a neighbor's efforts to shoot him; he had gotten a paw caught in a trap intended for woodchucks and somehow pulled it out—an experience that left him with a slight limp; and for a year we tried every ruse we could think of to lure him into a cage so the vet could put him to sleep. Through the summer, B. patiently kept moving a dish of milk closer and closer to the cage and, at last, into it, and one day she caught him inside, slammed the door shut, and had a ferocious, half-berserk cat behind bars. Our friend Perry happened by the barn just then, volunteered to deliver Evil to the vet, and loaded the cage into his pickup.

An hour later Perry returned with an empty cage and a story we could have predicted. "Just as I was lifting the cage out of the truck," he said ruefully, "that yellow cat squirted out between the bars and before I knew what was happening, he was gone. But don't worry," Perry added, "he'll never find his way home from eight miles away."

This summer, when the ever-optimistic Mamie had her three kittens—one yellow, one black, one gray—there were no other cats in the barn and they had the run of the place. But hardly a day passes that we don't look down the road half-expecting Evil to come limping around the bend.

After owning Guernseys, it took us a while to accept the Herefords' preference for staying outdoors in almost all weather. They seldom went into the open shed unless there was a cold rain; then they would lie inside, peering out at the world, so that what you saw on a dark, wet December morning was a sea of white faces punctuating the gloom of the barn. Now the shed is empty; so is the side-hill pasture, where they used to lie contented and uncomplaining at ten below zero, their breath forming miniature clouds of white in the dawn light. The cows and calves are no longer here; the herd has been sold to a farmer in Maine; and although the animals have been gone for six months there are ghosts on the place that will not be exorcised.

All small farms know a similitude of difficulties, and these days they operate ever closer to the brink of extinction. Held together figuratively (and sometimes almost literally) with baler twine, it is only a question of which knot will prove the weakest. In our case, there was not enough productive land to support the array of machines needed for an operation that was not small enough to manage without such equipment. Add to this the fact that the price you could ask for beef animals never rose in proportion to the cost of what you had to buy—grain, gasoline and oil, fertilizer, seed, baler twine, parts, repairs—and the problems were almost insurmountable. The two of us could have held our own with a small herd of registered beef cattle and made it a rewarding adjunct to another occupation. On a limited scale, this sort of operation can satisfy many needs—physical, intellectual, spiritual—while supplying a source of food and keeping land open and productive. But we could not handle it alone because of other demands on our time, and unhappily a small farm operation of the kind we had cannot support a full-time employee and make money.

What you begin to realize, after you've owned cattle for a while—especially if you're fortunate enough to have a rather small, select herd of animals maintained as breeding stock—is that each one has its own personality, its distinctive characteristics. At first we started naming cows for favorite friends, but we soon learned how awkward it was to tell Roz and Milly and Betty, when they inquired good-humoredly after their namesakes, that Roz and Milly and Betty had been killed by lightning; or to explain to Louise that Louise the cow had split herself on the ice and was sent to the knacker. Even so, some of the old cows remained in the herd almost to the end—sentimental favorites whose truly useful days were over but who, nevertheless, represented something important to us—a sense of continuity from the early days, and pride that some of our first decisions hadn't been so bad, after all. We couldn't bring ourselves to let the old 5X cow go until the last; she was one of the best mothers in the herd, the best-dispositioned animal we ever had, and even when she was so lame she could hardly walk, she still produced a better calf than two-thirds of the other cows. She came from our friends Wib and Marg Donaldson of Louada Farms in Ontario, as did another cow that proved to be a picture-perfect example of the breed; every professional who came to see the herd wanted to take that 272 cow home.

The longer we had the animals, the more we could see the definite individual and family traits, handed down from one generation to another. The 12A cow, daughter of a Penn State bull, was a loner, always off by herself, and she was a distinctive-looking animal with fluffy white ears. Her offspring were carbon copies—inevitably alone, easy to spot because of those same white ears. Some of the best cows we had came from our friend Charlie Heckler; they were related to each other, they looked alike, they were excellent milkers, good mothers, and they were gentle and easygoing. Until you tried to load them onto a truck. Then you could count on a real fight. When they first arrived to join the herd there were three of them, and they barged in like roughnecks from the next block, knocking heads in all directions to let the resident cows know who was going to be running things from then on. That very first day the 36 cow, who became our favorite, announced her primacy by displacing the old boss cow at once, and there was never again the slightest doubt who was in charge.

She was an unusual-looking cow, 36 was—huge, with soulful eyes and a Roman nose—and she was as alert as a hawk, always on guard, always first on the scene of a crisis or anything out of the ordinary. In fact, she was so eager to be ahead of all the other cows that she occasionally forgot her family responsibilities. Once, when we were moving the herd from the upper farm to winter quarters in the valley, 36 took off in the lead as usual and thundered down the road through the woods, not realizing that her calf had been left behind. (She was a positive thinker and undoubtedly assumed that the calf would follow as it was supposed to do.) It was late when we saw what had happened, so we decided to leave the calf in the corral on the upper farm overnight and pick it up in the truck next morning. But next morning, when we checked the herd, 36 was gone. She had cleared a forty-two-inch fence, found her way up the mountain road in the darkness, and was waiting outside the corral when we arrived to pick up the calf.

The business of raising registered animals is a world unto itself. You learn it slowly and mostly by experience, and you learn as you go that there are people in it you can trust and some you can't. You find that some breeders level with you about their animals' bad points, along with the good; they're the people who want you to come back again to buy, and you do. Then there are those whose only interest is in making a quick sale, and you learn to watch out for them. You buy two cows from a Yankee trader and discover that you really got only one, for all intents and purposes; each animal has a breeding problem and produces a calf only every other year. So you become wary—each year looking a little more closely at what is offered, each year wondering a bit more about the sellers' motives.

You learn too about the show world and how it can have as many con artists and bunco men as a carnival. You find out about the herdsmen who resort to a variety of cosmetic tricks to make an animal appear what it isn't; you hear of the fellow who gave shots to a rival's animals to make them logy and half-sick for the judging. You realize that some of the big prices paid for cows weren't really paid; that A gave top dollar for B's heifer at one sale, so B gives top dollar for A's heifer at a sale three weeks later. It dawns on you that no money really changed hands, that it was all part of a phony scheme to build up a particular bull's progeny records.

But this is not what it's all about, of course. You weren't really in it for the shows or money but for the satisfaction of raising superior animals that would be a credit to any farm. And you take pride in knowing that the herd you built so carefully was one of the best around. You made a lot of good friends, you learned something new almost every day, and you wouldn't trade the experience for anything. As a matter of fact, when spring comes, you might just head up the road to see if Everett Fillgate has a couple of those beautiful heifer calves for sale.

There is doubtless an element of truth to the proposition fostered by hunters that a deer herd is menaced as much by overpopulation and its attendant hardships as by hunting. And slow starvation during a hard winter, when there is not enough browse, is certainly far crueler for the animals than a quick death from a bullet. What strikes us as curious, however, is that so few humans apply the same logic to their own propensity for procreation, that they worry so little about the exploding human race and so much about the animals they want to kill. Perhaps the deer and the bear should have a voice in the discussion.

We own some woodland that we decided, many years ago, to keep open to the public for hunting and fishing. The decision was not an easy one to make—then or in the succeeding years. There are deer, bear, raccoon, rabbits, and numerous other small animals on the land, along with partridge, wild turkey, and woodcock, and we have even seen several fisher and a golden eagle—both protected species. We like knowing that the animals are there and have no wish or need to shoot them; but we also realize that many people in the community have hunted this land for generations—some of them, even today, with a pressing need to obtain meat for the table. Each passing year has seen the posting of more land in the valley, and today our woods are one of the few remaining places in this locale where a man may hunt. So, for various reasons, the desire to let people enjoy and benefit from the land has consistently outweighed other considerations.

Nowadays we close the gate to prevent damage to the woods' roads from jeeps and trucks. We like to think that anyone sturdy enough to prowl the mountain from dawn to dusk ought to be able to get a deer out of the forest without a vehicle. We wince every time we see the carcass of a deer or bear coming down the road lashed to the trunk of a car, but the results of keeping the land open have otherwise been satisfactory. (Ironically, though, our original purpose of enabling townspeople to hunt in the woods has failed. The pressure on unposted land has increased geometrically, bringing parties of hunters from as far afield as Pennsylvania, and we are told by local friends that they're afraid to use our land during deer season because of the army of out-of-staters roaming the woods.) Every year we see many of the same faces—men almost uniformly courteous, grateful for the opportunity of getting into some fairly wild country, and every fall brings smiling faces to our door, asking permission to hunt, or simply to walk the land. There are the occasional bad eggs, of course—those who shoot at the buildings and knock down pasture fences—but they are a minority, and for the most part we have no trouble whatever.

Our quarrel in this matter of keeping land open is not with the hunters but with the state. On the morning of the opening of deer season some years ago we decided to count the out-of-state hunters and concluded that there were at least fifty-five of them in the woods at that particular time. This figure did not include resident hunters, or other hunters who came on other days later that year or in other seasons. Even so, by the most conservative reckoning—using only a figure of fifty-five out-of-state hunters—the economics of deer hunting on our land look like a free ride for somebody—and it isn't us. The state of Vermont receives $40 for each nonresident hunting license. Multiplied by fifty-five, this means that the state collected at least $2200 for that one morning's count of hunters. To put it another way, by choosing to leave the land unposted, we annually make a gift to the state of Vermont of $2200, at the very least, for which we receive nothing in return—no tax credit or abatement, no legal support in the event a hunter sues us, no thanks of any kind. Not even a Christmas

card. (Indeed, by law "The owner ... of land who gratui-
tously gives another permission, actual or implied, to enter
upon such land for recreational purposes, shall owe that person no more than that owed a trespasser—excepting acts of
active negligence.")

At the same time, mind you, private land that remains open
to hunters is also assessed by the town (at the insistence of the
state) at what is called fair market value. Which means, to our
local assessors, that it must be treated as if a developer had
bought it and riddled it with tract houses. The result, in our
case, is an annual tax of $2500. When you add that figure to a
conservative estimate of the state's take from nonresident
hunting licenses, this particular piece of land annually produces about $5000 in revenues (actually a lot more, if you in-
clude fishing and other license fees)—all of which goes into
the pockets of the taxing authorities, with nothing for the
landowner.

Each year we ponder anew the question of whether to post the
land. Each year, so far, we have decided not to do so. But each
year finds us less sympathetic to the idea of keeping it open—
at least for nonresident hunters.

We have an idea that a great many property owners who
now post their land might change their attitude if they could
see some tangible benefit for doing so. And it seems to us that
the simplest way to achieve this is for Vermont—or any
state—to give them a credit against their property taxes in return for opening their land to the public.

But freeloading is not the only way the state misuses the
landowner's generosity. Seasons on certain game are continually being extended, while other open seasons are added, so
that there is virtually no time during the year when the property owner can call the land his own. Recently we marked off
the legal hunting days on a calendar and were startled to find
that there are now only three months out of twelve when
there is *no* hunting season, only three months of the year
when we can walk through the woods unconcerned, without

wondering if we will be hit by a stray bullet or arrow. And those three months happen to coincide with fishing season, when the state treasury is collecting revenues from yet another set of licenses.

We got to thinking about the state's attitude toward the property owner who chooses not to post his land, and were reminded of the old story about the Scotchman who ran a restaurant and served rabbit stew. One day a customer told the owner he thought he tasted horsemeat in the stew.

"Well," the Scotchman said, "it does have a little horsemeat in it, now that you mention it."

"How much?" asked the customer.

"Oh, it's only fifty-fifty," replied the Scotchman. "One horse, one rabbit."

Our trouble is, we don't even get one rabbit.

The distance from the house to the barn is not much, judged
by the number of steps between them; but on some days and
in certain seasons it has to be reckoned according to the emotional baggage you are carrying. The topography of the walk
is simple: down one small hill and up another, involving a
short stroll along the driveway, down a grassy pitch to the first
gate, then through a corner of the night pasture to another
gate, across the stream (where a progressively rotten bridge
plank makes constant mockery of our good intentions), up a
little hill, and into the barn. There are no chance encounters
along the route—only predictable ones: an ingratiating ankle
rub from Paul, the gray cat; the unblinking stares of ten suspi-
cious sheep, who are convinced, despite three years of daily re-
assurance to the contrary, that we have it in for them.

As always around Election Day, however, our thoughts are
neither on Paul's morning greeting nor the likelihood of yet
another rejection by the sheep, but on the future of the Republic. You might think, after nearly two centuries of fooling
around with self-government, that Americans would begin to
get the hang of it and would manage to put up the ablest and
wisest candidates for office, but each time we have gone to the
polls in recent years we have felt diminished by our choices.
There is consolation in knowing that we have somehow survived so many presumed lessers of two evils, but we wonder
how long our luck will hold out and we are reminded of E. B.
White's wonderful line: "I hold one share in the corporate
earth and am uneasy about the management."

We hear a lot about how Americans for Democratic Action
or Americans for Constitutional Action rate the political color-

ation of senators and representatives according to their voting records, but we wish someone would grade them on the strength of whether they've done anything at all—never mind if it was liberal or conservative. One of these days the people we send to Washington are going to discover that you can't run a country like this by voting *against* things. So if we seem to be ignoring party labels on Election Day, it's because we're looking for someone who has a clear head, a modest amount of vision, an interest in the survival of the human race, and a willingness to work.

We've never known whose idea it was to hold elections at this season, but we imagine he was a down-to-earth fellow who had learned from experience that the way you get through the winter is to face up to what has to be done early in November and then to set about doing it. The business of government has always struck us as a glorified kind of housekeeping, anyway, and our chief complaint about the men and women who have been running things in Washington for the last two decades is that they've forgotten how to make out a family budget and have fallen behind on the mortgage payments.

The winter that lies ahead of America is likely to be a long one, and perhaps our newly elected officials need to remind themselves that November's a time for counting chickens, for checking on what's in the freezer and the canning cupboard. If they do, they'll see what an infinite variety of blessings we possess. A lot of resources are stored away in the national closet—human resources, above all—and we can't afford to have any of them wasted.

Whoever the next president is, we hope he will not be as jittery on that morning in November as we are when we go down the list of what's facing us. There's the vegetable garden, begging to be covered with compost and manure and put to bed. By the time that's done, the ram will have been in with the ewes for a month; they'll be going into the second round of breeding. (Sheep tend to be furtive and nocturnal in their mating habits, and the way we detect their clandestine rendezvous is to smear the ram's brisket with red chalk—a difficult and thankless task—before he joins the ladies, and then to watch for telltale red marks on their backs. Three weeks later we alter the color scheme to green—the idea being that if any of the ewes have green on their backs the first effort was unsuccessful, and they've been bred a second time. All of which tells us when to expect the lambs in the spring.) It's multiplication time for a couple of goats, too, but with no need for colored chalk. Courtly romance is not exactly the billy goat's bag, and his trysts are all too visible.

The roses on the south side of the house have to be covered with dirt to a depth of twelve inches, the leaves need raking, the flower beds must be mulched, the cold frame has to be draped with blankets every night to keep the lettuce from freezing. Before there's too much frost in the ground we really should take soil samples from three pastures and the vegetable garden and send the little bags of dirt, with their accompanying forms, to the Extension Service.

Then there's the house: two chimneys and three stoves to be cleaned, kindling to be collected, more wood to be stacked, gutters to be emptied of leaves, storm doors to put on, and the tiresome task of sealing windows with Mortite. Each spring we painstakingly peel it off the casings and wind it around empty coffee cans, thinking we'll save money by reusing it in the fall. And each November we take one look at the hopeless tangle of gray, lint-covered clay and head for the hardware store to buy two new rolls. (One of the few certainties of life is that the moment the house is sealed as tight as a crypt we will have a week of glorious, hot, Indian summer weather, necessitating the removal of Mortite from six or eight windows in order to get some cross-ventilation.)

Let's see—what else? For one thing, we hope we'll remember what has to be done before the hunters start swarming over the property. All gates but one have to be left open so they can drag their deer out of the woods—otherwise they've been known to cut the wire fences. And once again we've promised ourselves to post one small area of the farm so we can have a place to walk in relative safety during hunting season.

Except for Christmas preparations, that's about it. (This was to be the year we bought the presents early and mailed the out-of-town parcels by mid-November; it was to be the year we ordered the Christmas cards and addressed the envelopes by Thanksgiving. But it won't be.)

It's difficult to imagine that even a president-elect has more to occupy his November, but we suppose that's possible. The problem is that presidents never *seem* very busy. Just wait—one of the first postelection stories out of Washington will describe how the president invited a group of congressmen over to the White House for breakfast and you'll see pictures of them, joking, talking, clapping each other on the back, looking as though they haven't a care in the world. (For some reason, politicians are big on breakfast—especially breakfast at the White House—and every president since Ulysses Grant seems to have operated on the theory that there's nothing a congressman won't do for you if you fill him with complimentary grits and red-eye gravy.)

It's our idea that the president could take advantage of this occasion and—by means of a simple but effective gesture—set the tone for the next four years, let the congressmen know how things stand with energy and the economy, and tell them ever so politely what we expect of them. After the senators and representatives finish the coffee and cigars and file out of the North Portico to be photographed before stepping into their limousines, the president would put a rake into the hand of each man, smile broadly, and say, "Boys, I've got a lot of leaves to rake on this big lawn and I'd sure appreciate it if you'd help me out."

It was one of those perfect December days—crisp and cold, snow on the ground that wasn't too deep for walking—and we hiked up to the pasture where we set out the spruce seedlings ten years ago. They're good size now, most of them at least five or six feet tall, with some individual trees that have taken off and grown to heights of ten or twelve feet or even more. And then there are the runts, trees that never went anywhere for reasons you can't understand. Some the deer have nibbled, cutting off the tops and stunting them, but mostly the trees have been left alone, and we go there every Christmas now to cut one, hating in a way to do it, but knowing on the other hand that the trees that remain will profit from any thinning we do. So we try to pick a tree that's good enough to decorate for Christmas, but one whose removal will benefit its stronger, better-formed neighbors.

The two of us were walking through the pasture when B. suddenly said, "Look!" And there, at the top of the field, standing inside the fenceline, were three deer—two big does and a fawn—that had caught sight of us and stood stock-still, staring, watching to see what we would do. We stood equally still, watching them, and it turned into something of a waiting game—we won't move until you do, as it were. Finally one of us shifted position, breaking the spell, and the three animals lifted their great flags and sprang to life, soaring over the fence into the deep woods beyond, their breath white in the frosty air, leaving us with the feeling of gratitude we always get from a glimpse of wildness.

From the high point of this old, overgrown pasture, where the deer had been, you can look south and west, and on a day such as this there is no feature of the mountains you cannot see in incredible detail. It had been bitter cold up there the previous night, and the trees across the valley, coated with rime, stood out against a blue, cloudless sky. Shadows were sharper in the clear, cold air, with every tree etched in extraordinary relief against the surroundings. It was one of those moments you wish might be preserved forever.

Heading down, we wandered back and forth across the hill in search of our tree. There's the one, we decided—that seven-footer with a poorly developed side, whose branches reached within a foot or two of a tree that will be an outstanding specimen some day, a tree that already outstrips all the others around it. While B. held the top we sawed the trunk as close to the ground as possible, experiencing a familiar feeling—the reluctance to end this tree's life, the growing sorrow with each stroke of the saw that this particular spruce had to die. It's ridiculous, of course: we know that the only way this stand, or any other stand of trees, is going to be improved is by culling the poorer specimens, the wolf trees, the halt and the lame—the ones that will prevent the best ones from achieving their potential. Yet we can't escape the momentary sense of remorse; we never cut a tree but what we feel the loss.

Then off we went, dragging our tree behind us, consoled by the thought of how much joy it would bring those who come to the house during the next ten days, and of how, once it was taken outside for the rest of the winter, it would provide shelter and a place for food for the birds.

On a recent visit to England, we were reminded of what centuries of overcutting can do to the forests, and of how fortunate we are that the process in this country was reversed before it was too late. Beginning in the Iron Age, Britons began using their axes on the ocean of trees that covered the land until, by the beginning of the nineteenth century, only 5 percent of the countryside remained wooded. It was one of the most savage destructions of timberland in history, and today, despite the determined efforts of Britain's Forestry Commission to establish plantations, only 9 percent of the terrain is forested.

As we turn increasingly to the use of wood for fuel, what happened in Britain is worth recalling. In Norman times the feudal villages began to expand their common grazing lands, and the wooded areas slowly shrank. Although many forests were set aside as royal domains or "chases" to ensure king and nobles adequate hunting, commoners retained certain rights in the woods—including the gathering of saplings for thatching and coppice work, the collection of firewood from boughs that could be reached "by hook or by crook," and, what was more destructive, the removal of seedlings for fuel. From the time of the Tudors on, and especially with the advent of the Industrial Revolution, Britain's forests were decimated. Shipbuilding, the making of charcoal for glassblowing and iron smelting, the cutting of timber for mines and canal works and other construction virtually denuded the land of trees, until the nadir was reached two centuries ago.

At about that time, it became fashionable for large land-owners to plant trees solely for aesthetic purposes—a movement abetted by the great landscape architects like Lancelot ("Capability") Brown. Sportsmen contributed their bit, too: concerned by the lack of cover for game, they planted copses on what was, in many areas, almost a treeless landscape. But these efforts replaced merely a fraction of what had once existed, and World War I made exorbitant new demands on the woodlands. Only since then has timber been regarded as a long-term crop, natural regeneration encouraged, and new species introduced.

Much the same sequence of despoliation occurred in America, of course, but happily the movement to promote forestry and timber culture began here before it was too late, as did public awareness that the dwindling forests should be protected. By 1827, all but 27 percent of the entire acreage in Connecticut had been cleared of woods; a century ago, Vermont's virgin timber was virtually gone, and only 20 percent of the land was left forested. This had happened within two centuries of the time when early European voyagers, approaching what is now the United States, reported their enchantment over the land smell that told them they were nearing shore—the perfume from the dense, unbroken wilderness that extended from the coastline to the Mississippi River. To those first settlers, America wore a mantle of apparently endless woods, and it was said that a squirrel could make its way from the eastern edge of Pennsylvania to the western boundary without ever leaving the trees, so thick was the forest canopy. Parts of that region were known as the "black forest" because the vegetation shut out the sun so completely, and it was little wonder that Europeans were awed by the sight—for hundreds of years none of their kind had seen anything to equal it, since woodlands had largely disappeared from the ancient world.

For a variety of reasons—most notably the changes that have taken place in farming—the forests of New England gradually made a comeback. We have an aerial photograph of our farm, taken in the thirties, showing that the land on the mountain was then almost entirely open—the effect of a century and a half of cutting and girdling, and of grazing by sheep and cattle. Today, those same hillsides are covered with trees. And the landscape of Vermont as a whole is a mirror opposite of what it was a hundred years ago: today, only one-fifth of the terrain is open, with the remainder forested.

As we trudged toward home with our Christmas tree on that sparkling December day, we thought of the miraculous cycle that begins with green plants, which utilize energy from the sun, combine it with water and carbon dioxide to create food, and at the same time liberate oxygen into the atmosphere. Man is the beneficiary of this process: we consume the plants, make use of the energy stored within them, and breathe the oxygen released by all the green organisms. And the question we must face is whether we will destroy, in our relentless and often unthinking conquest of nature, the chlorophyll cycle on which our existence depends.

On occasion they remind us of that scene in the manger so long ago, but as a rule the farm animals are not infected with the spirit of brotherhood or love. They can be lying quietly in the hay, contentedly chewing their cuds and meditating upon life's vagaries, but just let one of us enter the barn, remove the lid from the can of grain and fill the scoop, and there goes the peaceable kingdom.

The trouble, of course, is that animals—like the rest of us—have their pecking order, and the minute there is the slightest disturbance or hint of change, those at the top have to reconfirm the whole table of organization. Take the morning not long ago when we arrived for chores: the three goats and four ewes were standing around in the big pen not doing much of anything, just ruminating and minding their own business, but the moment they heard the rattle of the grain can, Dill—the boss goat—butted Popover, her eldest daughter, giving her a swinging head shot to the belly. Popover lunged at the baby goat—her half sister—and delivered a sharp knock on the rump. Upon which the little one belted the smallest ewe and sent her careening into the salt box. Unnerved by the commotion, the four sheep bolted out the barn door, scattering hay and salt behind them. And all the while Dill, the goat that had started it all, watched impassively, waiting as patiently as a goat can wait, knowing that she would get first crack at the grain.

We are sometimes asked what it is that prompts otherwise ordinary people to keep goats. Of all domestic animals, they are surely the least appreciated, the most suspect. Even though their milk, when properly handled, is the equal of anything a cow can produce, the offer of a glass of goat's milk is about as popular as an invitation to dine at the Borgias'. For centuries, goats have been the butt of jokes and the subject of caricature, and we have the uneasy feeling that a certain amount of this reputation rubs off on their owners, as with the man who is observed too often in the company of a known mafioso. Perhaps it has to do with the animals' strange yellow eyes, which have seen the dark places of this or some other world; perhaps it is the folk memory of the buck's repellent stench in mating season. No matter. Goats are indeed quarrelsome and perverse, they play tricks on you out of sheer deviltry, they devour rose bushes and shrubbery, girdle the young trees you have planted, and jump over—or onto—almost anything. Yet when you least expect it they will be as playful as puppies, following you on walks through fields and woods; they can be attentive, almost affectionate. (Heed, however, the slight, gentle tug at your sleeve; the goat is not nuzzling you, she is about to remove the button from your jacket.)

Goats can be uncannily smart. We are mindful of Harley Davidson, our billy goat that was afraid of the dark and turned the lights on in the barn every night—and off in the morning. But this is not to suggest that *all* goats are gifted. We once had a Nubian named Edna May Oliver, and we tethered her on the grass near the road in hopes that she would make lawn mowing redundant. Edna May did all right with the grass; the trouble was that she was afraid of cars, and every time one passed she would run at top speed in the opposite direction. Unfortunately, since she never learned that her collar was attached to a chain, and the chain to a stake, she would hit the end of the chain at a dead run and fly, heels over head, onto the ground. The result was a loud, whapping noise like a large salami sausage being slammed on a counter, but Edna May didn't seem to mind. She had escaped the automobile. She would pick herself up and immediately resume munching grass as though nothing had happened. Then another car would come along and the performance would be repeated.

It didn't appear to bother Edna May, this neck-snapping, but it did bother us and we finally went back to mowing the lawn.

We have never yet encountered a mature female goat that had what you'd call a full-time sunny disposition, but some are certainly more agreeable than others. The crossest animal we ever had around here was Brownie, a big Toggenburg with horns about ten inches long. On a rainy day—or for that matter any day when she was impatient to be fed or was just more ornery than usual—she would stand in front of the barn doors, lower her head, rear back, and butt her horns again and again, to a tempo about like that of the Anvil Chorus. All goats do a certain amount of talking, but when Brownie and the others were in the barn, in their pens, she talked most of the time—scolding this one, giving that one a piece of her mind, warning yet another what she was going to do to her when she got her outside. And every morning, when the goats were let out, Brownie went first, stood beyond the door, and unfailingly bopped each of the others as they emerged, to remind them who was in charge. Brownie went to her reward one midsummer day, mean to the very end. But wherever she is we can picture her, head down, banging on the gates, demanding admittance.

We never think of the goats and our relationship with them without recalling the December day when it came time to breed Dill. It was bitter cold—a dirty-looking day with snow falling fitfully and a big storm in the offing, so we did not dare proceed with the rendezvous we had planned with a prize buck, some fifty miles from home. The trip was risky on such a threatening day, and since it was already late in the season to breed Dill, and since a goat's heat period is a fleeting thing at best—waiting on no man or weather—we decided to take her down the road and breed her to Lil Baker's small buck. It seemed the sensible solution. So off we walked, with Dill trotting along on a leash just like a dog, sniffing adventure. Round the bend, she seemed to know, Mr. Right would be waiting for her. And sure enough, Mr. Right was waiting, only it was

Mr. Right, Junior—the smallest, most unpracticed, but eagerest little fellow you ever saw.

Our predicament was immediately apparent. Dill was a full-grown goat and Junior was not. In fact, the top of his head barely came up to her tail. Under the circumstances, it was clear that he would have to be assisted to his appointed station by some mechanical means. We would have to devise some sort of platform—a launching pad, as it were—from which he could operate. By now the snow was falling hard, the day had turned colder, and the only eminence in sight was a manure pile outside Lil's barn. We made our way toward it.

Mercifully, the story can be abbreviated. Five months later, Dill gave birth to a beautifully marked doe, the image of her mother. But we often think, when life looks darkest, that you don't know what trouble is until you have stood outdoors in a snowstorm, steadying a small male goat on top of a manure pile, in full view of neighbors and passersby, initiating him in the fertility rites.

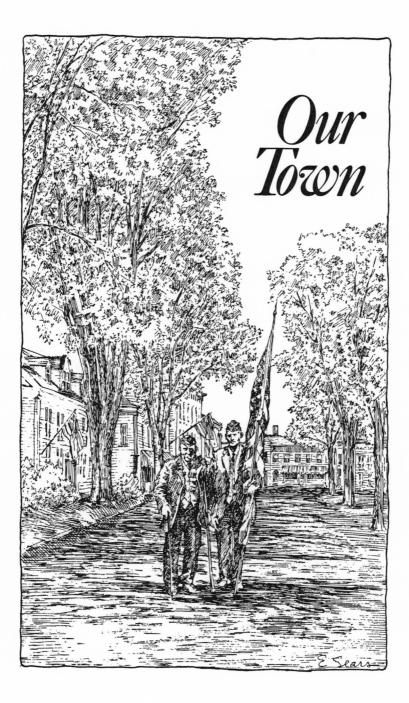

Our Town

Church Street on a still winter evening exemplifies the special quality of an old New England town. On one side of us we see the library, on the other the inn, between them the village green, and beyond, two uneven rows of white houses nestled in the snow beneath the arching maples and elms. Each house is an entity, an island of security and warmth, but what immediately gives this street and hundreds of others like it the appearance of a community is the way the yellow light from each house spills out across the snow to touch the light from its neighbors on either side. It's reminiscent of the opening call at a square dance—all join hands and circle eight around, or the nightly ritual for the westward-bound wagon trains of drawing up in a circle against the hidden enemy, ringing the communal ground. Here our community of souls holds hands, as it were, in league against the darkness and the cold and against whatever else may come.

There is a flagpole on the green and until this past summer, when a committee decided to tidy things up, an old World War I cannon sat there. The flagpole is nothing fancy—not much more than a white wooden pole—but somehow it and the anachronistic cannon struck just the proper note, somewhat shabby but simple reminders of the wars we have fought and the country we fought for.

It occurred to us the other day that nearly all the elements of our rural society are right there on Church Street. Halfway down the road is God's own house, constructed of Vermont marble by a prudent congregation after the old wooden church burned. There is the aforementioned flag representing the nation (and in our mind's eye—despite the committee's cosmetic work—we still see the cannon, token of the brave and the bold who kept us free). There is the green, symbol of sharing, of the life we have in common; the library, storehouse of the ideas and knowledge we have accumulated; the inn, which suggests our creature comforts; and the grocery store, which in this particular case is much more than shelves laden with canned goods, coolers filled with milk and butter and cream. It, and the post office, and the Rumneys' general store down the road, are the last daily meeting places in town.

For as long as we can recall, Perry's store has been the center of this community. It wasn't simply that Perry kept open six days a week from eight in the morning until six at night. It was that nearly everyone in town—natives and summer people—traded there and encountered one another there, and learned of the births, the deaths, and all the intermediate punctuations of village life. Because of the people who worked in the store—Perry's long-time partner Kimball, Ed and Morris, Charlene, Betty, Exina, Quince, and the others—it was an unfailingly friendly place. We could never quite figure out how many Perry had on the payroll or what the work rotation system was, for they were never all there at one time. But no matter: each one had the twinkle in the eye, the quiet humor, the air of friendliness that seemed a requisite for working in Perry's store.

To the best of our knowledge no one at Perry's ever tried to sell anyone anything. We can't imagine them doing it: the merchandise is there, they help you find what you can't locate, but no one is about to push something in front of you that you don't want. We have no idea how many people in town Perry supported in one way or another over the years. A few, in the old days, were simply ne'er-do-wells who couldn't or wouldn't hold another job, and Perry put them to sweeping the floor and taking cartons out to the trash because he knew there wasn't much else for them to do in the village. They couldn't possibly have earned what he paid them or gave them in groceries, but that didn't seem to matter. Then, of course, there were the sick and the hardship cases. How many people in town ran up long-standing bills at the store we'll never know; but we have it from a friend who was out of work and unable to pay that Perry carried him for nearly a year, never saying a word about his account, knowing that some day he would get his money. Which he did.

There were others from whom there wasn't the slightest chance of collecting money, and we remember thirty years ago seeing Kimball drive up the road in the twilight once or twice each week to stop in front of an elderly widow's house. He would get out of the car carrying a bag or two of groceries, walk up the path, and—without knocking—slide the bags inside the door and walk back to the car without a backward glance. It was all managed so as to spare the old woman the embarrassment of a meeting, and there was never a suggestion that he knew she might be inside the house, hidden behind a curtain.

Perry took over the store, which had been his father's, after World War I and he was there past the last working day of December 1976. For twenty-eight of those years he also served as town treasurer, but whatever else he did he was first of all the storekeeper—the one who could cut by eye from the great wheel of Crowley's cheese a slice that would vary only a fraction of an ounce from the pound you had ordered. When he ground the beef or sliced the steaks (and what beef and steaks they were) he always wore the spotless white apron and worked quietly, dapper in shirt-sleeves and tie, with the ever-present cigar in his mouth, intent on what he was doing. Perry was never one to make small talk. Once a city man appeared in the store, full of the news that he had just bought a house on the West Road and that he and his wife intended to live there year-round. He ran on about this for quite a while and when he finally finished talking, Perry took the cigar out of his mouth and remarked, "Winters are long," and turned back to his meat cutting.

Perry has left the store, to take the rest he has earned, but Lord knows we will miss him. It isn't often that a person has the knack of making a simple enterprise like a grocery store into an institution, or of serving his community so faithfully and well. For six decades he gave quietly of himself, making our town a place where people knew that someone cared.

A blacksmith shop might not seem enough of a symbol to pin a whole way of life on, but that's the way it struck us when we came here to live more than three decades ago. A good many smaller farms in the valley were still using horses, but you knew in your bones, even then, that it couldn't last long, and sure enough, it wasn't many years before Walt Jones quit shoeing horses and closed the doors of his shop. And the smithy was but one such establishment that passed from the scene as the industrial tide swept over the small towns.

All you need do to realize what self-sufficient places these villages once were is to look, as we have recently, at one of the county gazeteers of a century ago. In 1880, we find, the population of our town stood at 2199 (today it's only two-thirds of that). The village contained—as it still does—a church, a hotel, and two stores, but there were also two blacksmith shops, a grist mill, a wagon shop, a cheese factory, a marble-finishing shop for the local quarries, and a boot and shoe shop—all of them gone. The principal wealth of the town, it was said, lay in its "inexhaustible marble quarries"—all closed now. In those days the town had twelve school districts (now there is one central elementary school), employing three male and twenty-one female teachers at a cost of $1742.20, which works out to the handsome sum of $72.59 per teacher. The number of pupils enrolled was 1350, and the total monies expended for all school purposes was $1990.30, or an average of $1.47 per student. This year, by contrast, we have only 305 schoolchildren in town and we allocate $546,238.11 for their education—an average of almost $1800 apiece.

Less than a hundred years ago, in other words, three people

out of every five were schoolchildren, which gives you an idea how large the families were. And of 849 adults in the town, 189 were listed as farmers—one out of every five. Since only the heads of households (almost universally males) are listed in the gazeteer, the likelihood is that as many as four hundred people, or nearly half the adult population, were engaged in agriculture in some way, since women (not to mention the children) were vital to the functioning of every farm. It was early to bed and early to rise, and the governing philosophy was "Many hands make light work." When they could get away from their livestock, the farmers' travels were bounded by the distance they could go and come between morning and evening milking, and in the era of the horse this was ten or a dozen miles at best. Which meant that their village and its immediate environs pretty much comprised their world. That, and the fact that most people stayed settled in one place, made for strong community and familial ties. Families worked, prayed, and played together; the necessities of living required chores of each individual; and the closeness of their relationship was a direct measure of the need to make do.

At harvesttime this autumn you could sense what has gone from our farms. Where once the gathering of the crops occupied many hands (indeed, all hands, old and young, that were available), you now see a solitary man on an enormous tractor, as like as not wearing ear protectors to deaden the roar of his machine and the steady moan of the chopper spewing corn into a dump truck that tags alongside. The dump truck fills and speeds off toward the silo, to be replaced by another truck, and only rarely do the men inside the vehicles stop long enough to exchange a few words. It is a far cry—this noisy minuet of mechanical monsters—from the rhythmic swish of scythes as the reapers moved slowly along the rows, talking and sometimes singing, and the sight of women and girls bringing lunch baskets and jugs of switchel out to the fields. Someone once suggested that we lost the art of song when farming became a business instead of a craft.

This contrast between the harvest of old and what we know

today is the difference between many involved people and one lonely person and a machine, and it somehow symbolizes what has happened to the village as well as to the farm. If the easy, predictable cadence of the small town is largely gone today, so are the richness and diversity that once made them such vital communities. A century ago, virtually the entire business of a community like ours consisted of support elements for the farm. In the 1880 gazeteer, alongside the names of the householders, are listed their trades—blacksmith, carriage manufacturer, wagon maker, teamster, carpenter and joiner, cooper, shingle maker, machinist, harness maker, tanner, currier, cheese maker—each one directly or peripherally involved with the work of farming. (Among them is included an individual whose occupation is described as "pettifogger and grafter." He is a man we would like to have known, this shyster, for we imagine him contributing a note of villainy to the pastoral symphony. There are still pettifoggers and grafters in our midst, but none willing to own up to it.)

It is easy to believe that there is a relationship between what has happened to farm and village and what has happened to society as a whole; that the breakdown of institutions—farm and village, family, marriage, church, school—accounts for the feeling of rootlessness, the loss of what is called community. (A recent study reveals that only 16 percent of American families are intact, with both parents living at home with the children.) Our country is not alone in this, of course. In the Soviet Union, for instance, where the authorities are increasingly concerned about the rise in crime, its incidence is largely attributed to the movement of farm folk to cities, and to the effect of that move on people who leave behind the security and the values of family and village and are suddenly confronted by the unknown.

A good many of us have changed from being participants to being spectators, and the result is not unlike what happens to an athlete who gives up sports. Once he stops using certain muscles they atrophy, or he forgets how to use them, and before long the old skill is gone. Our community and others like it are the poorer for this, for we have today more and more passive people, people without a craft or trade, who lose their usefulness to society and to themselves, people whose principal activity is wondering how to put in their time.

Fortunately, some of the old ways persist. The village, almost in spite of itself, retains vestiges of the ancient rural pattern, recognizing the relationship between God, man, and the earth. The church is still the central edifice in town, overlooking the village green. In its shadow are clusters of houses, symbols of man's presence. And beyond, even today, are tilled and pastured fields where men and animals continue to work the land. Fortunately, too, a few people in our midst still possess the old skills. Dennis Troumbley, with a jack and what he calls his "teacle blocks" can right an old barn or replace a sill the way it was done when this village was first settled. Loyerston and Patty Bovey can do just about anything with a team of horses. Jack Stannard runs a trap line with all the cunning of an old mountain man. Paul Ferenc, a skilled mason, can teach you how to butcher a pig or steer. Abbott and Jennifer deRham have shown us how to make a clearing in the woods and build a house. The list could go on and on—and happily so, for these are the people on whom we are relying to lead us into the postindustrial age, along a path that may necessarily resemble a way of life annotated in the pages of the 1880 gazeteer.

There are also men and women around here who can tell you, from signs they observe, what sort of weather we are likely to have, predicting it far more accurately than the man in Albany who reads the most sophisticated instruments and reports from weather satellites. One fall a neighbor asked if the water in our pond appeared browner than normal. Yes, we replied . . . why? Well, he said, he had an idea that the tiny creatures that live in the pond, knowing that an early winter—and a long one—was ahead, were preparing for it in their own fashion, burrowing into the bottom and stirring up the silt. We remembered what he had said when the first heavy snowfall came in mid-December—a snow that was to remain on the ground until April. We don't know, and he doesn't either, if there is any scientific basis for his notion about the pond, but he was certainly right about the weather.

Like most small communities these days, our town is confronted repeatedly with the issue of change. Nothing very dramatic is going on here—no nuclear plant or corporate headquarters moving in—simply the rising pressure of refugees from city and suburb on a lovely New England town that offers sanctuary and serenity.

There are some ironies in all this. A local developer requests a zoning change that will enable him to build an industrial park, and we debate his request. We even accept the phrase "industrial park," not seeing that it suits our village as poorly as plaid doubleknits beneath the parson's robe. And while we argue about it, the construction of new homes goes on almost unnoticed, each one adding a proportionate burden to the demand for services, each one removing a little more open land from existence.

While our attention is riveted on a different proposal—this one an outside developer's plan to construct seventy or more single-family residences, which will increase the town's population by 15 or 20 percent overnight—still another local developer erects four houses, the first of ten or eleven that will occupy a once-beautiful meadow. And meanwhile there are rumors that a UN delegation (read "Arabs") is buying land, that a new luxury hotel is being planned, that a shopping center is in the offing. All this in a village of less than fourteen hundred souls.

The main effect of all the building will be most noticeable on the school budget, of course, since the school already takes 78 cents of every tax dollar. But the impact will also be felt by the town manager, the road crew, the listers, the constables, the town clerk, the volunteer firemen—by all who serve the townspeople in one way or another. And there are other, less obvious effects. Those places that have accommodated the community—some of them for generations—suddenly seem inadequate. The grocery store and the church, the post office and the hardware store, the general store and the room in the school where we hold town meetings, the club—even the cemetery—are filled to overflowing, and you find yourself wondering why. The service at the counter isn't as good any more and you hear customers grumbling. Who are all these newcomers anyway? Have you ever seen so many people you don't know?

Next, someone will be agitating for a new grocery store, possibly a supermarket. An enterprising couple will hear about that and decide that a gift shop next door might prosper. The school board will conclude that a new bus and another driver are needed, and they will call in an architect to discuss adding two classrooms. Before long, state officials will tell us we have to find a new source of water and build a sewage-disposal plant.

Even traditions that have nothing to do with buildings or services change. In our town, there's a ritual of waving to neighbors as two cars pass. It's taken for granted that when Hope and Linwood drive by, heading to the village, you and they will wave to one another. (Unfortunately, as these old eyes grow older it becomes increasingly difficult to see who the occupant of the other car is, and this often proves embarrassing, since we tend to wave at every passing vehicle for fear of being taken for a snob if we do not. It's also dangerous. We have to take our eyes off the road and peer intently at oncoming automobiles and their occupants, sometimes waving at women we don't know, who glower and drive on.)

This waving business can get out of hand; occasionally a friend will stop by the barn and talk for an hour and a half and then, when he gets into his truck to leave, he waves to you and you wave back, as though you hadn't seen each other at all. There are different kinds of waves, we've learned. One local man opens wide all five fingers of one hand, as if revealing it to a palmist. Another, crouched over the wheel of a van like a sinister Humphrey Bogart, lifts his index finger—slightly. There's a fellow who barely raises four fingers from the wheel, as though he's giving you a peek at a poker hand. And Bert Knowles, a veteran of World War I, used to salute as he drove by. But the point is that the wave, like a lot of other things in town, is beginning to vanish. After all, you can't wave continuously from our town to the next one at a steady stream of cars.

When you grouse about these things, the people who claim to stand for Progress remind you of the need for lower taxes, the need for jobs, and tell you that industry will provide both. And of course you want jobs for local people and houses for those who need them, and no one could possibly want taxes lowered more than you do. But these arguments for progress have been around for a long time, and there's no certainty that the introduction of a foreign element into a community—especially the unknown component of an industrial park—ever has the desired effect. What is clear is that industry and commerce bring more people to a community and that these people demand more and better service.

We need zoning here, you will say. Well, we have zoning—an imperfect set of standards, to be sure, but zoning nonetheless—zoning that was designed to preserve the kind of town we believed we wanted. But it doesn't always work the way people think it should.

Perhaps an answer for our town and for other communities similarly troubled lies in an ability to be flexible. Perhaps we need to change the rules from time to time, to recognize that zoning ordinances are not immutable, that they must be altered to fit the shifting tides of life in a community. Perhaps the people of a town need to reconsider and reassess their needs on a regular basis every few years, to ask the difficult questions that will reveal who they are and where they want to go and what kind of community they desire for themselves and their children.

A few years ago a little town in New Hampshire was the scene of much unexpected development and the selectmen were sufficiently alarmed to announce a radical decision. For one year, they declared, there would be a moratorium on all development so that the townspeople might decide what they wanted and what they did not want. Perhaps communities, like individuals, need time to think, time to catch their breath.

In our town, Memorial Day is something special. If you were a stranger here you might think this is so because it is the one time in the year we permit ourselves any military airs, but the truth of the matter is that we have allowed it to remain simple.

It begins at the church. There is a brief service with an invited speaker, as in days gone by, to remind the congregation of what the day means (or at least of what it means to the speaker), and then the honor guard and the veterans slide from their pews and file out. They are the same men we see around town every other day of the year—carpenters, plumbers, storekeepers—yet they wear a self-conscious air in church, almost as if they were members of a secret society sworn to silence and an unaccustomed decorum. When they emerge into the sunlight on the green the parade forms up, the members of the high school band—imported from a larger town—eager to get on with it, the former soldiers and sailors relaxed now that the formal part of the thing is over. A few fortunate ones can still get into their uniforms, and it comes as a surprise to see that the farmer down the road was a lieutenant commander in the Navy, that an elderly insurance broker was an Air Force colonel. But mostly the men are in civilian clothes, their only evident tie to the service a Legion or VFW cap.

The drums begin to beat, the mini-skirted twirlers and majorettes, suddenly deadly serious, go into their ritual movements, and the parade is under way. Up ahead at the intersection the town constable has parked his car, with the blue light flashing, and along the main street the older villagers are on their front porches or in parked cars; everyone else stands on the curb, peering toward the flashing light for the first glimpse of the flag-bearers rounding the turn.

Most of the marchers are out of step and you can see that a few of them are bothered by it, by the way they keep looking at someone else's feet and skipping to get back in the rhythm, but it is reassuring to realize how poorly the American takes to military cadence. After the veterans come the Scouts— boys and girls wearing their merit badges like rows of combat stars or honorary degrees; then the little 4-H clubbers, mostly giggling and looking for their parents along the route; and all these are trailed by children wobbling along on bicycles festooned with bunting. Bringing up the rear, two girls on horseback show off for the crowd by riding bareback, their mounts smooth and glistening as though this were a horse show.

The cemetery is one of the most serene and beautiful places in town, and suddenly Walt Whitman is here with us, for the lilacs—the flower he linked forever to the Civil War—are in bloom and their fragrance is everywhere. By now only the muffled tap of one drum breaks the silence and then there is no sound, no movement except the slow flapping of flags in the breeze while the minister says a prayer and a soldier lays a wreath on a grave. Someone calls the honor guard to attention and to order arms; there is the crack of rifles and then, from high on the hill, a bugler concealed somewhere in the ancient maples sounds taps. In this tiny cemetery lie the dead of all our country's wars, and somehow they are all comrades when those clear, heartbreaking notes float on the air, bidding them all "Go to sleep, go to sleep."

The day had its origins not long after the end of the Civil War. In 1868 the commander-in-chief of the Grand Army of the Republic, as the veterans of the Union Army were known, designated May thirtieth "for the purpose of decorating the graves of comrades who died in defense of their country during the late rebellion," and he expressed the hope that "it will be kept up from year to year."

So the custom began, and for years the occasion was known as Decoration Day. Even though the GAR decided in 1882 that it should be known as Memorial Day, for a long time Decoration Day was what the older generation called it.

By whatever name, it was a day that belonged to the veterans, and we are old enough to remember those fragile old men of the Civil War—long white hair under their blue campaign hats, their rheumy eyes fixed on some ancient battlefield, their thoughts on the tattoo of a distant drum—riding through the streets in open touring cars, headed for the cemetery where so many of their contemporaries lay.

It never rained on Decoration Day, and we used to sell lemonade from a big earthenware crock set up on a card table on the sidewalk, and it seemed to us—for we were very young and thrilled to a military band and the sight of the flag snapping in the wind—in those days it semed to us that war must be a very fine thing to be part of. War was a parade coming, and Father—who was the handsomest man in the neighborhood, if not anywhere—trying to get into a flight lieutenant's uniform and polished brown boots that no longer fit.

Someone suggested to us recently that Memorial Day is little more than a glorification of the military, but that's not the way we think of it in our town. Most of those who were killed, in whatever war, were so young and had no wish to die. There was a sweetheart or a young bride to come home to, a sugarhouse filled with steam and the sweet smell of boiling sap on a March morning, a barn warmed by cattle and the small sounds of contentment on a cold winter's night. By no stretch of the imagination could most of those young men be considered militaristic. They volunteered or were summoned, and they were the unlucky ones.

No, what we seem to be telling them, in our town at least, on this particular day in May, is that they are part of our youth that passed so quickly, so long ago. And here, for them, and for us to remember them by, is a spring day in all its perfection—the best we have to offer.

Soon the lilacs will be gone and we are reminded, as we walk away from the cemetery, that this is also the day we must plant the rest of the garden for the summer and winter that lie ahead. The earth will be warm now. It will take care of its own.

High summer was the time of that event we children thought of—always in capital letters—as The Family Reunion. The fact that we didn't really know many of the relatives who would be there, and cordially disliked a few of the young ones we did know, never dimmed the prospects of the occasion. For it was first and foremost an outing—an expedition, really, since it involved a train trip from Pittsburgh, Pennsylvania, to the little town in central Ohio, where Mother had been born.

What sticks in mind are the picnic baskets, filled to the brim with Grandma's unparalleled pies and Mother's similarly unparalleled cakes, a ham or turkey, potato salad, relishes and preserves, homemade rolls and biscuits, and heaven knows what else. There was the excitement of entering the cavernous railroad station and waiting while Dad purchased the long strips of tickets that had to be folded again and again before they would fit into his pocket; then struggling out to the train platform, laden with baskets, suitcases, and all the paraphernalia required for the trip. The train shed may just have been the most exhilarating place in the world then, with half a dozen gigantic engines hissing steam, the echoing clang of metal as cars were coupled and uncoupled, firemen shoveling coal into the boilers, engineers in their blue-and-white striped caps and overalls leaning casually out of the cab to gaze imperially on the passengers walking below—their goggled, sooty faces breaking into grins when a child waved and called a greeting. From inside the stationmaster's bay-windowed office came the insistent click of a telegraph key; trainmen with long brass oilcans made their appointed rounds; and down the long line of passenger cars you could see the white-jacketed Pullman porters standing beside little yellow stools, helping people up the steps, smiling, joking, giving helpful directions. Then came the magical moment when the conductor bellowed "B-O-O-A-R-D!" signaling the last embrace between visitors and passengers, and the engine delivered several long sighs, *whooshed* loudly once or twice, and then moved slowly out of the train shed, chugging through the smoke-filled tunnel, picking up speed as it emerged into the sunlight and crossed the river, and finally swung into the rhythmic *chook-a-chook-a-chook-a-chook* of the open countryside.

The trip is only a blur at the back of the mind now—ghostly images of children's books and puzzles and endless games of Rummy, trips to the observation car to watch the tracks vanishing in perfect perspective to the horizon—and we have no recollection whatever of arriving at our destination or of anyone meeting us. There is only the memory of being in a park by a slow-moving stream and seeing the long row of plank tables beneath the shade trees, dappled with sunlight and a sea of food, surrounded by a sea of faces, most of them old and unfamiliar. We were always relieved to catch sight of jolly Uncle Milt and Aunt Elva, cross Aunt Agnes, pretty Cousin Fern, and Clark and Cecil, who were nice to us even though they were older. And we counted on shaking hands with the elderly gentleman everyone called "Gen" or "General." We were never certain who Gen was, except that he was a relative of some sort, but we do recall Dad's snort of laughter when we asked what war he had been a general in. "Why that old jaybird," Dad hooted, "he never got closer to a uniform than the Army-Navy store. He was *christened* General George Washington Davidson."

Nearly all the relatives lived nearby in small towns or on farms, and came to the reunion in Model T's or Model A's or by horse and buggy. Except for Mother and her family, it was a short journey for most of them—short enough so they could tarry in the park, there by the river, laughing and talking with their kinfolk into the long summer evening. When darkness began falling they would say their good-byes, round up the sleepy children, light the lamps on their buggies, and the slow procession would wind out of the park for home. We came from the city, of course, and stayed overnight in the house where Mother had lived as a child, where our great-grandfather with the snow-white beard still lived, and the next day we would be taken on a tour of the neighborhood—to see the little town and the hardware store Great-Grandfather had owned. Somehow the sight of it reminded Grandma of the pair of high-stepping black horses he used to drive, and her wonderful rich laugh would ring out as she told how those blacks ran away with him every time he took them out. We would visit the farm owned by Uncle Ray, which had a noble barn like those Louis Bromfield called typical of this part of the country: ". . . a big, red barn built in the days when farmers were rich and took a pride in their barns . . . barns which are an expression of everything that is good in farming . . . barns with great, cavernous mows filled with clover hay, two stories or three in height with the cattle and horses below bedded in winter in clean straw, halfway to their fat bellies. . . ." Approaching Uncle Ray's farm we crossed a plank bridge over a lazy little stream, and Grandma told in a hushed voice the tragic story of how Uncle Ray's father and mother were returning home one night in a terrible rainstorm, and how this little creek was swollen with a flash flood, with water rising over the bridge. Uncle Ray's brother was in the barn, worrying about his parents, and he hurried down through the storm to lead their horse across the bridge. But he was too late: they had already started to cross when the terrified horse shied, and horse, buggy, and the old man and his wife were swept into the raging yellow waters. Their son leaped from the bridge to try to save them, and he too was swallowed up by the flood. Despite the story, we children came away from Uncle Ray's place with a love for farming that time has never diminished.

We remember that long-ago reunion sometimes when we read what has become of families in America. Once they were so close, so united—ready to help out when there was trouble or

sickness or death. Now it seems that there is not enough time
for families to be together, time to cement the ties that blood
creates but cannot bind. Perhaps the day of the family reunion is passing—and we cannot help wondering if the family
itself is heading in the same direction. We have put so much
space between ourselves that we can only get together by
long-distance telephone. We have managed to create an economic situation that increasingly requires both parents to
work outside the home in order to make ends meet. We have
even contrived a system of taxation that makes it advanta-
geous for certain working couples to get a divorce in order to
save money on income taxes.

Until two generations ago, a substantial number of Americans lived on farms, and it is interesting to hear about the close
family ties and the working relationship that characterized
their lives. In *The Family Farm,* Maisie and Richard Conrat
quote a middle-aged man who grew up in rural Wisconsin:
"When I was a boy," he said, "it seems like families were so
much stronger . . . we all worked together, you know. Us kids
all worked. . . . It was like a whole little world right there—
everybody working together and wanting to make things
good, everybody putting in his share. . . . I guess I never
really thought much about families and such things before my
own kids started growing up, and I'd be going off to the job
. . . and we'd all be going off in different directions." Husband
and wife (and children, too) worked in those days, but it was a
shared arrangement, a partnership in which the tasks were in-
tertwined and interrelated, directed toward a common goal.
When America moved away from farming, when the husband
spent all day at a job away from home and unrelated to it, he
began imagining that what his wife was doing there was not so
essential. And valuing her work less, he lost her and his family
to a new world.

So we think of that extended family assembled in a park in
central Ohio, and we still recall the feeling of warmth that existed in that grove of trees by the river. The stars and the
fireflies are beginning to shimmer in the gathering dusk, there

is a hum of laughter and talk, and then someone at the far end of the table begins to sing, "Just a song at twilight . . ." One after another, the members of the family join in, and the words and the melody of love's old sweet song float across to us on the soft evening breeze.

It was the ninetenth century and the nation was still young, bristling with confidence in the future and pride in a brief past. Well into the first third of that century the memory of independence and what it meant was still green, and on speakers' platforms festooned with tricolored bunting, a few white-haired old men, honored veterans of the Revolutionary War, nodded sleepily in the morning sun while orators droned on about the Founding Fathers and the deeds of men made to seem like giants.

On Independence Day every New England village sprang suddenly to life to the shrill of fife and the beat of drum. There they came—all the men who had uniforms or some claim to military address (one more venerable than the others), parading along the dusty street past the village green to the delight of small boys released from chores. It was a day of fireworks and ringing church bells, watermelon and lemonade, the celebration of summer and freedom.

One of New England's worthiest representatives to the Second Continental Congress, who cast his vote for independence on July 2, 1776, had urged that that day be commemorated as the moment of deliverance, ". . . solemnized with pomp and parade, with shows, games, sports, guns, bells, bonfires and illuminations, from one end of this continent to the other, from this time forward, forevermore." As it turned out, John Adams did not have his way about the date, but nineteenth-century New England remembered his message.

Today the spirit of the village and of what once used to be called the Glorious Fourth have all but vanished from many a community, and we suspect that their passing is something many Americans view with a sense of sadness and concern, not knowing what can be done about restoring them, yet wishing nonetheless that the values they represented were still part of our national life.

One of the time-honored institutions in these parts is the common—a piece of land held for the use of all townspeople, originally for grazing their livestock. Equally familiar was the town forest, which was also for the communal use of town residents. Over the years both of these traditions have fallen into disuse, but we believe a case can be made for reviving them.

What better celebration of freedom could a town have than to purchase and set aside a parcel of land for the use and enjoyment of all its residents? Whether it be a pasture for grazing cattle or sheep, a park or community garden, footpaths, a scenic stretch of river or a wooded mountaintop, a farm, even a vacant lot where children can play ball or sit and dream—what more appropriately suits the heritage of the town or the horizons of its citizens?

Recently we saw the results of a poll, indicating that more than half of the people living in cities of more than fifty thousand said they wanted to move to the country. Before these newcomers arrive, it might be well for the present residents to set aside some open space that will be with us, as John Adams hoped for his proposal, from this time forward, forevermore.

It is all very well for Horace Sutton to write, as he did in *Saturday Review,* of "the luxury of high-speed trains roaring from city center to city center on retina-popping time schedules," while a computer keeps an electric eye on the controls. Or to tell us of the new German train "that operates by magnetic levitation . . . a railroad car that will wrap itself around a single-beam elevated guideway" and travel at speeds up to 250 miles per hour. Or even to mention the Budd Company's self-propelled diesel-powered railway car that "can attain speeds of 120 miles an hour and is an ideal people-mover for resort travel. In Vermont," he goes on to say, "it could run to ski resorts on unused tracks."

For a man who lives in what was, not so very long ago, a horse-and-buggy town, which is leaning in that direction again (provided we can locate enough horses and buggies), those are heady thoughts. Too heady by far. We will settle for less exotic forms of public transportation. It is true that nothing would please the operators of our ski resorts more than the reality of those sleek Budd cars rolling through the countryside at 120 miles an hour. The trouble is that a good many of the unused tracks have been torn up or paved over, while those that remain have been allowed to deteriorate to the point where only freight trains dare risk passage over them, and then at top speeds of 20—not 120—miles per hour.

People here are beginning to fret about how they will get around in the postpetroleum age, and as a result, our local community college and the chamber of commerce sponsored a lively forum on public transportation. This is a resort area, where most local businesses depend heavily on tourism, and those businessmen are understandably concerned about how the tourist will get here as gasoline supplies dwindle and the price of gas climbs beyond the reach of the average person. And, the business people ask, even if the tourist does manage to get here by bus—which is the only form of public transportation serving the community—how does he move from hither to yon, once he's arrived, in a town that boasts two taxicabs? Apart from the tourists, residents of the community are beginning to worry about how they'll get around themselves—whether it's to and from the job or the grocery store or the Elks.

It was an interesting notion, this forum—which saw concerned citizens of a community facing up to a problem that isn't yet serious, but that will become more so with each passing year, to see what can be done to solve it now, while there is still time. Vermont's lone U.S. Congressman came to talk, as did representatives from Amtrak, from Vermont Transit, the bus company, and from the state energy office. It was clear from the outset that rail transportation was the sentimental favorite with the audience, and the least likely to reappear in an area where passenger service was abandoned years ago. In Vermont, as elsewhere, most passenger lines—especially the numerous short lines that once crisscrossed the state—have long since fallen victim to our love affair with the automobile, and can only be resuscitated with massive doses of federal and/or state money. (It occurred to us that this is one of the most unsettling ailments of our day—the idea that so many of our problems can only be solved by spending the taxpayers' money. Where, we wondered, is Commodore Vanderbilt when we need him? The Commodore, you may recall, did rather well with railroads: when he died, his fortune was almost exactly equal to the amount in the federal government's treasury.) As a means of transporting goods and people, the efficiency of the railroad has never been equaled, and it is interesting that most of the world's industrial nations—except for the United States—have recognized that fact and are investing in research on and development of railroads. In this country, of course, the railroad long ago lost out to the automobile's power, glamour, and the way it granted access to personal freedom (regardless of the consequences). The result is that most American communities are completely oriented around the automobile, more than 90 percent of all personal travel is by automobile, and we have more than 100 million cars on our highways—one for every 1.9 people.

Given the realities of the situation, what struck us as the most interesting and promising aspect of the conference on transportation was van pooling. Here in Vermont van pooling has been the baby of a dynamic supersalesman named Lee Perkins, of the state energy office. There is some difference in age between Perkins and his young associate, Mark Niemiec, and the latter finds it hard to believe that Lee grew up in a world without television. Reminding Mark of that, Lee observes, "You'll tell your children, ten years from now, that you used to drive alone in your own car from your house to the office. And they won't be able to believe you."

Perkins, who has been instrumental in making Vermont's rural van-pooling program the most successful in the country, has concentrated on selling the concept of multiple riders, and then on helping van poolers get started, by assisting them to lease or purchase a van, holding workshops to explain the functioning of the operation, aiding them in setting up records, finding neighbors to ride with them, getting them preferential insurance rates—in short, reducing as many barriers to van pooling as possible. He likes to point out that it now costs 27 cents a mile to operate even a compact car, assuming that you drive 12,000 miles a year and keep the automobile for three years. For someone making a round-trip commute of thirty miles, that's $8.10 per day, or $178.20 a month if he drives alone, with no one to share costs. By contrast, a typical van-pool monthly fare for the same distance comes to $44.00, for a monthly saving of $134.20. There are additional benefits: the van that travels from Glover and Barton to Newport, Vermont, not only saves its riders money—it eliminates eight vehicles from the highway and the parking lot, and conserves five thousand gallons of gasoline each year.

There's another wrinkle to the van-pooling concept. Rather than have their vans sit idle during working hours, a number of van operators are making their vehicles available for other uses between commuting trips. Some vehicles are utilized by municipalities, some by health-care agencies, some for other purposes, and whatever earnings are received are passed along to the van-pool members, to reduce their monthly fares. The more we heard about it, the more we liked the idea of the twelve- to fifteen-passenger vans (which, incidentally, boast the best accident-free record of any form of transportation and are insured accordingly), and we wonder if the concept couldn't be expanded considerably. We envision vans with wheelchair ramps for the handicapped, vans for the elderly, vans for shoppers, sightseeing vans, vans for charter by small groups for travel to parks and recreation areas, to railroad and airplane terminals, to museums, theaters, and ball games. Who knows? The local delivery van may even make a comeback, and we might see the return of the day when the fruit-and-vegetable man, the egg man, the butcher, the cobbler, the milkman, and the dry cleaner all made the rounds of the neighborhood, bringing goods and services to every door. It sure beats having everyone pile into their cars to drive to the shopping mall.

What we remember best about a certain magical time of childhood are the long July evenings after school was out, when all the children in the neighborhood played together until the last glimmer of daylight was spent. In those days you made your own amusement or you didn't have any, and we recall that it was a great era for swings; nearly every household had one—a porch swing, a glider, a tire hung from a tree, or more rarely, a child's set with swing, slide, and seesaw. Our favorite was a green, wooden-slatted affair in which two seats faced each other, where as many as six of us would glide back and forth in the twilight, singing. One of our early recollections is of that swing and a big girl named Mimi, who always chose the songs because she was nine and the rest of us were six or seven. Anyway, one of the songs she taught us was the doleful tale of a maiden who apparently had nothing better to do than languish in a hammock, and one afternoon while she lolled there a slick operative with a waxed mustache (that's the way we imagined him, at any rate) sidled up, sat down beside her, played his guitar, and then "smoked a cigar, smoked a cigar, smoked a cigar. . . ." We have only the dimmest memory of how the song went, but ever since then we have regarded guitar-playing, cigar-smoking men with deep suspicion, since, as we recall it, the pretty young thing in the hammock ended up crying (". . . oh, how she cried") and then dying.

We had regular playground swings at our house—two of them, with a trapeze—and that made it a regular gathering place until all of us were about fifteen and far too sophisticated for such stuff. But until then we would sit and swing and exchange the important confidences of youth, usually while one of the gang hung upside down from the trapeze, his face growing redder and redder as the conversation wore on.

Night after night we would play games—Kick the Can, Prisoner's Base, Release, Capture the Flag—all of them much the same, of course, in that one team tried to capture those on the other team, meantime hoping to prevent any uncaptured enemy from touching home base and releasing the prisoners. As many as thirty of us were often involved in such games, and since the extent of our play area was The Neighborhood, this usually meant that the game never ended but was called off on account of darkness. In the meantime, from each house you would hear its special family whistle, calling first the littlest children, then the older ones, to bed, so that at last only a handful of players remained on each team.

Looking back on it, we realize that we were never captured in any of those games and the reason was that we had discovered the perfect hiding place. Halfway up a big maple tree in our yard, a large limb angled off from the trunk in such a way that it made a comfortable perch, and there we could sit for hours, screened from view by the dense foliage of the tree and by the fact that no one passing directly beneath us ever looked straight up—which was the only way we could have been detected. We recall the thrill of holding our breath while the Dickey brothers stood at the base of our tree and discussed a plan for catching us—Bob to go this way, Bill that—never suspecting that their quarry sat ten feet above their heads.

But mostly what we remember, at this remove from that long-ago childhood and the soft summer evenings, are the sound of cicadas singing and the fireflies, or lightning bugs as we called them, punctuating the dusk around our maple tree with little pinpricks of light. Oftentimes we children would catch one of them and hold it loosely inside a closed hand, enchanted by the way it would glow, on and off, shedding a greenish-yellow light through the fingers. Or we might put a few of the little insects, with some blades of grass for sustenance, inside a bottle, thinking we might keep them all summer and show them to Miss Schmeltz, our nature-study teacher, in September.

We learned recently that fireflies, like just about everything else, have come a long way since our day. Certainly it never occurred to us (or maybe even to the lightning bugs) that they could be put to any good use, least of all to turn a profit. We always supposed that lightning bugs had nothing more important to do than illuminate the twilight of our childhood, but we find that in certain tropical countries they are collected, put into bottles, and used as lanterns. It is even said that men who move through tropical forests at night attach fireflies to their boots to light the path (presumably this sort of thing goes on in countries where the flashlight has not yet been invented). And Cuban women, we are told, put luminescent click beetles in their clothing or in pendants, apparently hoping to attract members of the opposite sex with the seductive, flashing green light.

While Cuban women are busying themselves thus, two companies in the Midwest—Sigma Chemical of St. Louis and Antonik Laboratories of Elk Grove Village, Illinois—have been paying children (and, presumably, adults who have nothing better to occupy their time) to catch and deliver lightning bugs to them. Some years ago it was discovered that two chemicals in the firefly's tail—luciferin and luciferase—were activated by a compound called adenosine triphosphate (ATP), which is present in all living cells. So, while the male firefly idly squanders this combination of chemicals advertising his presence to females, scientists are removing those same substances from the lightning bugs and introducing them into other organisms for such wondrous purposes as diagnosing heart attacks, detecting diseases in infants, gauging the germination probabilities of certain seeds, counting the bacteria in water, and even determining which hogs are susceptible to stress. Sigma and Antonik pay up to a penny a lightning bug, and last year Antonik bought a million and a half of the little arthropods, reselling them to doctors, scientists, and chemical companies for as much as $20 a gram.

Just as we were wondering if all the fireflies in the Midwest would vanish into the maws of Sigma and Antonik, we heard a touching story about the lightning bugs of Japan. For centuries, the firefly was admired as a fragile and beautiful symbol of summer by the Japanese, who take pleasure in the smallest wonders of nature. Years ago, parents told their children that each firefly was the spirit of a fallen samurai warrior who had returned to continue the battle, and in some households the children would release lightning bugs inside their mosquito netting and drift off to sleep watching those tiny moving stars twinkling overhead. But the day of the Japanese firefly is done; they have been almost entirely destroyed by the fumes, the poisoned water, and the spreading concrete of that highly industrialized society.

There are still those Japanese for whom the firefly is a reminder of an innocent, departed past, and they engage in what struck us as a heartbreaking commentary on modern man and his longing for what he has lost. The Edogawa district in Tokyo spends $15,000 a year and allocates the part-time labor of fifteen government employees to breeding and raising a batch of fireflies so that once a year the people of the neighborhood may experience a moment of special wonder. The date has to be kept secret, lest the crowds get out of hand. And at dusk of a July evening, Hisashi Abe, who is in charge of the Edogawa firefly project, opens a box and hundreds of the tiny winged creatures drift out into the night air, blinking their lights against the darkness, while all the children exclaim "Oooh" and "Aaah" just the way their parents did in the old days, when there were lightning bugs all over Japan. "Sometime in everybody's life," Mr. Abe says, "he must chase a firefly in one form or another."

We are not much good at spotting trends. On the rare occasions when we go to the city and wonder why it is that passersby smirk at us, we realize it has something to do with the haircut, the narrow necktie, the wing-tip shoes, and the straight-arrow suit that make us look like something out of a Dick Powell movie. We recall laughing at the Beatles when we first heard them and telling our children that that kind of music was a flash in the pan. We told friends not to worry, that long hair and beards wouldn't last through the first hot summer. We bought stocks at their thirty-year highs and put a house on the market the day the bottom fell out of real estate.

One of the few movements we *did* see coming was the revival of crafts, and it's a wonder, considering our record in gauging the future, that it's managed to survive as long as it has. What pleases us about this particular trend, even more than the astonishing variety of objects being wrought, is an attitude that goes along with it—an attitude that might be described as pride of workmanship, the satisfaction that comes from doing things properly. And it's our belief that some of this enthusiasm for excellence might (just might, mind you) rub off on other members of society, which would be a good thing for everyone concerned.

We hold to an outmoded view that every worker—not only the artisan—ought to take pride in what he does, whether he happens to be writing articles or throwing pots, repairing automobiles or weaving, bank-telling, fixing a leaky faucet, or frying chickens or stringing beads.

Some time ago we came across a calotype—an early print

made by the English pioneer of photography, William Henry Fox Talbot—and it struck our fancy because it suggests the way things were done a century and more ago, when people in many walks of life regarded work as something of an art. It was a picture of a hayrick, taken about midway into the nineteenth century. And what a hayrick it was! We always supposed that nothing could be more mundane and workaday than a stack of hay—indeed, we have the uneasy feeling that if we were compelled to put one up, it would resemble last year's bird's nest, wisps of hay going every which way, all a-jumble, the whole thing leaning precariously to one side. But the art and skill that went into this wondrous pile combined simplicity and utilitarianism and beauty in a way our forebears took for granted.

To shed water, there was a sloping thatched roof neatly stitched along the eaves, nearly vertical sides, and a beveled bottom—not a hay out of place, as it were. We doubt if much hay in this particular rick spoiled, and it must have been sheer joy to behold it as one rounded the bend of a country lane. Quite apart from the artistry involved, this structure spoke volumes for the farmer who built it. We can see in our mind's eye his sleek, contented cows munching happily in the clean, tidy barn. And we would bet our last dollar that that farmer was prosperous: a man who took such pride in stacking hay had to find equal satisfaction in turning a profit.

Ever on the alert for portents of progress in our own day, we wish to report on a sign we saw in front of a filling station on the way to the office the other morning. There it was, in brave letters:

WE

WASH

WINDSHIELDS

It took us back to a time when an ambitious young fellow literally ran out the door to greet you at the gas pump, tipped his cap, gave you the big grin, and was washing the windshield before you'd even had a chance to ask directions to Newton Center. Horatio Alger was written all over him, and you had the feeling that before long he would be vice-president in charge of sales and marrying the boss's daughter.

We are old enough to remember when the automobile salesman stopped by the house on Saturday with the latest model—gunmetal gray with snappy red trim and spoke wheels—and said, with a smile, "Why don't you take it for a spin tomorrow and see how you like it? No obligation, of course—I'll pick it up on Monday." And before long he had an order, and you were wondering if you had really needed a new Nash.

The most heartening news to come our way lately, though, concerns Walter Sherwood, the dump-master of West Tisbury, Massachusetts. Before this rather specialized job fell into his hands, Mr. Sherwood was a barber on the mainland, and barbering, as we all know, is not what it once was, when customers dropped in each morning for a shave and once a week for a haircut. Well, the long and short of it is that Mr. Sherwood was out of work until an agency of the federal government bestowed a modest sum upon Martha's Vineyard for the purpose of creating new jobs. One of them was that of dump-master for West Tisbury, and Mr. Sherwood applied successfully for the position.

By all accounts, the West Tisbury dump was a real dump—garbage and trash all over the place, overrun with rats, stinking to high heaven. Then Mr. Sherwood went to work.

A man with a talent for organization, he began by cleaning up the place and he put up signs instructing townspeople where to pile their refuse—garbage here, trash there, lumber over yonder; colored bottles on this pile, clear glass on that. And in case anyone missed the message implicit in the dump itself, he posted a sign reminding them of life's transitory nature: "Be Good—the End is Near." No man to idle, when he was not patrolling his domain, dispensing philosophy, or assisting people, Mr. Sherwood turned his hand to building a dump-master's cottage, a tiny, windowed structure entirely fashioned from scraps the West Tisbury natives had thrown away. One local resident likens this bungalow to "a little Japanese teahouse," which may be overdoing it a bit, but there's no doubt that it is as much a product of ingenuity and pride as the dump is. Mr. Sherwood's own description of the building is what sticks in our mind, somehow recalling that marvelous nineteenth-century hayrick: he calls it "the dump-keeper's love cottage."

That puzzling matter of property rights has been on our mind recently. The tradition of the sanctity of private property—the idea that a man's home is his castle and that he could junk his armor in the backyard if that suited him—goes back into the dim recesses of history, to a far simpler time when there was ample space for all. If you didn't like the smell of the boiling oil your neighbor poured from his battlements or didn't approve the location of his moat, it didn't matter much, since most country houses weren't cheek by jowl. But times have changed.

The other day a friend of ours attended a selectmen's meeting in town because his neighbor was applying for a permit to dump sludge from septic tanks on an open field he owns near our friend's house. On the face of it, the solution appeared simple: let the fellow put the sludge somewhere else. But the problem is no easier to dispose of than the sludge, as it turns out. We do have septic tanks, they do have to be cleaned occasionally (usually in the dead of winter when the ground is frozen solid, if our experience is any guide), and the man applying for the permit makes a living at this nasty but essential job. Obviously he has to dump the sludge somewhere, and the town provides no such place. But just as obviously, our friend doesn't want the stuff upwind from his front porch.

Another instance involves a veterinarian who is trying to create what he calls a "wildlife wonderland" in a rural setting nearby. Promotional labels aside, this is what used to be called a zoo in the old days, and he planned to fill it with exotic animals which would (the veterinarian hoped) attract droves of tourists. Now, the neighbors haven't taken kindly to this proposition. Understandably enough, they don't want their quiet country lanes overrun with out-of-state cars; they don't want the hordes of sightseers; they don't relish the anticipated smells and sounds associated with those animals. In short, they don't want to live next to a zoo, even if someone calls it a wonderland. When the veterinarian decided to jolly them along by offering to substitute ordinary farm animals for elephants or ostriches or whatever he originally had in mind, the neighbors asked why a "wildlife wonderland" was needed under these circumstances. Why not let the folks from the city visit an honest-to-goodness working farm?

Where *do* property rights begin or end? Does a landowner have the right to do anything he wants with his property, no matter how it may affect the neighbors (and, presumably, the value they place on their property)? In a good many towns, of course, some sort of zoning regulation has been laid down to deal with these questions. And although zoning is probably necessary, things being what they are, we confess we don't care much for it. It smacks of the city and suburbia, of regulations and bureaucracy, and it seems a denial of what country living is about. We always figured that if we want to put a dormer window on the house or build a garage, that's our affair—so long as it doesn't hang over the property line.

The thought of zoning reminds us of the New Jersey couple we read about who bought three or four acres about fifteen years ago in order to keep horses. They love horses, and the family's life has revolved around the animals until recently, when the authorities passed an ordinance that zoned the horses right out of town. Now the family has to pull up stakes and try to find another place where they can keep animals. Fifteen years of love and care went into that property, all of it wasted as far as they're concerned.

We don't pretend to have answers to these problems, but we do feel that most zoning ordinances and the people who are charged with carrying them out could be more responsive to the real needs and sensitivities of their neighbors. It's an awesome responsibility, when you think about it. The members of zoning boards are vested with enormous power, and a community ought to put a lot of thought into choosing those people.

In our opinion, zoning is a matter for local concern. Each community has a different mix of problems and aspirations, and these should be provided for at the local level by giving the citizens of a town an opportunity to determine what they want. And when they go to select the members of their zoning board, let them seek out men and women with vision—people who have in their mind's eye at all times a picture of what their town wants to be. When an application comes before them for a project that may alter the character of their town, they had better ask themselves—and their fellow citizens— whether they *want* their community to change. We know of one village where the authorities gave an unqualified blessing to a condominium development because it met all the requirements that had been set up, even though the development would substantially increase the local population and sorely tax every existing facility—school, highway department, stores, post office, even the cemetery. Yet at the same time the same authorities were wrangling interminably with one resident over the placement of his garage. It's a matter, obviously, of distinguishing the trees from the forest.

Another thing these zoning-board members ought to keep in mind is whether the proposal before them offers a genuine service to the community—a service not to outsiders, not to the promoters of the facility, but a service to their present neighbors, the people who have made their homes in the town. Will it provide local jobs if jobs are what is needed? Will it perform a service the community requires? Which brings us back to the dumping ground for the septic sludge and the wildlife wonderland.

We don't want the sludge deposited beyond our bedroom window, but we realize it has to go somewhere, so the town had better find a place for it. On the other hand, if we were in charge of dealing with the zoo, we would first of all ask to hear from the animals. Do they really want to live in a wonderland?

Or would they just as leave stay where they are, lackluster though the old place may be? It strikes us that this project has a lot in it for the promoters, for the tourists the townsfolk don't want, and for the vendors of souvenirs and spun candy, but very little for the elephants or the neighbors.

Many's the October day we went to pick apples in Rufus Gilbert's old orchard, and mostly we enjoyed the view as much as the picking. When you're up on a ladder, reaching as far as you can for that glorious, fat red apple that's just beyond your outstretched fingers, there isn't much to see but foliage—the dappled canopy of green that surrounds you. But when you emerge from the branches and look around to decide which tree you'll tackle next, your eye crosses the valley to the open meadows and mountainside beyond and, though you may have seen it hundreds of times before, you marvel at the sight of a Vermont hillside in the spectacular raiment of full autumn. There isn't anything to equal it, especially here in the Taconic range, where the soil is so congenial for hardwood trees, where the hard and soft maples, the beech and birches and ash, in combination with dark-green conifers and the light-green mountain meadows, weave an incredibly rich and wondrous tapestry—a tapestry that changes colors with each shift of sunlight and shadow beneath the scudding white clouds.

In the orchard, the bees work more industriously than ever, knowing that time is running out, while the grasshoppers, oblivious to the future, dance and sing in the long grass. There's a special sadness in the air, concocted of summer's passing, the golden beauty of autumn, the sound of insects, and the felt knowledge that the sun's rays are weaker, that winter is coming and death is at hand. In such a cruelly short time the green world will vanish, done in by hard frosts and November's storms.

Rufus planted the McIntosh trees here in 1924, and he says the flavor of these apples is far superior to those from trees set out in later years—"Better stock." But he hasn't been up to spraying this orchard for the last two seasons, which means there aren't any decent apples to pick. Sad, but the same thing is true everywhere around us. Twenty-five years ago, the hillsides on both sides of the valley were covered with producing apple trees, but now only one commercial grower is left. We wondered why and decided that Rufus was the best one to ask.

We sat on his porch in the morning sun and talked about why the apple business had collapsed. There wasn't a single reason for it, he said, but many. Growing fruit commercially had taken hold here in a fairly big way just after the turn of the century; before that time every farm and household had trees for its own use, but few apples to sell. Then Ernest West and others had begun planting orchards and there had been good years in the twenties and thirties and forties, when apples were probably the best agricultural business to be in. "We got a good price," Rufus recalled, "and if we'd saved our money instead of putting it into new equipment and setting out more trees, we'd have been a lot better off.

"I think it was the number of other fruits that became available that hurt us the worst," he said. "Why, at times apples were selling for ten cents apiece in the stores, and nobody's going to make applesauce at that price." So people bought oranges or grapefruit or some other fruit—canned or frozen as well as fresh.

"More than a hundred people used to come here very year to pick," Rufus continued. "They came from all over—Pawlet, Granville, everywhere in the valley. And on the first day of picking there'd be cars and people swarming all over the orchard. My goodness, what we had to do to get ready for them—ladders, baskets, barrels, you had to think of everything—and just when things were organized and running smoothly, it was all over. Two weeks of it and you were done.

"Nowadays there are only two ways to make a go of it with apples," he went on. "One way is to be big—the way Byrd does it down South, with orchards all over Virginia and the Carolinas and an integrated operation that takes the apples from the trees through processing and packing plants and onto the trucks. The other way is to have a small orchard and produce maybe two thousand bushels of apples that you can sell at your roadside stand, along with other fresh produce, at the retail price."

We hadn't the heart to tell Rufus what the apple business of the future is going to be like if the U.S. Department of Agriculture has its way. Since the USDA has very little to offer the small farmer these days, it probably will surprise no one to learn that the department is developing, with our tax dollars, a machine that may make it possible for the commercial apple to go the way of the commercial tomato. According to Dr. Bernard R. Tennes, an agricultural engineer, "The day of the square apple tree is coming. Instead of designing equipment to suit the shape of fruit trees, we should shape the trees to suit new, more efficient machines."

Dr. Tennes, we see, is a creature of his time. Make the apple tree suit the machine—just as the tomato was made to suit the machine, with results that are all too familiar. In the case of the tomato, taxpayers' money was also used to develop a machine to harvest on a large scale. The trouble was that the machine had a heavy hand and most of the tomatoes got bruised. So what did the agricultural engineers do—design a machine that wouldn't bruise the tomatoes? Not on your life. They bred a tomato with a skin so thick you can barely cut it, so that it would take the rough treatment from the machine. And the devil take the consumer.

According to Dr. Tennes, apple trees of the future "will have to be small, uniform, and of a predetermined shape." One possibility he suggests is a cube. Another is a tree with two widely separated layers of limbs. A third looks like a three-dimensional Y. And we'd better get cracking, Dr. Tennes warns: ". . . the quicker we develop the technology and gain the information we need to develop management systems, the better off everyone will be." Everyone, that is, except the folks who like a tasty apple.

Dr. Tennes and his associates at the USDA's Agricultural Research Service are working on an over-the-row machine—"an inverted-U-shaped power unit," they call it—which has a pruning attachment that prunes the trees and collects, chops, and deposits the branches as mulch; a spraying attachment that meters chemicals at rates proportional to ground speeds; and a picking attachment. Since one operator will be able to handle all these tasks, the inverted-U-shaped power unit will presumably do away with quite a few jobs. And from the look of it, the machine will probably cost $30,000 or $40,000. Even if anyone around here could afford one, we doubt if it would behave properly on a steep New England hillside. Which means that it will be most suitable for the orchardist with plenty of capital and plenty of flatland. Chalk up another one for the USDA and agribusiness.

"Imagine, me buying apples!" Rufus had said. "But Ethel likes an apple in the evening and I picked up three pounds at the supermarket not long ago. Why, at the price I paid, they're getting sixteen dollars a bushel. Imagine that! Just before we went out of business it cost us two dollars for every bushel we packed, and we were only able to sell them for a dollar fifty."

The other day we drove by Rufus's orchard and tried to imagine how those big, unruly McIntosh trees with the wonderfully contorted branches would respond to a management system and an over-the-row machine that turns trees into topiary. We wondered, too, what would happen if the U.S. Department of Agriculture ever turned its attention to the small farmer and to helping him survive.

The storm signals went up on Martha's Vineyard in the autumn, the moment McDonald's announced plans to open a fast-food franchise on the island. As one would expect in a place that has always prided itself on its distinctive offshore charm, the immediate response to the news was the formation of a No-Mac Committee; and in December the islanders were scurrying about, collecting funds for legal fees, a press campaign, and the impending battle. "If every member of the Island community were to send a contribution equal to just the cost of one meal at McDonald's," one appeal read, "we could stop the Big Mac attack."

In January the Board of Health denied the franchise applicant a permit for a septic tank, but many anti-McDonald's people had the uneasy feeling they had not heard the last of restaurant chains.

What they are up against, of course, is a huge corporation with revenues of about $3 billion a year and an annual advertising budget of $100 million. Not satisfied with some 5000 outlets, McDonald's had announced its intention to build one new restaurant every twenty-four hours for the next decade. (McDonald's is the name. Growth is our game.) That comes to another 3650 hamburger stands, in case you were not counting, causing one to wonder if the Golden Arches will eventually soar over every hamlet in America.

The messages coming in from the Vineyard had a familiar ring. In our town, a few years ago, rumors began to be heard, followed by confirmation that McDonald's would soon come to Manchester. Most people's reaction was, "Isn't it too bad? But there's nothing we can do." A few felt otherwise, and they got together one evening and decided that they could and *would* do something. A friend of ours who calls herself the Town Crank wrote a starchy letter to the local newspaper, calling attention to the issues raised by McDonald's plans, and others followed suit. Members of the group talked to neighbors, organized a public meeting to discuss the problem, and quickly realized—since the matter would undoubtedly wind up in an environmental hearing—that they would have to raise money and retain a lawyer.

A succession of hearings followed, before a bewildering array of committees and commissions, both local and state. The citizens' group and their attorney had concluded that the most telling argument against the restaurant was the potential traffic congestion at the particular site chosen by McDonald's—property bordering the narrowest section of the main highway through town, just south of a major route intersection already so plugged with traffic during the height of the tourist season that cars are sometimes backed up, bumper to bumper, for a quarter of a mile.

Then the local selectmen decided to oppose McDonald's. Traffic experts brought in from Montpelier and from Maryland averred that vehicles turning into the Golden Arches would indeed create hazards and recommended that the highway be widened (at McDonald's expense) to accommodate two additional turning lanes for those in quest of a Big Mac and a milkshake. The upshot was that McDonald's decided to drop its option on this particular site. Now the citizens' group is waiting for the other shoe to fall. The town, McDonald's spokesman added, continues to represent "a viable economic opportunity for the corporation," and a new location will be selected. So while the first round goes to the anti-McDonald's forces, the fight will almost certainly be resumed one day at a new battleground of McDonald's choosing.

What strikes us as heartening in all this is that a small, determined band of sixteen people (out of the area's population of three thousand) had the strength and the will to take on an enormous corporation on an issue of very real local concern.

Vermont's environmental laws being what they are, the only matters that come to adjudication are those that have opponents. In other words, if you are against a development, you have to stand up and be counted; only then is there a contested hearing. So the citizens' group gets the credit for belling the cat.

As is often the case, other issues were lurking in the wings. One might ask, for example, by what right a giant corporation imposes itself and its plastic-wrapped sandwiches on a community if that community doesn't want them? Or, conversely, by what right a small, vocal citizens' group sets itself up to speak for the community? The citizens of Manchester were not asked to vote on the matter, so no one can say with certainty what the public attitude is; but one clue to that sentiment appeared in a poll of 270 local high school students, when 37 percent voted for McDonald's and 40 percent against, with the rest undecided. Those in favor gave as their reasons that they liked the food, that the town needs the employment the company would provide, and that the taxes paid by McDonald's would increase the town revenue. Those opposed believed that the advent of McDonald's would alter the character of the town and cause it to lose its identity, that there was no need for a McDonald's here, and that the increased tax revenues would be inadequate recompense for other problems the fast-food outpost would create.

A factor that weighed heavily on people's minds was the potential effect of a McDonald's on local businesses—small restaurants, especially. What would happen to them if the fast-food chain moved in? How could Jack Green at the Double Hex, who was then paying $1.60 a pound for top-quality beef for his hamburgers and selling them for $1.00, compete in price with a company that has its own colossal herds of beef cattle, that is the largest consumer of meat in the United States outside the armed forces? Would the likely loss of customers and tax revenues from the small, owner-operated restaurants cost the town more than it might gain from a

McDonald's? And would the character of the town indeed be permanently changed, as Burger Chef and the Colonel and others moved in on McDonald's heels?

One thing that gives a town character is diversity—a healthy mix of small businesses that provide meaningful jobs and an opportunity for entrepreneurs to have their own business and the heady feeling of independence. Character, in a community, is variety—a range of different styles, as opposed to a strip of fast-food emporiums serving up the same indistinguishable assembly-line food, varying only in the garishness of their façades and the colors of the plastic tabletops.

And there is the question of how much revenue a typical McDonald's actually *does* bring to a community. According to the Institute for Local Self-Reliance in Washington, D.C., more than 75 percent of all the money taken in by a representative McDonald's may leave the community immediately. (That includes advertising, payments to the corporation for land, rent, service and legal fees, other corporate expenses, food and paper products, and management costs and salaries.) Something like 15 percent of the total sales volume goes for labor at the restaurant, and less than 2 percent is paid in local taxes.

The citizens of a town had better concern themselves with questions such as these, for it may be argued that the most important role they can play is to ask questions, to determine what sort of community they want, and to shape their plans accordingly. Every community needs its quota of Town Cranks—the burs under its saddle, the questioners.

As our friend Harvey Carter observes, a fast-food mentality has taken hold of American life these days—at all levels. Somehow the notion has arisen that everything should be quick and easy and in disposable packages. And for those of us who prefer that products be made well, fashioned with artistry and care, it is distressing to witness the decline of interest in craftsmanship in any field. Perhaps the most we can hope for is that choices will remain—that the fast-food restaurants will go where they are wanted (though, one wishes, in buildings designed by someone other than the Golden Architect, and offering a product where the food itself, and not the grossly wasteful packaging, is paramount), and that the good local eating places will continue to prosper, thanks to food and surroundings as distinctive as the individuals who have created them.

Our earliest, most enduring memories of Christmas are of the kitchen smells that filled the house when Mother was baking the wondrous array of cookies we would deliver to friends all over the neighborhood, and of the ritual of Christmas Eve, when we hung up the stockings and Father read "A Visit from St. Nicholas" in front of the fire, just before we were sent to bed. It came to be a family ritual that persisted for nearly fifty years, because he would read it whenever children or grandchildren or great-grandchildren were present for the occasion, repeating the story in exactly the same way, with a twinkle in the eye and the voice, pausing now and then before the last word in a line of verse to let the small listeners fill in the rhyme and to shout with joy and laughter because they remembered and because he, apparently, did not.

When we grew older he occasionally told of the man who had written the poem, and there was something about the way he spoke that made us aware of the impermanence of life. Here was a poem, he would say, that had been repeated in households such as ours for a hundred Christmases and more—a poem that was as familiar to us as any piece of verse we knew—yet scarcely anyone was aware of the name of the man who had written it.

Clement Clarke Moore, we learned, was born midway through the Revolution and died seven days after the Battle of Gettysburg, his eighty-four years bridging the birth and breakup of the Republic. As the son of an Episcopal minister, he grew up in a gentle, courtly world that was virtually unchanged from pre-revolutionary days. His grandmother on his mother's side had left his parents her handsome, three-story house, called Chelsea, on a wooded hill overlooking the Hudson River at what is now Twenty-third Street between Eighth and Ninth avenues in New York City. (She also bequeathed them a salt meadow in New Jersey, four slaves, and lands in upstate New York that had been part of a 400,000-acre patent from the Crown.)

Moore's particular interests were language and religion; after graduating from Columbia College he began work on *A Compendious Lexicon of the Hebrew Language*, hoping no doubt to whet his countrymen's interest in the study of Hebrew. In 1819 he gave part of his estate to the Protestant Episcopal Church, thereby making possible the building of its General Theological Seminary, where he became professor of Biblical learning and for a quarter-century taught Oriental and Greek literature.

Inevitably, the passing years brought change to the area surrounding Chelsea. Twenty-third Street became a bustling thoroughfare; brick row houses sprang up where once there had been open fields; woodlands and the marshes vanished; and eventually the only reminder of the Moore house was the name Chelsea Square.

In December of 1822, as a gift for his family, Moore composed twenty-eight couplets of a ballad, and on Christmas Eve read it for the first time to his five children. Members of the family immediately recognized themselves, as well as the protagonist, who was modeled, Moore said, on "a portly, rubicund Dutchman living in the neighborhood," and perhaps they sensed even then that the verses captured more than what was familiar to them, more than the love and warmth of the household at Chelsea; that they told of innocence and wonder and simple belief, of the breathless anticipation of childhood; and that they belonged not only to the Moore children but to every family that cared to listen.

A relative who was at Chelsea that Christmas Eve copied the poem into an album; a friend of hers from Troy, New

York, read it, copied it again, and gave it to the editor of the *Troy Sentinel,* who printed it a year later, in the issue of December 23, 1823. He admitted, "We do not know to whom we are indebted for the following description of . . . Santa Claus, his costume, and his equipage, as he goes about visiting the firesides of this happy land, laden with Christmas bounties." Not only was the poem's author unknown but it had no title, so the editor set a line of type over it reading, "An Account of a Visit from St. Nicholas," followed by the words Clement Moore had composed for his children:

> *'Twas the night before Christmas,*
>   *when all through the house*
> *Not a creature was stirring, not*
>   *even a mouse;*
> *The stockings were hung by the*
>   *chimney with care,*
> *In hopes that St. Nicholas soon*
>   *would be there. . . .*

Each year a few more newspapers repeated the poem around Christmastime, and although the author had never thought it worth publishing, it was printed in the early 1830s as a little book with illustrations by Myron King, a Troy engraver who brought Moore's spry old elf to life. In 1844, when it appeared in a collection of his poems, Moore observed in the preface that it was only one of many "mere trifles . . . [that] have been often found to afford greater pleasure than what was by myself esteemed of more worth."

And of course it is what Moore called mere trifles that stick in our minds from Christmases past. Not the elaborate packages or what they contained, but the ornaments the children made the year they were sick in bed—ornaments that still decorate the tree. The annual struggle to hang the strings of beads so that they draped naturally. Caroling in the falling snow as dusk closed in on the village. Neighborhood children appearing at the door to present a wreath they had made. The visits from grandparents, the hanging of stockings. The family dogs and their bewilderment by squeaker toys that emerged on Christmas morning. The recollection of having to assemble toys that came knocked down, in a kit; setting up the electric train in the small hours of the morning when the house was still at last; the picture of bright little faces appearing beside their parents' bed long before the sun rose, wondering if it was yet time to go downstairs to see what Santa Claus had brought. Glimpses of a little girl dressed as Mary, of an equally small boy playing Joseph in a pageant, of a midnight church service when the choirboy standing next to ours suddenly got sick and threw up all over his neighbors in the middle of "Hark, the Herald Angels Sing."

This year, once again, when the tree is trimmed and the wreaths are hung, we will go to the church on the village green, to sing the carols and hear the old story of the shepherds and the wise men and their visit to the manger, while we await the best moment of all—the moment when the lights in the church are turned out and the minister steps down from the chancel bearing a single candle, to light a small taper held by one of his parishioners. From that one, another and another and another will be lit, each member of the congregation passing the flame along to the next person until the entire church is aglow with soft, shimmering light and everyone begins singing that loveliest of carols—"Silent night, holy night. . . ."

Then it will be time to return home, to the fire and the Christmas tree, covered with ornaments fashioned or contributed by so many generations of the family, some dating back to Christmases in Ohio in the homes of great-grandparents we never knew. And it is then that we will remember once more the picture of a kindly man with laughing eyes, holding a little child in each arm and a book between them as he reads:

'Twas the night before Christmas,
  when all through the . . .
"HOUSE!"
Not a creature was stirring, not
  even a . . .
"MOUSE!"

One of the many reassuring aspects of a democracy is the obligation its elected officials have to submit regularly to a reappraisal by the voters. The Ins, in other words, have to take their chances on becoming Outs. Presidents run the risk of becoming ex-presidents, mayors ex-mayors, and the trial by ballot extends right down the line to second constable and fence viewer. Those we throw out go back to being lawyers or merchants or dentists or whatever they were before fate made officeholders of them, while those who are reelected are granted one of life's rarest privileges—a second chance. Whatever the shortcomings of those who are returned to office, it is their good fortune to start over again with a clean slate—absolved, as it were—with another opportunity to accomplish all the things they probably ought to have done in the first place. One can only hope that the next time around they will give thought to their constituents' hopes and fears and attempt to come to grips with both.

We have been thinking a good deal lately about political campaigns and it occurs to us that this democratic tradition of renewal—the clean break with the past—is one that we non-officeholders ought to practice, just to see how well we would fare. After all, we expect our elected officials to have brains, looks, 20–20 foresight, a witty and intelligent spouse, attractive, straight children, sane parents, the demeanor of a television anchorman, the confidence of a cardinal, and God knows what else. If we require that and more of them, the least we can do is ask ourselves now and again if we are headed in the right direction—or if, indeed, we are headed anywhere at all. Ideally, we suppose, an individual's life might be viewed as a series of long, flat steps or plateaus, each higher than the one that preceded it, each representing a greater challenge and demanding a wiser response than the one before. So the purpose of this self-questioning would be to ask if it isn't time to move along, to take another upward step.

Despite the inherent hazards, self-examination sometimes leads to surprising and salutary results, and no time is better for such stocktaking than January, the cold season of new beginnings and good intentions. If we permitted ourself to dwell upon the year just past it would be evident that someone was trying to tell us something—three of our best cows killed by lightning, crops spoiled or lost because of rain, the upper farm road and four bridges washed out by a hurricane no one could have foreseen. But no, in the manner of innocents since time began, we put the past behind us and face the future with hope, confident of better days ahead.

For many years now we have had a New Year's Eve party at our house, and some time ago our friend Louise—who is a great one for games and keeping people busy lest anyone doubt that he is having a good time—instituted the custom of handing each guest a slip of paper and asking for a written prediction for the coming year. Sometime after the old year has slipped away, these unsigned forecasts are drawn from a hat and read aloud, and they tend to follow a certain pattern. There are the inevitable gags, there are the predictions that are meant to be taken Very Seriously, and then there are the few scribbled lines that represent hopes or dreams rather than expectations, and these are the ones that interest us most because they occasionally go to the heart of things. Often someone records on a slip of paper the promise that we will all be here together a year hence, and everyone smiles confidently, not really imagining that one of us might be missing.

There is nothing out of the ordinary about this particular New Year's Eve celebration unless you count it unusual that some of the young adults who are here first came to the party as small children, or that we have all been together, parents and children and friends, talking and arguing and laughing and singing our songs and loving each other for as long as anyone cares to remember. The food is always good and there is plenty to drink, but the food and drink are not what brings the people together—something else does. We like to think that it is the moment that comes each year a minute or two before midnight, when something special happens among this assemblage of all ages, making tangible the sense of community everyone feels. We form a large circle around the perimeter of the living room, each one clasping tightly the hand of the person on either side while we sing "Auld Lang Syne," and it is then that you see tears shining on the cheeks of these friends—tears of sorrow for those who are no longer here despite the brave predictions of the year before, tears of joy for the friendship and love we have shared.

And sometimes before the evening is over those of us who like singing harmony together, having done all the show tunes and popular songs we can remember from our parents' and our own and our children's youth, know that we will have to wrap it all up with "Good Night, Irene" and, finally, "Now the Day Is Over," with those marvelous parts everyone has been waiting for hours to sing. Then the last friend is out in the driveway, climbing into a car and calling good night and happy new year, the snow is crisp, the air and the stars incredibly clear, and you know that this is one of the magic moments of life.

Feeding
the Stove

This winter we returned to school, in a manner of speaking, to audit a noncredit course in bookkeeping. We took pains to avoid this arcane subject in college, but now that we understand the basic principles involved, we realize that it holds no hidden mysteries. In the final analysis, everything comes down to the difference between income and outgo, and only the most rudimentary intelligence is needed to see the mounting pile of debits at our house—the backwash of the energy crisis.

Each month we tot up the havoc: oil bill nearly twice what it was last year; electric bill up horrendously; the cost of driving an automobile double what it used to be. Each week we emerge from the grocery store with a lighter bag of food for which we have spent more money than ever. Our personal balance sheet reflects not only the widening gap between what we are able to take in and what the necessities of life cost; it testifies also to the declining reservoir of the world's natural resources.

As if this were not enough, one recent invoice shows how the wind is beginning to blow. Examining the latest *billet-doux* from the power company, we noted an unusual item called "Customer Service," which—upon investigation—turns out to be a charge for reading the meter and billing. Now, despite outward appearances, we are not without some experience in business affairs. We recognize that every transaction requires an exchange of cash for goods or services rendered. But this is the first time anyone has come out flatly and said they are billing us for having to bill us, and it takes a utility company, with its gift for public relations, to define the monthly inconvenience as Customer Service. It occurred to us that when we go into a store to buy a pair of overshoes we are not charged extra for the time the clerk spends writing up the sales slip, and the longer we thought about this, the clearer the message seemed. In a spirit of generosity and thrift, we offer our solution to the power company to help them through the difficult days ahead. We will henceforth read our own electric meter, multiply the kilowatt hours consumed since the last reading by the rate, and send a check for that amount to the company, thereby eliminating the need for them to charge us $5 additional each month.

What John Cole of the *Maine Times* has called the postindustrial revolution is upon us with a vengeance. So many of the old verities we used to take for granted—including the supposedly unlimited supplies of cheap power—are gone or going, and for a while this winter, every time we carried in a load of logs to stoke the stove's dying embers we cursed the Arab sheiks for what they have done to us. Then, no less angrily, we took to cursing ourselves for being so prodigal, so unseeing, so like the grasshopper in the fable who would neither think nor plan ahead.

Perhaps, we found ourself thinking, if we had never known or experienced the wonders of an industrialized society, we would be better off. Just imagine—if a one-time New Haven Railroad conductor named Edwin L. Drake had never demonstrated that reserves of petroleum exist beneath the earth's surface . . . Or better yet, if we had been sealed in a time capsule around the middle of the nineteenth century—*then,* we said to ourself, we would be able to cope, able to live off the produce we had grown, able to warm body and home with the wood we had cut and split a year in advance. We imagined ourself heading backward in a time machine to take our place in that spartan, uncomplicated world, satisfied with the slow pace of horse and buggy, content for our entertainment with visits from neighbors, happy to take each day as it came in the slow, orderly progression of the seasons.

Somehow we find a certain satisfaction and peace of mind in

such rumination. It isn't—as friends have accused us—that we yearn wistfully for the past as though the present didn't have a great deal to offer. It's just that we think the time has come to shuck off the unnecessary frills that add little to the quality of life. There is an old saw to the effect that what our fathers regarded as luxuries we accept as necessities, but the time is nigh when necessities will be luxuries again.

Take our national mania for packaging. We are told that the definition of fair market value is the price a willing buyer will pay a willing seller, but we are continually being confronted with merchandise that makes an unwilling buyer of us. We will always remember this year as the one we first saw an acorn squash wrapped in plastic. Now, if there is any vegetable we know that does not require the magic of modern packaging, it is the acorn squash. It always seemed to us that nature had done herself proud with this vegetable, compensating for the plain, undistinguished interior by endowing it with a superbly efficient outer garment—nothing beautiful, mind you, but virtually indestructible and germproof. We found that we were filled with resentment over a marketing system that had manufactured that plastic and caused it to encase a humble squash.

The upshot of this discovery at the supermarket is a resolve to nurture our hills of acorn squash with special care this summer. It may be that the produce will cost as much as what we can buy at the supermarket, but we don't care; we anticipate gleefully the sight of those squashes mounded neatly in our root cellar—wearing a few traces of dried mud from the garden, to be sure, but with their skins unsullied by the cosmetics of modern packaging.

Certain straws in the wind suggest that something is happening to traditional buying habits in this country. For two years in a row now, the total volume of food moving through commercial channels has declined, even though the nation's population has continued to increase. On the face of it, this might suggest that per capita food consumption is decreasing, but we doubt it. We suspect that something more significant is at work. The figures collected by the U.S. Department of Agriculture do not include any estimates of food consumed from home gardens, nor do they take into consideration purchases made directly from roadside stands operated by farmers, truck gardeners, and orchardists. Could it be that America's eyes are turning once more to the land?

Now and then a well-meaning visitor from the city inquires what we do with our spare time here in the country and we are hard put to answer. There is no spare time anymore. The carefree hours once devoted to reading, visiting, walking, or just lolling around are consumed in ministering to the cast-iron companions of all our waking hours—the woodstoves. Even now, with the snows of winter nearly gone and April here, there is only a pause in the wood-heating season—a pause occupied by what is known as the wood-cutting-hauling-splitting-and-stacking season.

On the strength of our winter's experience, we can offer a few observations based on nourishing four stoves and one fireplace.

BUILDING THE FIRE   There are several schools of thought concerning the proper laying up of logs for a fire, but the important thing is to *get a fire going.* Unless this first principle is observed you will put match to paper, close the stove door, turn to other chores, and return fifteen minutes later to find a pile of black, smoldering logs and a cold firebox. This discovery necessitates removing the logs from the stove. Since there is no place in most rooms to deposit charred, smoking sticks of wood, you have two options: (1) put on a pair of asbestos gloves (*see* "Asbestos gloves and potholders," below), lift out the logs, and dash to the nearest exit and throw them into the snow, where they will lie, unfit for use until the following season; or (2) carefully pry up the logs with a poker and, with another poker (there are never two pokers at hand beside a stove, so you send your wife or a child to fetch another), stuff additional newspaper and kindling into the space below the logs, light them, and stand by whistling cheerfully, hoping for the best. In windy locales like ours, downdrafts are a frequent menace. To compensate for a downdraft (which you will recognize when smoke from the stove billows into the room), throw open a window, grope your way through the smoke back to the stove, open the stove door wide, and wait for an updraft to take effect—hoping, meanwhile, that no sparks fly out onto the rug. The temperature in the room will drop noticeably while this procedure is going on. The smoke will disappear eventually. The smell of smoke will not.

DAMPERING   The technique of what we call dampering eludes many a novice with his first airtight stove, but it may be summarized briefly. The idea is to get a good draft going through the fire and to keep it blowing until the fire is burning fiercely enough so that you can damper it down. In our particular airtight model, once the fire is blazing with the doors open, we carefully and somewhat surreptitiously—so as not to let the fire know what we are up to—close one door with the right hand, slowly opening the rear damper with the left. If this is done too hastily, smoke will pour from the rear damper, filling the room. But assuming things have gone as they were supposed to, we just as carefully and surreptitiously close the other door, simultaneously opening the other rear damper. With luck, the fire will not go out (which is what it wants to do) while this maneuver takes place. Then we let the fire roar like an inferno for about twenty minutes—until the stove attains a healthy red glow or until the temperature near it is sufficient to singe the hair on our legs (we are doing this first thing in the morning, remember, attired in bathrobe and slippers), and then close the dampers about halfway. If we find that the stove is still glowing red, or if perchance we have started a chimney fire, we close the dampers all the way. When all danger has passed, we go upstairs to shave.

ASH REMOVAL   At our house, ash-removal time comes around every Saturday morning. Knowing this, we do not fire up the stoves on Friday night, which means that the house is about the temperature of a crypt in winter when we arise. And since ash removal takes a while, the house remains at that temperature until the job is done. So it is generally done quickly. Our method is to bring in a small galvanized garbage can, used only for this purpose, from outside, set it alongside the stove, and ever so cautiously shovel ashes into it. As the garbage can has been sitting outside since the previous week, the bottom is covered with snow and ice, but we do not realize this until the snow and ice begin melting on the dining-room floor. After mopping up the water we take great care in removing the ashes. No matter how painstaking you are, however, a fine cloud of dust will hover over the stove, float around the room, and settle gently onto the furniture. The ash removal is followed—as soon as the stoves are clean and fired up again—by a general dusting and vacuuming.

STOVEPIPE CLEANING   Mercifully, this operation takes place at less frequent intervals than ash removal. About every three or four weeks, that is, or when chunks of hardened creosote begin to work their way out of the joints in the pipe. The way to begin this job is to have a complete edition of the Sunday *New York Times* (preferably last week's) on hand to cover the floor. This done, you may proceed to dismantle the pipe, thereby showering the newspaper (and several triangular-shaped sections of the rug, where the paper has shifted slightly) with a substance resembling lampblack, only gooier. The sections of pipe are then taken outdoors, to be cleaned with a wire brush or other instrument. When reassembled, they do not fit the way they did before they were taken apart.

ENTERTAINING AROUND A WOODSTOVE   Since all the assembled guests will be discussing their woodstoves, conversation is never lacking. But one of the most difficult tricks for the host is to get a seat on the far side of the room from the woodstove after the company arrives. Since you want the room cozy and welcoming for friends coming in out of the cold, the woodstove will have been building up heat for some time. In fact, the temperature by the chairs closest to it is 115°F. When the women guests enter, shivering, and take these seats, they soon find that one arm and the side of their face nearest the stove are turning an alarming pink, and they lean dangerously away from the stove, pretending to be carried away with laughter. Uncle Fred, who has been through all this before, has quickly preempted a chair at the opposite side of the room, where the temperature is a comfortable 70°, and the trick is to dislodge him so you can slip into his place. Usually it is necessary to ignore his empty glass, forcing him to get up and make his own drink while you leap for his chair.

In addition to these general remarks, it may be useful to list a few items of equipment we have found essential to the proper operation of woodstoves.

ASBESTOS GLOVES AND POTHOLDERS   It is well to have at least one of each beside every woodstove—not that you will remember to use them, but to have in readiness after you have burned your hand and remember that that's why they are there.

ALOE PLANTS   For reasons not altogether clear, this plant with the fleshy, spiny-toothed leaves has medicinal powers highly beneficial to the woodstove operator. When you burn the back of your hand or wrist on the stove, which you will do regularly, reach immediately for the plant, break off one of the tips, and squeeze the juice onto the burned area. Relief is almost immediate. Friends who are unaware of the plant's healing properties often ask why none of our aloes have points on the leaves and we reply simply that we are hybridizing a new variety.

HUMIDIFIER   Any household in which a woodstove or two is used for heating should have a humidifier. The model we have holds four 2-gallon pails of water, and it is a relatively simple task to haul this water from the kitchen sink to the humidifier every morning, after we have carried in three loads of wood for the stoves.

WATERING CAN   Even with the humidifier going full blast, the moisture content in our house approximates that of the Gobi Desert, and the houseplants are in constant need of water. We try to give them a drink every other day, fitting this chore in between loads of wood for the stoves and trips to the humidifier.

NEEDLE, TWEEZERS, AND MERTHIOLATE   The need for these handy little items will be readily apparent. The only question is whether to have one central first-aid station for the removal and treatment of splinters, or one by each stove.

COMBUSTIBLE MATERIALS   Paper, kindling, and wood—these are the three essential ingredients for the woodstove.

(1) Paper. Subscriptions to *The Wall Street Journal,* the daily and Sunday *New York Times,* and two weeklies provide just about the right amount of paper to start the fires in four stoves and a fireplace. We have found that *The Wall Street Journal* burns best, the *Times* next best (except for the Sunday Magazine Section, which is almost worthless), and the weeklies worst.

(2) Kindling. No matter how much kindling you have, it is never enough. Since very few items come packed in crates these days, it is necessary to become something of a scavenger, picking through dumps and other likely sources of supply, skulking around sawmills for odd scraps, collecting dry twigs when you walk in the woods, and buying the occasional pickup

load from a supplier whose price is right. But you will not have enough.

(3) Firewood. The countryman who used to be judged by the condition of his barns and fences, the appearance of his livestock, and the size of his milk check is known today by the size and dryness of his woodpile. The burning properties of various types of hardwood have been widely described, so we will not cover that here. Suffice it to say you must have a very large quantity of dry, split hardwood—preferably maple, ash, oak, apple, and the like—to feed your stoves. A *very* large quantity. What we have learned, to our sorrow, is that each of our four stoves and the fireplace requires a different size log. The Glenwood, which has a minuscule firebox, likes an eighteen-inch stick (and not a fraction of an inch longer), split rather fine. The American-made airtight works best with two-foot logs, with the larger ones split at least in half. The fireplace will take unsplit two-footers handily, but could accommodate something longer. The Franklin prefers eighteen-inchers, only split a little larger than those for the Glenwood. And the Scandinavian airtight will accept nothing longer than fifteen inches.

You are beginning to get the picture. Ideally, we should have five separate woodpiles, each with logs cut and split to the dimensions of its particular stove. But we do not. We have a single woodpile at the house, from which we must select carefully (always on the coldest night, when the wind is blowing hardest) the appropriate logs for each stove. It is an operation that doubtless lends itself to computerization, but somehow we are not equal to that, and on winter evenings you will find us shuffling around the woodpile, pulling out a log here and a log there, cursing when the pile shifts and a chunk of rock maple cascades down onto an instep.

We sit by the stove writing this. Outside the wind howls, but here in the room it's toasty and warm and a teakettle bubbles merrily. Under such circumstances it seems almost sacrilegious to say so, but we're awfully glad another wood-burning season is drawing to a close.

April's a quirky time, an in-and-out month. The neighbors are irritable and squabbling, out of sorts with one another and with us. The dead hand of winter hangs on, clutching at our sleeve, clinging like a garrulous old man at a wedding reception.

There were occasions, these past months, when we sat looking out at the dark encircling hills that have brooded over ten generations of Vermonters and asked ourself how in heaven's name those old-timers managed to keep warm. We think we've done a day's work when we fell a big maple tree with a chainsaw, cut it up, and haul it to the house in the pickup truck. And then we think about the people who had to do the job with an ax and bring the load down off the mountain through the deep snow behind a team of oxen. We have a tight house, well-insulated; theirs must have leaked cold air like a sieve. Our woodstove functions efficiently; their fireplace probably lost as much heat as it gave off. In a pinch, we can turn on the oil burner or an electric heater; they had nothing to fall back on.

We have been—all of us, in this land—beneficiaries of the age of technology. Longer life, more leisure, bountiful harvests, a rising standard of living—these are only a few of the blessings the child of the twentieth century has known. We grew up believing that nothing was impossible, that the future was unbounded, limited only by our imagination. If we said we could put a man on the moon, we could—and did. We pick up the telephone and talk with a friend in London. We flick a switch and see and hear what is happening in Kabul and Karachi. But suddenly the future is here and we are running out of gas.

One man who saw it coming was Anwar Sadat. In the wake of the Iranian revolution and the Soviet invasion of Afghanistan, the president of Egypt quietly observed that "The war for the oil has begun." As indeed it has.

The production of domestic oil in the United States peaked in 1970 and has been declining ever since. Indications are that we will probably have exhausted all of our economically usable oil by the end of this century. How much we will be importing by then, or how much we will be permitted to import, is anybody's guess. But the question may be academic, since at the present rate of consumption, the world's supply of oil may not last a lot longer than our own.

The story of energy in this country has been the exchange of one form for another, the transition from an increasingly expensive form of fuel to a cheaper, more abundant, more convenient source. So we have switched from wood to coal, from coal to oil and natural gas, and the idea was that we would move ultimately from oil and gas to nuclear power. What comes as a shock to us now is that there is no more cheap energy in sight. We have used up all the readily available resources, and what remains of the world's supply is going to become scarcer and more expensive. Although Americans represent only one-sixteenth of the planet's population, we have—in only fifty years' time—consumed more than half the producible oil created by nature over hundreds of millions of years. And as long as we continue to equate progress with growth, we will go right on demanding and producing more of everything. As long as Gross National Product is our measurement of success, we will need more energy to produce more goods.

Here, then, is the terrible economic dilemma of our time, to which labor and business leaders, politicians, philosophers, artists—all of us, must address our attention while there is yet time to do so. In a nation whose goal and whose god have been growth, where do we turn when the resources that make growth possible no longer exist? What do the factory workers do when the boss shuts off the boiler for the last time?

Blessed with such natural resources as no other people in history have known, we have always operated as though there were no tomorrow. We cut all the timber in New England, but that was all right because there was plenty more in Michigan; by the time that was gone, we had spotted the big trees in Oregon and Washington. We planted cotton and tobacco and wore out the soil because we could always move west to virgin land and plant more cotton and tobacco. Even today, faced with the dwindling reserves of petroleum, we pin our hopes on a new find off Alaska or comfort ourselves by saying we have coal enough for a hundred years, maybe a thousand. But a lot of that coal is too deep to mine, or lies in veins that are too thin to extract economically. And who will mine all it takes to satisfy our demands? How will we transport it around the countryside: on the railroads we have been neglecting for forty years? or in trucks, until the trucks run out of fuel?

Recent experience has been rude for supporters of nuclear power. The events at Three Mile Island revealed that human and mechanical errors are going to occur in nuclear plants in spite of all we can do to prevent them, and that when they do there is no predicting the consequences. In the meantime, one utility after another has announced that it is abandoning plans to build (or in some cases, to complete) nuclear power plants, because the costs of construction have become prohibitive, the problems of waste disposal monumental, the environmental risks too great.

There are other potential sources of power—solar, hydroelectric, waste products—but none is capable of supplying more than a fraction of our current needs. The problem is not the technology. The problem is our appetite. And the first step toward a solution is conservation. It is predicted that by the middle of the present decade—by 1985—we will require almost twice as much energy as we consumed in 1970. But no one seems to know where it is going to come from. That sort of supply simply does not exist.

There are times when we believe we would be better off without quite so much energy anyway. For instance, we just received an announcement of a new plastic chair, molded in the shape of a giant human hand—"impervious to water and moisture . . . ideal conversation piece . . . perfect for poolside and hot tub areas," available in yellow, orange, sandalwood, chocolate, and antique white. That's one of the items we hope to do without in a petroleumless world. Another is the pocket calculator that is programmed to remember Dad's birthday, giving you the hour, date, and Dad's telephone number, accompanied by an alarm sound. If American industry could get away from producing poolside conversation pieces and concentrate on making things we really need, it would be off to a good start.

Who knows but what we may find it possible to do without a lot of other items we've taken for granted? If we have no fuel to propel our airplanes, rockets, and naval vessels, perhaps we'll get around to signing an arms-limitation treaty, or even abandoning war altogether. Since our present means of agricultural production relies almost entirely on petroleum —petroleum to run the machinery, petroleum to supply the fertilizer—and since the system expends nearly twenty calories of energy to produce one calorie of food, maybe we'll have to learn something from the Chinese. Their population is, unfortunately, nearly a billion, and approximately 85 percent of those people are directly involved in agriculture, concerned with feeding themselves. Just now, by contrast, only 2 percent of the U.S. population is directly involved in feeding the rest of the country (plus millions of others elsewhere in the world). But it looks as though this will have to change. A lot of our friends in the city had better learn something about hoes and potato hooks and planting schedules.

One of the more encouraging words we've had recently comes from Gardens for All, in Burlington, Vermont. In 1979, they say, 33 million American households—which is 42 percent of them—grew some of their own food in home or community gardens. The retail value of that produce was $13 billion—all from plots of ground whose median size was less than 600 square feet, which the average gardener spent $19 to cultivate and plant. Three out of four of these gardeners, by the way, preserved some of their harvest, and the average yield was $325 (not to mention quality or healthfulness). Not a bad return on a $19 investment, is it?

That, as we say, is the sort of news that gives us hope. At this time of year we find ourself identifying more with the robins than with any other creatures. Like us, they're victimized by the vagaries of April. After wintering in the south, out of touch with reality, they finally get bored and fly north, eager to tidy up the place before the little ones arrive. Sure enough, they come too early, bouncy and full of energy, as chesty and confident as a new-car salesman, only to find themselves plodding through a couple of inches of snow in search of worms. We watched one of these robins rather closely the other day, feeling sorry for him, and the more we looked the more we realized that the weather didn't really seem to bother him. In fact, he seemed to be enjoying it.

We decided he must know something we don't know.

As an addition to the language, the word "retrofit" is right up there with "audible-ize," which Howard Cosell gave us one memorable Monday night. But the practice of retrofitting—by which old houses get a face-life of sorts and thereby become more energy efficient—is something most of us have come to accept, however reluctantly. Late last fall we visited a community where we spent many happy years, where a number of people live in large, turn-of-the-century arks, and where we found all our friends bustling about, trying to put their houses in order for winter.

Barbara and George were closing off the back wing. Mary—if she can find a place to put all the linen and papers that have accumulated there—was planning to seal off her third floor. Ann and Joe were switching from oil to gas. Bob, as pleased as Punch with his giant new storm windows, had discovered that they had been put in backwards and was reinstalling them. And the talk in the neighborhood, which once centered on politics and books, is now of R-factors and stackpacks, of thermal mass and triple glazing. Ironically, these people probably reached the decision to modify their homes grudgingly, when forced to it. Most of them, nearing retirement, had doubtless expected to let their houses join them in the slow, downhill slide into the Golden Years, with expenses kept to the minimum required by occasional cosmetic maintenance.

So it goes these days, in every community we know. The house Liza and Casey built the summer before the Arab oil embargo is a good example of how a place has been altered under the influence of necessity. The new additions include three solar panels on the roof, to heat the domestic water. Heavily insulated pipes from these panels have preempted the wall formerly occupied by their bed, and pass through the living room en route to the basement. Above the big windows in the kitchen and the study are large rolls of what looks like padding—quilted insulated shades that are pulled down every night to keep the heat in and the cold out. The living-room fireplace has been sealed off and in its place is a woodstove (an arrangement that caused Santa to enter by the front door this year). Between the kitchen and dining room stands yet another big woodstove. Outside is a new woodshed. The front porch is stacked high with wood, and down by the barn next year's supply is drying.

We sought some professional advice on our own house, which was built during the fateful winter of 1973–74, and the recommendations made us wonder if we had done anything right. Replace the thermostat. Insulate the sills. Remove the domestic hot water from the oil-fired boiler and install a solar-heated, electrically backed-up system. Put reflectors behind all radiators. Caulk the doors and windows. Add storm sash to the existing double-glazed windows. Replace radiator under window seat with "fan coil unit." Install fan-vent between dining room and living room for better heat transfer. Add thermostatically controlled zone valves to heating zones. Insulate basement walls. Close up doorway off cellar. Replace oil-fired burner with wood-fired boiler or thermal electric storage system. Build vestibules outside the front and side doors.

Since the estimate for this was only somewhat less than the original cost of building the house, we had a further question for the consultant:

"How many cords of wood do you suppose it will take to heat this place if we change over to a wood-fired boiler?"

"Hmmm . . . I'd say between fifteen and twenty."

We scratched the wood-fired boiler from the list and decided to wait until they perfect the technology for burning wood pellets.

———

At the same time we heard about what must be the ultimate in retrofitting. The City Council of Winooski, a town in northern Vermont, recently authorized the community's development office to apply for a $3.4 million federal grant for an innovative, "multi-functional energy proposal." Four items compose the package: $2.5 million to construct a hydroelectric facility on the site of an old woolen-mill dam; $800,000 for insulation and hot water solar-heat panels, primarily for residents with low and moderate incomes; $45,000 to study the feasibility of creating a municipal power authority; and— here's what made the headlines—$55,000 to determine the possibility of erecting a dome that would cover all or part of the mile-square community and its 7500 residents, a solar-collecting roof that would conserve energy and make possible a controlled environment within.

The idea brought back memories of the 1939 General Motors Futurama and other heady visions of the future, which leave us feeling vaguely uneasy. Although the details are fuzzy, what sticks in the mind are moving walkways for "pedestrians," multilane superhighways on which automobiles and streamlined buses shoot in and out of buildings at various levels, towering apartment houses of chrome and glass, downtown heliports, and—surrounding the city's limits—a vast agribusiness complex.

Clearly, Winooski has no such scheme in mind, but since the past decade has witnessed the blossoming of the indoor shopping mall, we suppose that today's planners may be contemplating the next logical step, in which an entire community, encased in plastic and lulled by Muzak, lives out its unchanging days and nights undisturbed by pollution or changes in the weather or season. We can see the pale denizens of some future Sealed City, dressed in leisure double knits, strolling across their Astroturf lawns, admiring the plastic geraniums, happy in the knowledge that their unvarying temperature and climate are the equal of Miami's on a clear day, without the hazards of hurricanes or falling coconuts. There will be no acid rain, no radioactive fallout, no plagues of locusts; but neither, unfortunately, will lovers swear upon an inconstant moon nor poet remark a bright particular star, so dim and diffused will the light from those heavenly bodies be. No snow or sleet will obstruct these covered streets, but neither will bird, bee, nor butterfly brighten the morning air. And what of Mrs. O'Reilly, over on East Main, cooking O'Reilly's plate of stew on a Saturday afternoon: will the odor of onions linger inside the dome for weeks? Will condensation from the plastic bubble drip continuously, creating a tropical rain forest below?

But these are niggling doubts, for someone else to reckon with. What is important is that the people of Winooski and other towns are talking, working together. Americans' minds are being challenged, their ingenuity stimulated, and they're thinking and behaving like members of a community rather than a collection of isolated individuals. The neighbors are getting acquainted again, and we suspect that this coming together may be the best thing that could happen to us, with results far more significant in the long run than any saving of energy. The people of Winooski would be the first to tell us that it takes more than a plastic dome to create a community. Whatever is required to achieve that end is worth the effort, as the citizens of yet another Vermont town—St. Johnsbury— noted in the preface to their Town Plan:

> There is need for intimate human relationships, for the security of settled home and associations, for spiritual unity, and for orderly transmission of the basic cultural inheritance. These the small community at its best can supply. Whoever keeps the small community alive and at its best during this dark period, whoever clarifies, refines, and strengthens the vision of the small community, may have more to do with the final emergence of a great society than those who dominate big industry and big government.

As November and the unmistakable signs of winter approach, we find ourself thinking more and more about a trip we made through northern New England one summer and of how reassuring it was to find people everywhere—most notably the young—facing up to the crisis in energy. How sensible and ingenious they are, and how determined to find means of licking the problems that loom so large. It put us in mind of those master tinkerers of early New England—Eli Whitney, Samuel Slater, Eli Terry, and the rest, who made this region synonymous with invention and industry.

We are, we must keep reminding ourselves, at the end of the pipeline. No major gas or oil reserves underlie the stony crust of New England's soil, we have no refineries or deepwater ports, and while we are 75-percent dependent upon petroleum to power our utilities and heat our homes, factories, and public buildings, we pay more for oil than any other section of the nation. We were first made aware of this painful truth in the wake of the Arab oil embargo, when New England's energy bill increased by 139 percent between 1973 and 1974 alone—three times the national average. We are, in short, terribly vulnerable, and it is no comfort to see those bumper stickers in the South, with their grim message for us: "Let the bastards freeze to death in the dark."

So what can we make of our location and our sparse resources? Housing, they tell you at the Shelter Institute in Bath, Maine, is inefficient and prohibitively expensive, so they have done something about it—and they showed us half a dozen of the many homes their students have built for themselves at costs ranging from $4000 to $20,000. This, mind you, when the *average* dwelling constructed in the United States cost $55,000 and when a modest new mobile home sold for $12,000. Consider also that the houses spawned by the Shelter Institute have substantially more space than any mobile home, that they have been designed by the owners to suit their particular needs, and that they are extremely stingy in their consumption of energy (we saw several two- and three-bedroom residences that were heated in winter with less than three cords of wood plus heat collected from the sun). What's more, a number of these houses have been erected by people who never did anything of the kind before, who learned—through the institute's intensive three-week course—the essentials of construction and afterward built their own place, using native materials and a remarkable lot of ingenuity and imagination.

We saw a solar house designed and built by the lively group at Total Environmental Action in Harrisville, New Hampshire; and now, every time the oil truck pulls into our driveway we think longingly of that house's rows of solar collectors, its passive heat-collection devices (including a solar greenhouse), and all the insulating and heat-conserving tricks that have been incorporated into the structure. In Falmouth, Maine, we visited the Maine Audubon Society's handsome new home, a light, airy building where the sun's rays are collected, stored in a heat sink of crushed stone, and used in combination with a wood-burning furnace. We had a conversation with Albie Barden, who is working these days on a modification of the so-called Russian stove—a masonry furnace and chimney introduced to this country by Russian immigrants. Barden is part of a growing network, he tells us, of people dedicated to finding answers to the dilemmas posed by the shortage of energy—answers that will make particular sense in New England's inhospitable climate.

We hear often enough, as Saul Bellow once reminded us, that it is closing time in the gardens of the West, but more likely it is really closing time for some of the old ideas, some of the old habits of thought. One dinosaur that comes to mind is the Army Corps of Engineers. Having fixed a baleful eye on Maine's Saint John River more than a decade ago, the Corps is still pushing relentlessly for the vast Dickey-Lincoln hydro-electric project—an immensely expensive power complex that will operate only two and a half hours a day, since that is all the volume of water in the river will permit. And the Corps persists in the face of a study made by the Massachusetts Audubon Society that reveals some rather startling facts. To wit: if the same amount of money that is to be spent on Dickey-Lincoln were used to purchase wall insulation for homes, it would save seven and a half times the amount of energy to be produced by Dickey-Lincoln. Or, those same dollars, if spent on storm windows, would save four times the energy Dickey-Lincoln will produce. Or, if we were to take the money destined for Dickey-Lincoln and use it to buy nine-inch Fiberglas insulation for New England's attics, we would conserve forty-three times the energy to be produced by Dickey-Lincoln. All this without reference to the eighty-nine thousand acres of timberland that will be flooded by dams in the Dickey-Lincoln complex. Those forest lands, if left alone, will produce forty-thousand cords of wood each year.

The trouble with most of us is that we don't open our minds to new ideas and to new ways of thinking. Happily, though, a few do, and we are at once reminded of a couple that seemed in some respects the youngest and most energetic people we saw on our travels. Scott Nearing is entering his ninety-eighth year; his wife Helen is in her late seventies; and you get the feeling that they take delight in learning something new every day. When we caught up with this vital nonagenarian he was loading a cart with five-gallon cans full of water and wheeling them up a hill to water his blueberry bushes (Maine was unusually dry, we realized). His face crinkled in a broad smile and he paused to give us an animated description of their garden and of what was going on around the place, but he is not a man whose affairs you like to interrupt for long; his days are filled with so much activity of so many different kinds—physical, intellectual, cultural—it seems shameful to detain him from what he's about any longer than necessary. Seeing the Nearings certainly makes you realize how good "The Good Life" has been to its two champions; for four decades or more these remarkable people have gotten along almost without resort to the support system we all take for granted. From what we could see, they have no appliances other than a freezer, no machines, no tools but hand tools, and all—or nearly all—the food they eat year-round comes from their own garden and their own fields, to be stored away in row after row of jars for the long winter ahead.

This astonishing pair has built a new house—a house plus a garage-workshop-storeroom, in fact—both buildings constructed of local stone, stone laid up by Helen using cement mixed and hauled in a wheelbarrow by Scott, and they have started housekeeping there all over again, undertaking a new garden from scratch, settling into the new home. All this, of course, when he is at an age most of us will never attain, much less equal in vigor and liveliness. The wonder of it all is that they are unafraid of new beginnings at their time of life. And we recognized that this is the lesson all of us must learn.

The world in which we find ourselves is subtly but unmistakably different from the one that we knew in the more innocent springtime of 1973—a few months before the Great Awakening, when we came to the realization that the Organization of Petroleum Exporting Countries, chiefly the Arab states, control most of the oil on which our way of life depends and that they planned to get tough with us. As a consequence, we stand somewhat apprehensively at the threshold of a new era—a more eventful time, possibly, than any that has gone before in this country, for suddenly the resources on which we have depended to become the world's foremost industrial power are running out. Not only oil but a lot of the earth's other treasures, including not least the fertility of our soil. And the result is that, in almost every sense, the daily lives of Americans are bound to change.

Some of us may not look the part, but we're a little like those Americans who headed west in their covered wagons a century and a half ago, not knowing exactly where they were going or what unforeseen perils lay along the trail—certain only that they were bound for a new and distant land, and that others would follow along behind and join them there.

If you are lucky enough to own a place in the country, you immediately become aware of the importance of renewable and nonrenewable resources. And you develop very quickly a fresh set of values, a different outlook. For example, shelter. A lot of us have had, or will have, energy audits made of our homes—cold-blooded assessments of how much heat we are losing through the skins of our houses, critical examinations that tell us where the leaks are and what must be plugged up.

We know, as John Anderson liked to remind Americans during his campaign for the presidency, that "the cheapest, most effective way to replace a barrel of oil is not to use it," so we are adding insulation to our ceilings and walls, putting double and even triple glazing on the windows, looking into insulating curtains and off-peak electric storage heat, wind machines and heat pumps, solar greenhouses and wood-burning stoves and furnaces. In 1973, we venture to say, none of these options had occurred to most of us.

Our habits are changing. The hours we used to devote to tennis each week are now spent working up wood for the winter ahead. Instead of practicing our backhand, we cut, saw, split, and stack, feed and tend the stoves, check and clean the flues. And we gain, in the process, a deeper concern for our resources and how we must husband them for succeeding generations. This winter a logger told us how many thousand board feet of timber he could cut for sawlogs without damage to our woods; then we spoke with a professional forester, who concurred with the logger's estimate but reminded us that on those steep slopes, in that thin soil, it might take up to a hundred years to grow trees of that size again. So we cut with care and with caution, saving trees that are sixteen inches in diameter for the children and grandchildren to take when the trees grow to twenty or twenty-four inches in girth.

No sooner is the firewood season over (can it ever really be over?) than we turn our attention to the garden—starting plants from seed, tilling the soil, planting, weeding, cultivating, picking and gathering, freezing, canning, putting the produce into the root cellar. Friends whose closest approach to the source of a hamburger was once a supermarket cooler are raising chickens and sheep, milking a goat, fattening a steer, discovering the joys and the occasional heartbreaks of keeping animals, slowly and painstakingly learning the ancient art of husbandry. Intimately involved in these pursuits is the quest for information—how to accomplish a myriad different tasks, from raising a better tomato to transforming the raw wool from a sheep's back into a sweater or an afghan—and what cannot be ascertained from old-timers in the neighborhood we seek in books or periodicals or government pamphlets.

We used to walk into a ski shop and select a parka on the basis of color or fabric; now, before buying one, we read an article on the various features we should look for and put the shopkeeper through a third degree before deciding—on the strength of our newfound knowledge—which one is most likely to keep out the cold and wind, to shed the snow and rain. We look for garments made of cotton and wool nowadays, knowing that they are in many respects more practical than synthetic fabrics and produced from renewable sources. What is fashionable in vehicles is no longer a factor of styling or power or speed, but of fuel economy, durability, and practicality. And for the short hauls, we take to the bicycle and dream of an electric car. It used to be that you traded up for a tractor, but people are thinking smaller these days, wondering if they can get by with the model with fewer horsepower, or sizing up walk-behind machines that require even less fuel and more human energy. Suddenly hand tools are back in style, too—the bow saw and the one-wheel garden tiller, the scythe, the push lawnmower.

All too often, in recent years, the press has conveyed the impression that the argument over a new dam or a power plant is merely one more tiresome confrontation between the environmentalists and the business community, but gradually we are realizing that all of us—environmentalists and businessmen alike—must question, on its own merits, each project that involves our resources. A classic instance is Georges Bank—the offshore area east of Nantucket where, the Department of the Interior estimates, there may be 123 million barrels of oil. But suddenly we are waking up to the fact that at the present rate of oil consumption in the United States—some 20 million barrels a day—all the oil from Georges Bank will last us for only *seven days.* So the choice comes down to this: will we invade what is probably the world's greatest fishing grounds and risk destroying the abundant marine life there in order to run our automobiles for another week?

In twenty years, an official at the World Bank tells us, we will be able to produce only enough food for ourselves, with nothing left over for the rest of the world. So, which will mean more—seven days' worth of oil from Georges Bank, or the fish that will continue to multiply there for hundreds of years unless we destroy them?

The great divide at which we find ourselves was described a quarter century ago by E. B. White in an essay on Thoreau. The sage of Concord once observed that "This curious world which we inhabit is more wonderful than it is convenient; more beautiful than it is useful; it is more to be admired and enjoyed than used." If Thoreau were here today, Mr. White remarked, "He would see that . . . ten thousand engineers are busy making sure that the world shall be convenient even if it is destroyed in the process, and others are determined to increase its usefulness even though its beauty is lost somewhere along the way."

We were reminded of this thought one day recently when a group of us were talking about politics and of what we *wished* presidential aspirants would discuss. "If you could somehow mastermind an election campaign and insist that the candidates talk about certain subjects, which topics would you pick?" someone asked. Our friend Jake was the last to speak, and it was apparent from the way he hesitated that he had no faith that most candidates would ever come to grips with matters of genuine substance. All right, we pressed him, but just suppose you could set the rules, what would you require?

"I would have them speak about the environment and what they are going to do to save it," he replied. "Because if we destroy the earth there isn't much point in worrying about other problems, is there?"

Travel

Decided to go to Florida. Difficult undertaking from Vermont. Too far to drive. Hate flying: friend calls planes "death tubes," girds for flight with three martinis, codeine, penicillin. (Martinis to induce stupor, medication in case of crash—codeine for pain, penicillin for injuries.)

Heard jingle on radio: "Easy does it, Amtrak does it." Made reservations on train. Won't it be nice, friends said. Just like old days. Great way to relax. Fare from New York to West Palm $120 more than plane, travel time twenty-three hours instead of three. But it would be nice. Catch up on letters and reading.

Boarded bus at Manchester, Vermont, at 6:21 a.m. In Albany terminal saw woman on floor. Barely breathing. Reported her to dispatcher. "We've already heard about her," he said. Announced next bus.

Arrived in New York ten minutes ahead of schedule. "Port of Authority," driver told us. Time from Vermont, four hours, fifty minutes.

Taxi fare to Penn Station $1.90. Lost 75 cents in quarters before finding locker that worked. Put bags inside. Three hours until train time. Sunday. No familiar restaurants open. Taxied to St. Regis hotel, $2.75 including tip. Lunch, $24.00 for two, including fashion show. Another taxi to Penn Station, another $2.75. Lucky to find redcap willing to put bags on Silver Meteor. He seemed pleased with tip. Probably too much. Train departed on schedule, 2:50 p.m.

Roomette smaller than what we remembered. Porter had English accent. Asked where he came from. "New Jersey."

Where did he get English accent? "Not English," he said, "British." Seemed offended.

Began writing letters. Illegible. Roadbed rougher than what we remembered. Watched countryside rushing past. Mostly trash, junk cars, scrub growth, pharmaceutical plants. Went to lounge car for beer, 65 cents. Noted price of drinks— $1.40. Glad we brought bottle of Scotch. Back in roomette sampled bottle, anticipating difficult night.

Walk to diner a nightmare. Silver Meteor living up to name, rocketing along, caroming passengers from one wall of aisle to other. Diner shorter of amenities than what we remembered. Only one spoon in place setting, but less soot. Roast beef, salad, beets tasteless and gray. Dreaded return to sleeping car but dreaded prolonged stay in diner more. Suffered minor contusions on walk back.

Pulled berth out of wall in roomette. Room seemed even smaller. Pushed berth up into wall again, got out bottle of Scotch, hoping to encourage drowsiness. Dark outside. Lights flashing by. Hypnotic effect.

Down with berth again. Shorter than what we remembered. Discovered impossibility of stretching out full length. Tried diagonal position but hated having head in corner. Claustrophobia. Feet hung over end of mattress. Blanket too short: covered either shoulders or feet. Not both. Settled for feet. Turned off light, hoping to gain illusion of space.

Terrible rattling noise overhead. Turned on light. Located trouble. Glass cover for ceiling light not screwed in tight. Opened closet door to look for Swiss Army knife in trouser pocket. Found on floor of closet, tricky to reach. Stood on berth to tighten screws. Awkward position, banging from wall to wall like squash ball. Debated ringing for porter, decided against it. Didn't want to grapple with berth again in order to get dressed. Experienced feeling of weightlessness, felt like fool standing on berth monkeying with light. Screws finally secure. Rattle no better.

Decided to remove screws. Difficult to find slot while bouncing around on mattress. Should have put on glasses.

Screws out at last. Glass cover dangling from hinges. Rattle worse.

Couldn't get screws back in again. Said to hell with it. Put two suitcases in overhead rack, wedged shirt and two towels between suitcases and glass cover of ceiling light to hold it in place. Rattle stopped. Back to bed. Light off.

Relief premature. Rattle began again, louder than before. Resources and patience exhausted. Tried sleeping with pillow over head. No good. Claustro. Got up, pushed berth back in wall, found Scotch.

Dozed off during stop at Richmond. (Rocky Mount?) Awoke to find train under way again. Stared out window. Close to tears. Watch read 1:40. Continued to doze and wake with start. Each time watch read 1:40. Assumed night would never end.

No more heat in car. Air conditioning now. Must be in Sunny South. Cold became penetrating. Pulled down berth, got in. Spread Sunday *Times* over blanket. More fitful dozing. Papers rattling.

Light in sky. Watch read 1:40. Got up, pushed berth into wall, shaved, dressed, headed for diner. Banged head en route.

Crew stirring in diner. Clock on wall read 6:30, thermometer 86 °. Complained to steward about heat. Nothing he could do about it. "It's controlled outside," he said. Mysterious. Coffee lukewarm. Heard steward say he'd been making this run for eighteen years. Asked him if we could get a newspaper in Jacksonville. "Never been there," he said. Puzzling.

Back to sleeping car. Lots of bony cattle and orange groves outside window. Florida at last. Asked porter why we were moving so slowly now. "We're ahead of schedule," he said. "Engineer has to loaf along, lose time."

Arrived West Palm Beach twenty minutes late, result of loafing along. Thirty-two hours from Vermont. West Palm hotter than what we remembered. Faced with decision of how to make return trip. May stay here.

Our infrequent visits to the metropolis are invariably occasions for one small adventure or another. No city dweller could possibly regard these humdrum episodes as adventures, but for one whose companion is as often as not a cow, or a bird that is just passing through, a little excitement is a heady experience.

We always know we have reached the city when we hear the noise. Not surprisingly, on the farm the sounds that are most offensive to our ears have a mechanical origin. We particularly dislike the high-pitched whine of the corn chopper, but at most one hears that a few days a year, in September, and then there is all outdoors to absorb it. The only nonmechanical noises that might be called obtrusive come from the cows and their calves at weaning time, and from the goat with the nastiest disposition and the biggest ego problem—who blats incessantly at the other nannies to remind them of her tyranny (as if they could ever forget it).

So accustomed have we become to these pastoral sounds that we are not really equipped to deal with something as deafening as a city subway. Nowhere, we suspect, is the chasm separating rural from urban America delineated in starker terms than on the subway, where fear and bedlam ride side by side. This terrifying form of locomotion assaults all the senses simultaneously—cars hurtling through dark, subterranean passageways that lead God knows where; the unearthly, ear-shattering clatter; the stench—mostly of human origin; the crush and clash of angry, alien bodies; the threats, real or implied, that emanate from one's fellow passengers.

We have read enough about crime in the city to believe that

a subway is synonymous with danger. And so, assuming the worst, we begin an underground journey by slipping adroitly into a role we have devised for just such an occasion. In the belief that we will be spotted as an easy mark by thugs (alerted to our arrival in town by the underworld grapevine), we know that the first task is to put adversaries on the defensive. Pulling our coat collar up around the neck, we jam both hands into the pockets and do our best to look like a Mafia hit man just in from Detroit. This involves narrowing the eyes to slits, skinning the upper lip back in a sneer, and turning the head slowly from side to side, sweeping everyone on the station platform with a withering look.

What destroys the illusion, of course, is the necessity to board a train. It is impossible to maintain the cool of a hit man while being shoved through the doors of a subway car with your arms pinned to your sides and your hands locked inside your coat pockets. And, anyway, it is at this point that we remember our wallet and clutch for it with both hands—a movement that, if done suddenly, can throw the sacroiliac out of place.

On a recent visit to Boston, we found ourself standing on the Arlington Street platform in company with three other people. They were obviously unnerved by the sneer we gave them, but other than that each was minding his own business, patiently awaiting the next train's arrival, when the loudspeaker began to squawk. Like all loudspeakers in all public places, this one was virtually impossible to understand, but after the message had been repeated several times it came through to us: "Guard your pocketbooks and wallets," the Voice of the Subway was saying. "A pickpocket is on the platform."

Immediately everyone was a potential thief, everyone a likely victim, with four people edging ever farther apart, trying somehow to look innocent and unconcerned and on guard at the same time. What finally saved the situation was a train, thundering into the station. The four of us leaped aboard and dispersed, to vanish among the other riders.

At Park Street we changed trains, continuing to glance back furtively, half expecting to see a pickpocket approaching. We looked for signs to Harvard Square, found them, and began following the colored line that leads to the train. Only one other person was heading that way—a little girl, perhaps twelve or thirteen years old, wearing a jumper and a worried look.

Poor kid, we thought. Probably terrified. All alone, trying to get across town on the subway. What's the matter with parents these days anyway? My God, a nice little girl like this . . . *alone* . . . after *dark* . . . on a *subway* . . . in the *city?*

Suddenly she turned left into a passageway and started to run. What's the matter? we wondered, glancing nervously behind us. Uh-oh, maybe she heard a train coming in. So we began to run, too. Neither of us actually knew that a train was in the station yet, since we couldn't see one, but there is something about walking at a normal pace toward an invisible incoming subway train that proves impossible. At some stage you simply have to run, whether a train is actually in the station or not. So we ran—convinced that we might miss a train that might not even exist. We hoped the nice little girl wouldn't think we were chasing her.

Yep, there's the train, all right—there in the station.

The two of us ran onto the platform just in time to see the doors slam shut and the conductor leaning out between cars to see if everyone was aboard.

"Wait!" we shouted, waving at him.

The conductor ignored us and the trained pulled out.

The nice little girl looked as though she would cry. Uh-oh, we thought. Better reassure her. Tell her another train will be along in a few minutes. There, there . . . don't worry. That sort of thing.

We walked toward her, smiling an avuncular smile, and were just about to say something comforting when we realized that she was watching the train disappear into the tunnel and was yelling at the conductor.

What the nice little girl was yelling was a four-letter word.

———

A couple of hours later, two friends walked with us from the restaurant where we had eaten to the Harvard Square subway station. We heard footsteps pounding behind us, turned, and saw three policemen running toward the kiosk.

"They're at it again!" one cop shouted to the others as they trotted heavily past.

We reached the subway station shortly after the cops did and observed them—three big men in blue, each with a walkie-talkie, a drawn revolver, and an inscrutable expression that possibly comes from holding a radio to one's ear. Their radios were squawking but we couldn't understand them.

"What are they saying?" we asked our friend Marcia.

"There's been another holdup down on the platform," she said, "and they're not sure if the guy got on the train or if he's still down there."

It was plain, from the way those three cops were standing there, waiting for a message on the walkie-talkies, that they had no more intention than we had of descending the steps to see if a holdup man was on the platform.

We took a taxi back to the hotel.

The cement that binds New Englanders together is an unstated article of faith, a credo we hold in common regardless of race, religion, color, or place of origin. Part of the regional folk memory, it is an absolute as ingrained as Plymouth Rock and the Mayflower Compact, taken for granted and never questioned.

So it came as somewhat of a surprise to see that what every man, woman, and child here has known since the day the first Model T chugged into town has been trumpeted as news by *The Wall Street Journal.* The ancient canon learned at our fathers' knees is now public knowledge: Massachusetts drivers are the worst in the United States. Maybe in the world.

A warm, smug glow filled us to think that the world at large has finally caught up with a conviction held so stubbornly by New Englanders. We often take a stretch of road frequented by automobiles with bumper stickers that read, "Pray for us—we drive Route 7," and any time we see a long line of cars stacked up behind a vehicle that is traveling at eighteen miles an hour and weaving along capriciously to the left of the center line, it is a foregone conclusion that the car in the lead bears the dread *"blancs-et-rouges"*—the red-and-white Massachusetts license plates that terrorized a French visitor during his recent stay here.

If a man who has been exposed to all that goes on on France's highways is shaken, what of Massachusetts officialdom? Well, one functionary reports ruefully that the reputation of Massachusetts drivers is legendary among his fellow safety officials around the country. The Bay State's secretary of transportation told the *Wall Street Journal* reporter that there is indeed "an anarchic tradition" on Massachusetts roads. And a fellow at the Massachusetts Registry of Motor Vehicles, while claiming that "We aren't any worse than anyone else," admitted grudgingly that Bay State motorists do scare nonresidents to death. If further indictment is needed, it exists in the rates imposed by insurance companies on Massachusetts drivers. They pay the highest premiums in the nation—two and a half times those in Detroit, for example—and the reason is simple: more cars are damaged there than in any other state. (Perhaps not surprisingly, considering the chaos that characterizes Bay State highways, more cars are stolen in that state than anywhere else—almost twice as many as in New York, for instance; the number of auto thefts rose 43 percent between 1973 and 1974, as compared with a nationwide average of 4 percent.)

One reason for these anarchic conditions is the apparent tendency of Massachusetts police to look the other way, where traffic offenders are concerned. As Richard McLaughlin, a former secretary of public safety, puts it, "Massachusetts drivers represent the third or fourth generation of drivers who have had little or no police control." To make matters worse, the state has "the most obsolete and nonuniform driving laws in this country and every other country in the Western Hemisphere," according to the executive director of the National Committee on Uniform Traffic Laws. Even behavioral scientists are troubled by the phenomenon: one of them shakes his head sadly and states that Massachusetts motorists "exhibit more erratic behavior" than those anywhere else.

The highways and byroads of Massachusetts, in other words, may be likened to a massive Dodg'em arena in an amusement park, a horde of maniacal drivers at the wheel, automobiles caroming into and off each other as far as the eye can see (with those temporarily not in motion being stolen).

With the Labor Day weekend upon us, the leaf peekers cannot be far behind, and for the benefit of visitors who have never engaged in car-to-car combat with Bay State motorists, we provide the following public service message. This is our impression of the operators' manual that must govern Massachusetts license-holders' conduct in the open country:

1. Drive as though your car is the only vehicle on the road. Pay no heed to other motorists—let them look out for themselves.

2. Do not signal before making a turn in either direction. This will confuse motorists behind you and teach them to keep their distance. On interstate highways, however, switch on your turn indicator and leave it on so that following traffic will not know which exit you are taking (if any).

3. Disregard stop signs, blinking lights, and red lights when entering a main artery from a side road. Maintain normal speed or, if possible, accelerate while joining oncoming traffic. Your sudden entry into the stream of cars will give other motorists a chance to test their brakes.

4. On narrow, winding roads where there is no opportunity to pass, position your vehicle athwart the median line and maintain a steady speed below 20 mph. This will allow the drivers behind you to enjoy the scenery and to contemplate the mistakes they have made in life.

5. While passing a historic marker or scenic view, slam on the brakes and come to a full stop in the highway. This is a good time to eat the sandwich you brought with you.

6. Whenever possible, follow the so-called Plymouth Convention laid down by our forefathers. Simply stated, this calls for traveling at double the speed limit in restricted zones and at half the limit in high-speed areas.

7. Remember, the honor of the Commonwealth is in your hands.

"Vive les blancs-et-rouges!"

We called it The Lemon. Not, as will be seen, for its color but for other reasons. From the beginning, the vibes were bad. It was a Detroitcar, ordered in a rage when we could not obtain parts for our European automobile, ordered because we like the local dealer, respect his skill as a mechanic, and believed that he would be able to iron out all the kinks and quirks Detroit might have built into the vehicle.

This particular dealer has no showroom, so we went to his garage, leafed through catalogues, and selected a four-door sedan with six cylinders (to save gas) and manual transmission (to save gas and because we like it better in the snow). The color we picked was a kind of silver-gray, with a light-blue interior trim, and in a burst of recklessness we ordered a radio with tape deck.

Three months later (we know exactly how long it was because we had been driving the foreign car for three wintry months with no rear windshield; it had one of those electric-coil defrosters and one morning, after an ice storm, our son turned it on and the windshield shattered into four trillion pieces; no replacement windshield could be found in the entire United States of America, and the Europeans were in no hurry to send one). Anyway, three months later the new Detroitcar arrived. The dealer called to say it was here and then, after a long, pregnant pause, he asked, "Are you in a good mood this morning?"

"Of course we are," we replied testily. "What does that have to do with the car?"

"Well," he said softly, choosing the words carefully, "you ordered a silver-gray car, didn't you?"

"Right."

"Well, ah . . . Well, when I filled out the order I thought that S was the code letter for silver-gray. But it isn't."

"No?"

"No. S stands for Florentine Red."

"You mean we have a Florentine Red car? With light-blue interior?"

"Right." Then there was a long sigh. "I'll repaint it at my own expense, since I made the mistake."

"Well, don't do anything till we look at it."

We went, looked, and took the car even though we hated the color. We just didn't feel like driving without a rear windshield anymore that winter.

The first day we had the car we went shopping, locked the car, and when we came back from the meat market and tried to unlock the door, nothing happened. Neither key unlocked either front door. We called the dealer.

He came to the parking lot, jimmied a window, reached inside with a clothes hanger, and opened the door. "There you are," he said, smiling.

"Is that the way we'll always have to unlock it?" we asked.

"No," he said, "we can probably find a key that will work. But it's funny the ignition key doesn't unlock the doors. I wonder if you got a Monday car." And off he drove.

"What's a Monday car?" we asked when we caught up with him at the garage.

"Any car that's made in Detroit on a Monday is automatically screwed up," he explained. "Those guys on the assembly line make so much money they don't care if they work more than three or four days a week, so they just don't show up on Mondays. They call in sick. The auto companies have to have a whole standby crew that works only on Mondays, on account of the absenteeism. And I guess they're not all that good. Anyway, if this is a Monday car, you've got trouble."

We had trouble, all right, and the keys were the least of it. For instance, during the first month or two we noticed that the new car burned a lot of oil. About a quart each five hundred miles. When we took it in for a checkup we remarked on this to the dealer.

"Normal," he assured us. "As soon as she's broken in you'll notice a big difference." What we noticed was that forty thousand miles later she was still burning a quart of oil every five hundred miles.

Another problem we observed right off was the way the car didn't always start. "She's a slow starter, isn't she?" the dealer said one morning when he came to the house to start it with jumper cables. "Real slow."

About the time the novelty of being a new-car owner wore off, we began calling it The Lemon (The Florentine Red Lemon, sometimes), and gave up complaining about it to the dealer. By then we were resigned to the knowledge that the rubber gasket on the right front door would never fit, and that anyone riding on that side would get wet if it rained. (If no one were sitting in the right-hand seat, of course, the water merely soaked the seat. For days.) We found that the windows in the car were constructed in such a way that if they were open while the car was moving, it was impossible to hear another person talk. To surmount this acoustical barrier, each passenger had to roll up his or her window whenever anyone wanted to speak; then roll it down for a breath of air; then roll it up again so that a reply to the first speaker could be heard. The procedure made for a good deal of exertion on a long trip, and as the passengers became overheated the defroster had to be kept going continuously to clear the steam from the windows.

Although it may sound like a trivial thing, the windshield wiper on the driver's side was what bothered us most. As best we can describe the noise it made, it went "ffft" on the out-stroke—a smooth, efficient sound; followed by a kind of death rattle on the return—"eh-eh-ehk." It got so we dreaded the onset of a rainstorm and the thought of being trapped inside the car listening to "ffft, eh-eh-ehk; ffft, eh-eh-ehk; ffft, eh-eh-ehk. . . ." The first time we heard the noise we turned on the radio, thinking we could drown it out, but the radio antenna was embedded in the windshield and this caused the wiper sound to be magnified through the speaker, producing an ear-shattering "FFFT, EH-EH-EHK; FFFT, EH-EH-EHK. . . ." Ah, you will ask, why not play the tape deck? Because, dummy, the tape deck shredded the tapes we put in it, that's why.

The engine was like everything else. There was no way to get a smooth ride at speeds under 25 mph, even in first gear; at the other end of the spectrum, there was no hope of passing another vehicle on the open road unless you were on a downgrade and had picked up momentum for two or three miles. Then there was the rust. Just before we traded the car we asked the dealer if he didn't think it had rusted out unusually quickly. "Yup," he said, "about as fast as any car I've seen. Let's see, she's a '73, isn't she?"

"That's right."

"Thought so. That's the year they tried using recycled metal. It won't hold paint worth a nickel."

Well, The Lemon has gone now—traded for a foreign car—and we can speak frankly, without fear of reprisals. It seemed the final irony that, on the car's last morning with us, we opened the glove compartment to remove maps, registration, matchbooks, pencil stubs, and the detritus of three years, and as we did so the lock fell out of the glove-compartment door. The Lemon had struck again.

Now we have a new foreign car—sort of a silver-blue, with four cylinders (to save gas) and manual transmission (to save gas and because it's good in the snow). Just the other day we were driving along, thinking how much better this was than The Lemon, when we heard a funny clanking noise up there under the hood. It seems to be getting worse.

As one of the few middle-aged Americans who has failed to finish or to win a marathon this year, we are hardly in a position to write about running. But the proliferation of books and magazines on the subject makes the temptation difficult to resist, especially so now that we have picked up some of the jargon. In our way, we have been running quite a lot lately—if a mile and a half can be construed as quite a lot and if running can be defined as moving, in a more or less erect position, at a pace faster than walking. As a matter of fact, we have something of a reputation to uphold when it comes to performing at substandard speeds. Our children and their contemporaries used to express considerable wonder at the length of time it took us to negotiate a downhill ski run. We would ride up the lift with them and then begin our "run," if we may dignify it by that term—a series of slow, rather stately traverses on a route nearly perpendicular to the slope of the hill, punctuated with long pauses between turns to enable us to study the lay of the terrain below. While we were thus engaged, the young ones often made three or four round trips, waving and catcalling each time they schussed past.

Our philosophy about running is a good deal simpler than that of most writers and may be simply stated. We hate it. Marathoners have an expression—"hitting the wall"—to describe the utter exhaustion they experience somewhere around the twentieth mile, the moment at which they have used up all their physical resources and have to finish the race entirely on willpower or guts. Well, we usually hit the wall at a point that is precisely 163 feet from the kitchen door, before we even get out onto the road, and from there on every inch of ground we cover qualifies as an act of pluck and dogged courage.

For as long as we can recall, we have found running boring. In the days of our youth, there were occasions that demanded prolonged rapid movement; more often than not, it was the sight of the Rezler brothers heading purposefully in our direction from the school yard and it always seemed prudent to pretend that we had an urgent errand to attend to at home and to head as speedily as possible in that direction. Usually the result of such exertion was a painful stitch in the side or shin splints. Or both. Oh, we ran often enough at other times, but usually in short, quick bursts—to beat out an infield hit, say, or to retrieve an opponent's lob in tennis—and somehow there was always a moment in which to catch your breath. But not with running for running's sake.

The vision of running you get from most books and articles is of slim, willowy athletes floating effortlessly and endlessly up hill and down dale. ("Running easily," Jim Fixx writes, "I glide along the edge of the sea, through marsh grasses and then along a beach. Soon I am home again, breathing lightly and feeling both spent and exhilarated.") And as often as not they manage to carry on a long, thoughtful conversation with a companion. But that's not the picture around here. Our neighbors must see us as a man old enough to know better, lurching along the road in all kinds of weather, gasping for breath, perspiring heavily, looking just about the way Pheidippides did when he croaked out his final message to the Athenians. On our chilly morning runs, friends drive by and smile indulgently. Even the birds seem to be laughing at us: crows call contemptuously, a woodpecker looks up from his drumming long enough to stare in wonder, and a flock of grosbeaks chatter raucously and pelt the road with droppings.

According to William P. Morgan, writing in *Psychology Today,* your run-of-the-mill jogger engages in a kind of self-hypnosis called dissociation to keep his mind off the agony of it all, often whiling away the miles by reciting poetry or repeating his mantra over and over; whereas your elite, world-class runner spends his time monitoring bodily signals of respiration, temperature, heaviness in the limbs, and that sort of thing. We are not exactly a world-class runner, but we do know that our entire run is occupied with monitoring anxious calls from a thumping heart and querulous muscles, listening for the telltale signs that our homeostasis, or internal function, is breaking down. Meanwhile, the incessant pounding on limbs and joints, bone and cartilage unaccustomed to such foolishness is beginning to tell. Severe pain is spreading through the lower vertebrae and down along the insides of the knees, and we detect a prominent bone spur developing in the metatarsal area of the left foot. The upshot is that the money we once spent on cigarettes now goes to a cadre of specialists, to Dr. Scholl, and to the pharmacy for liniment and various unguents.

Another fault we find with running is that it has turned us to cheating and, what is worse, to self-deception. Although we are up with the birds each morning, neighbors are already on their way to work and for some unaccountable reason we don't want them to see us out on the road in a sweatsuit not running. We may have decided to slow the pace to a fast walk in the interest of getting the old heart back to a more normal beat, but just let us catch sight of a car in the distance and we start moving faster, to prove that we are a jogger and not an indigent ragpicker. Passing the barn we hear the derisive bleating of goats and sheep, and as we reach the small hill by Blanche Park's house we slow to a gasping walk (ignoring Fixx's advice that "running uphill strengthens the quadriceps"). Arriving at the crest we begin jogging again and catch sight of two snarling dogs racing to the attack. We manage to pant, "Good doggie, good doggie" just as they prepare to spring. Taken aback by the flattery, they trot off to lie in wait for us on the return trip.

By the time we pass McWayne's cornfield we are breathing hard ("sucking air," in the lingo) and wondering if the fumes from the fresh manure are really all that good for the system. We glance furtively up and down the road to see if anyone is watching and begin to walk so that we can breathe again. Nothing wrong with a brisk stroll, we say softly, and before you know it we have convinced ourself that walking the next hundred and fifty yards will amount to the same thing as running. We are comforted by the memory of a line from Fixx's *Complete Book of Running:* "If you feel that you're running, no matter how slow you're going, no one can say you're not."

Finally we turn and head for home, tense about the dogs and wondering if our glycogen supply has been exhausted or if we're suffering from paresthesia (a tingling of the fingers and toes, followed by muscle tetany). We recall the words of an older, wiser friend who once told us of his plan to start an organization called Exercisers Anonymous. The idea was that each member would have at his side at all times the phone numbers of other members so that whenever he felt the urge to exercise he could make a call and engage in diverting, sympathetic conversation until the mood had passed.

Even before the end of January the winter of 1977–78 had been one of the cruelest in memory. In Buffalo, a series of blizzards had smothered the city with more than ten feet of snow by month's end, and more was on the way. In Vermont, the first snows came early in December and there had been no thaw. Across the nation, newspapers and magazines were calling it the Winter of the Big Freeze; even in Miami and Palm Beach snow flurries had been seen. Fuel supplies were running short; schools had closed (245 of them in southern Illinois alone); the Ohio and Mississippi rivers were frozen over for miles; in Iowa, the frost had penetrated six feet into the soil; there was eighteen inches of ice in the Hudson River. The brutal, unrelenting cold had brought personal tragedy and a national crisis. It was another reminder, if we needed one, of how vulnerable modern man is—despite any illusions he may have of controlling his environment—to the whims of nature.

The prediction was for more snow when we left Vermont for New York City, so we packed long johns and took the train. We arrived on Sunday evening, and the next morning we felt at once the eerie silence that hung over Manhattan. Snow was falling heavily. No traffic was moving. Only a few pedestrians were in the streets. Over radio and television came dire predictions about the weather, warnings to people in the metropolitan area of the impossibility of travel, of stalled subways and buses, nonexistent taxis, businesses and schools and stores closed. It looked as though we might have the city to ourselves.

Late in the morning we called on a doctor, a friend of more

than thirty-five years, and shoveled his walk for him (he would reduce his fee, he said); then we enjoyed the luxury of talking leisurely for an hour, and he served us tea. We suspected it was a morning like no other in that usually busy office.

What the newscasters, promising calamity, missed completely was what fun it was for a lot of us. People stood in the middle of Fifth Avenue, staring in awe at the empty streets, listening to the silence—it was so quiet you could hear a sneeze a block away. Hundreds of parents and children were sledding in Central Park. A man with whom we had a lunch appointment arrived at the hotel on cross-country skis, and when we greeted him we could hear the sound of singing in the streets. Only the happy ones were out, someone suggested; a foot of snow tended to discourage muggers and malcontents. Those who were abroad were there because they reveled in the taste of the elements, the unexpected holiday. They said hello to passersby; one man, picking his way through the deep snow arm in arm with his wife, called "Merry Christmas!" and we all laughed. Waiters in restaurants were suddenly friends and neighbors, people whose destiny you found yourself caring about. "Where do you live?" was the question everyone asked. "Is your subway running?" It came to us that the city, suffering under the worst blizzard in years, had become by this accident of nature a place of manageable proportions, the way it had once been.

All day Monday and through the night the snow continued without letup. Nothing moved but the people on foot. On the side streets lumpy lines of automobiles were buried beyond recognition. The movie theaters were half-empty; we heard on the radio that tickets for the Metropolitan Opera performance that night would be reduced to $4, even though Beverly Sills was singing (as it turned out, enough people walked to the concert to pack the house—Beverly and the bargain price were too good to miss). All evening hardy souls drifted in out of the storm to warm, friendly havens like P. J. Moriarty's; it was the sort of night everybody talked to Bill the bartender, wondering how he would get to his family on Staten Island.

Out of all this came two immediate impressions—one sensory, the other an inner awareness. The first was of silence, the beauty of the streets, the wonder of the whiteness when the lights came on at night, the almost incredible gentleness and cleanness of a city that is normally so harsh and angular and dirty. The other—a response to how few people were in evidence—was an appreciation of smallness and of the joy that is possible in a community where the pressures of business suddenly vanish, giving people time to care about each other, to communicate, to smile and to laugh.

Next morning you could sense that the spell was about to be broken. People still walked in the middle of avenues and streets in all sorts of attire, some wearing skis, heading for the parks; but the signs of ill humor set in as the day wore on and apartment dwellers located and exhumed their cars. Slowly, taxis and buses got moving again and the snow turned to pie dough and then to slush, with deep unfordable pools of icy water accumulating at every corner. Then the trains began to run, and two friends rode in from Westchester to see us and the buried city. That night, once again, the mood at Moriarty's was mellow and warm.

Wednesday morning's papers reported that the storm was over. For forty hours it had raged, paralyzing city and suburbs with almost eighteen inches of snow, enormous drifts, and the task of digging out that would take weeks to accomplish. The accidental holiday was over. Now there would be thankless drudgery for those who had to do the digging and yet another inconvenience for those who live in the city to add to their list.

There are times when you realize you are lucky to live where you live, and this was one of them. We could board a train and leave to the New Yorkers their monumental problem, while we returned to a small town where the road crews are used to dealing with winter storms and where they have the equipment and the space for disposing of snow. Our highway crews are a lot like firemen—expecting the worst, they're almost always ready for it when it comes. Most of them do their job so well everyone takes them for granted, and it's probably a rare day when anyone thanks or compliments them. We were thinking about that as we drove along the expertly plowed road that leads to home, admiring the long rows of snow piled so neatly on each shoulder.

No matter where you live, life presents obstacles with which you have to cope. But it strikes us that more options are open to an individual in the country than in the city, and that those options are more within the person's power to control. More choices, more freedom of action. The electricity goes off and we light the kerosene lamps and cook on the wood stove; the water line freezes and we can break the ice in the stream and haul buckets; if the road to town is impassable, we have meat and vegetables in the freezer, more food in the root cellar. One of the requirements of country living is a state of mind, which might be described as the need to be prepared for all possible eventualities. It's a variant of Murphy's Law: anything that might happen probably will, and you'd better be ready when it does.

Just when most people were beginning to get the message that the world's supply of oil is finite and that we are consuming it at an unparalleled rate, along came the government with a report that was three years and God knows how many dollars in the making, proclaiming automobiles as the wave of the future. For those who missed this remarkable document, we summarize. A bipartisan panel of senators, representatives, and transportation executives—known as the Transportation Policy Study Commission—concluded that the automobile's place in the scheme of things will increase greatly between now and the year 2000. This judgment was based on several premises: there will be half again as many additional households in the United States by century's end; there will be a notable rise in affluence; there will be a "huge growth" in the ownership of automobiles (Americans are expected to triple their present investment in cars); and there will be an 80-percent increase in individual travel. Representative E. G. Shuster, chairman of the commission, declared further that the nation's highways are wearing out faster than they can be repaired, which means that most of the federal transportation budget will have to be devoted to replacing them—including $40 billion for "critically deficient bridges" alone.

The president summoned Detroit's auto executives to the capital and called on them to "reinvent" the automobile. As Transportation Secretary Brock Adams put it, we need "to establish for the American people the kind of car they deserve to have."

(In fairness to Mr. Adams's challenge to Detroit, we would be all in favor of reinventing the automobile if we could be certain the federal government would have nothing to do with its design. We have no faith that Washington could even reinvent the wheel. The dinosaur, maybe—but certainly not the automobile.)

Meanwhile, at the end of a month during which 750,000 Americans were turned away in the rush to trains, the administration announced that it was cutting back Amtrak rail service by 12,000 miles—or 43 percent. This, in the face of two other extraordinary statistics: that for twenty-two consecutive months the use of public transportation systems increased; and that 25 million more Americans rode mass transit facilities in the month of April 1979 than twelve months earlier. Even in California, land of the three- and four-car family, the use of public transportation was up by 25 to 40 percent in a number of cities.

Late in June, faced with the hue and cry over gas shortages, the Department of Transportation relented to the extent of grudgingly recommending an increase in the appropriation for Amtrak. Temporarily. But Secretary Adams, speaking with the calm assurance of a man who knows all the answers, stated that certain Amtrak routes will nonetheless be cut back. "We stand with our original plan," he stated. "People simply do not ride trains now." (Nor will they be riding buses much longer, it would seem. General Motors, the largest manufacturer of ground transportation equipment, has annnounced that it will produce no more intercity buses, while AM General, one of the last three companies in the field, is closing its bus-manufacturing shops.)

Now all of this came to pass before President Carter had second thoughts about where he and the nation were going, before the speech in mid-July in which he announced sweeping new energy goals and spoke feelingly of America's crisis of confidence. Well, just so he knows where we stand, our own personal crisis of confidence has been kindled by the kind of backward thinking that produced the Transportation Policy Study Commission report. It almost defies belief that the people we pay to run things in Washington can be so oblivious to reality, yet what they are saying is that the automobile means more to the American than anything else (including, presumably, his freedom and economic security if we continue to bankrupt ourselves buying foreign oil), and will encourage the manufacture and sale of cars at the expense of other means of transportation. Except the airplane, that is. Airplanes, the commission tells us, will replace trains and buses on short- and medium-range hauls. Down with buses and trains, they say. Down with mass transportation systems. The federal government will support the two least cost-effective methods of getting from Here to There. (Not to mention commercial aviation's reputation among many as a step backward in every respect but time. Flying, after all, requires that you spend both time and treasure getting to the airport, arriving early enough to wait in line and have your luggage and your person searched, after which you are strapped into a seat like a condemned man, sold high-priced drinks, fed plastic food, bumped around, exposed to the possibility of being hijacked to Cuba or Ghana, terrified on takeoff and landing, and as like as not set down at a destination you never had in mind, while your baggage is routed to another city halfway across the continent. If a more uncivilized and humiliating mode of transportation has been devised by man, we are not familiar with it.)

We live in a town that is, like many others in New England, dependent for its livelihood on tourism. Which is why we deplore any effort to eliminate Amtrak's Montrealer—the one passenger train that serves New England, tying it to Canada, New York City, and Washington. It is why we oppose attempts to reduce bus service in the area. Automobiles there will continue to be, but operating—we would bet—at levels entirely different from what we know today.

Consider the scale of our present reliance on cars. There are more than 117 million of them on U.S. highways. At a price of $1 a gallon—which was the national average in 1979—Americans spent $82.5 billion a year for gasoline— more than $700 per passenger car. If you add to this figure the cost of all the new cars purchased each year (11 million of them, at an average price of $6500, or a total of $73 billion), and the annual cost of repairing these vehicles (some $50 billion), you have an expenditure of more than $205 billion annually on automobiles. Without even considering the cost of insuring these cars or subsidizing the roads on which they run, we spent in 1979 on automobiles alone $930 for every man, woman, and child in the United States. To put this figure in perspective, it is more than the combined per capita *income* of Egypt and Algeria, and our total outlay of $205 billion is equal to the combined *gross national product* of China and Norway, with their combined populations of nearly 870 million people.

Being, as Christopher Robin said of Winnie-the-Pooh, a bear of very little brain, we have difficulty comprehending the size of a billion dollars, but recently we ran across an illustration we like. It is this: if you had spent $1000 a day since the day Christ was born, you would not yet have spent a billion dollars. Far from it, in fact. You would still have more than a quarter of your billion left—enough to go on doling out $1000 a day for another 760 years. That's how much a billion dollars is. So think of that amount, multiply by 205, and you have an idea of how much money we are spending in a year's time on our pleasure cars.

Money aside, in electing to endorse the automobile at the expense of other forms of public transportation, what do our federal officials propose to do about the elderly widow who has never learned to drive, or the young people not yet of driving age, or the lame, the halt, and the blind? What of those millions of Americans who cannot afford—or simply do not choose—to own an automobile? What of others who can neither afford nor find the gasoline for a long trip, or for their daily commute to and from the job?

Alas, Washington often seems more concerned with effect than with cause. We were reminded of this peculiar governmental talent not long ago when we read a news release from the Forest Service. To provide "for the comfort of boaters,

water skiers, and others" on Pyramid Lake in southern California, the Forest Service has launched two floating restrooms
there. These lake-going outhouses, we read, "will relieve the
normally crowded conditions at the lake's shore-based facilities
and shorten recreational 'down-time' necessitated by frequent
and time-consuming trips back to shore." We do not know
what these floating outhouses cost the U.S. taxpayer, but we
wonder if anyone in the Forest Service—or elsewhere in the
federal government—has read a newspaper lately or is aware
of priorities more compelling than recreational down-time and
the calls of nature of water skiers.

Week in Florida. Sounds great till eve of departure. Packing ordeal reminds us of friend's aged aunt, preparing for trip. "Bruce," she said, "I can either get ready to go or I can go, but I can't do both."

Decide to try on lightweight clothes. Uh-oh. Cleaner has shrunk trousers around waistline. Funny how green linen jacket seems dated. Has odd, cinched-up look when buttoned.

Vowed to carry only one suitcase this year. Having made rule, have to conform. Clothes don't fit into one bag. Dump them out onto bed, try again. Still no go. Up to attic for larger bag. No luck. Discover it's possible to squeeze everything into two suitcases—same two we carried last time. Heavy as lead. Suddenly remember tennis racquet and sneakers. Jam them into large bag. Zipper breaks. To basement for clothesline. Tie suitcase shut.

Discuss when to get up. Drive to airport takes three hours (longer than flight). Better allow four, just in case. Decide to set alarm for 4:15 a.m. in order to get off by 7:00. B. likes to leave house in apple-pie order. Wants countertops and sink clean in case she doesn't come back.

Turn off lights at 11:15. Look outside. Snowing hard. Tell B. not to worry. Say it will probably clear. B. not fooled.

Alarm goes off at 4:15. Pitch-black. Turn on outside light and peer through ice on windowpane. Snowing hard. Six- or eight-inch accumulation. Wonder if road crews have been out all night plowing. Probably not. Always snows or rains when we fly. B. suggests calling airport for weather report. Grumpy voice says no snow in Hartford. Seems surprised we asked.

Try U.S. Weather Service. Metallic, recorded voice reports no snow in Hartford area.

Leaving house fifteen minutes past self-imposed deadline creates nervousness, tension. Still snowing hard. Windshield wiper collecting ice. Glad we allowed extra hour. Decide to take longer, roundabout route to avoid mountains. Farther south, snow tapers off. Roads clear.

Arrive at "Valet Parking" for airport. Apologize to attendant for amount of luggage. Mistake. Ask if car will be safe in open lot. "Look, mister, we got police dogs patrolling the place," he reassures us. "Jeez, those are heavy bags you got there, mister." Holds out hand. Unsmiling young woman with extraordinary amount of hair drives mini-bus to terminal. No one talks.

Check luggage at ticket counter. Clock indicates hour to kill. B. buys chewing gum for cracking ears when airborne. Looks unsuccessfully for something diverting to read. Book-racks loaded with mayhem, sex. We step into bar. Order martini. 10:30 a.m. Half an hour till departure.

Uniformed woman at security check resembles Ilse Koch. Tells B. to unpack carry-on bag. Culprit is small metal hair dryer. X-ray device sees it as dangerous hand weapon. B. repacks, smiles apologetically. Other passengers eye her suspiciously. Ilse Koch glowers.

Stewardess with thick Southern accent and martyred look welcomes us aboard aircraft. "It's *real* bumpy today," she says. "I'll be *real* glad when this trip's over, I can tell you."

We locate seats. Squeeze into them. Hold hands. Watch oncoming passengers in order to spot potential hijackers. Most look furtive, foreign. Plane taxis to runway. Realize too late we got seats next to emergency exit. Recall story of man sucked out of plane at forty thousand feet when emergency door opened accidentally. Look around anxiously. No empty seats left.

Jet lifts off. Very bumpy. Hot smell like burning kerosene fills cabin. "What's that hot smell?" B. asks (B. always asks about hot smell and squawking noise made by retraction of landing gear.) "What's that squawking noise?" she whispers.

Stewardess with Southern accent explains "safety features"—especially use of seat cushion for flotation, in case of emergency landing in ocean. Describes evacuation procedure by which passengers slide from aircraft through chute into water. Demonstrates inflation of life preserver. Warns against inflating it until immersed. We try to imagine fastening plastic flaps of life preserver beneath crotch while under water, then blowing it up like balloon. Too much. Think instead about martini while safety lesson goes on. Stewardess points out emergency exits. We lean away from ours. Wonder whether to slide head first or feet first through chute into water. Wonder if women and children go ahead of men. "In the unlikely event of cabin pressure failure," stewardess continues, "your oxygen mask will drop into position automatically. You need only reach forward for the mask, put it over your mouth and nose, and breathe normally." Sound of abnormal breathing distracts us. It is B. Eyes are closed.

Now that safety drill has ended, captain comes on intercom. Lazy, relaxed voice. Conveys impression of man in shirt-sleeves with feet on porch railing, sipping highball, chatting with next-door neighbors. Apologizes for bumpy takeoff. Laughs. More just like it ahead at Newark, he chuckles. (Newark? Travel agent said flight was nonstop.) Be sure to secure seat belts, captain warns. Heavy crosswinds predicted. Weather at Atlanta (Atlanta?) windy, warm. Eighty-five degrees at Palm Beach. Sit back and enjoy ride, says captain. Signs off. Wish he would pay attention to his driving.

Lunch arrives. Green beans, salad, mystery meat, mystery dessert. Meat proves to be chicken. Dessert remains mystery. Salad dressing is from Oakland, California. Cream substitute manufactured in Union, New Jersey. Contains sodium citrate as "stabilizer." Ingredients listed on small packet of salt include "salt, sodium silico aluminate, tri-calcium phosphate, polysorbate 80." Wonder what happened to old-fashioned salt. Pepper packet contains pepper. Flatware wrapped in plastic. Everything else plastic—trays, plates, cups, drinking glasses, interior of airplane. Maybe food, too.

Only good thing about Newark stop is chance to buy another martini after takeoff.

The World Outside

We have had chickens much in mind lately. We have never shared the enthusiasm for these fowl that some countrymen have—notably E. B. White, who, in writing of his attachment to the hen, said that he had been "faithful to her in good times and bad" for nearly four decades. So it was gratifying to have him confirm what we had supposed ever since reading of Chicken Little, that "a hen is an alarmist. . . . She has a strong sense of disaster, but many of her fears seem to me well founded: I have seen inexperienced people doing things around hens which, if I were a hen, would alarm me, too."

Our own sense of disaster is probably not as strong as that of Mr. White's hen, but something tells us that these are parlous times for chickens. We've come a long way from the day when every farm—not to mention many households in town—had a small flock; so few people keep hens now that it's a rare person who knows the taste of a freshly laid egg. Not many Americans who have been inoculated against swine flu know, either, that the killed virus from which the vaccine was made was grown in fertile chicken eggs. In the normal course of events, vaccine makers use about 5 million eggs a year; but in 1976, thanks to the federal government's vaccine program, there was a demand for more than 100 million eggs. And who supplied them? Well, the Kerr Hatcheries of Frenchtown, New Jersey, for one. They managed to put some two hundred thirty thousand hens under contract—hens belonging to Amish farmers in Lancaster County, Pennsylvania, who keep a close eye on their flocks, feeding them and gathering the eggs by hand—and the hatchery hoped to obtain an average of ten dozen eggs from each hen.

With more than two hundred thousand eggs arriving at the hatchery every day, the situation soon reached the stage where the general manager, Bob Wills, said he was ready to start cutting out paper dolls. Despite the precautions that were taken, there was bound to be a certain amount of breakage, not to mention the occasional bad egg, and mechanical failures like the day an incubator dumped fifteen trays of eggs on the floor. According to Wills, 5 percent of the eggs arriving at the hatchery were broken when received. Now that doesn't sound like much, but 5 percent of two hundred thousand eggs is ten thousand broken eggs a day—plus another 10 percent, or twenty thousand eggs a day, that were discovered when candled to be cracked or of poor quality. And what do you do with thirty thousand bad eggs a day? Well, at Kerr Hatcheries you have a 1500-gallon septic-tank-cleaning truck stop by five times a week, pick up the eggs, and cart them away for land-fill. That's right, landfill. Smelly landfill.

Of course if we look at this business from the standpoint of the chickens, we can probably assume that Frenchtown's landfill problem is of less concern to the hens than what becomes of them when their selfless tour of duty with Uncle Sam is over. It takes an unusual effort to lay just the right sort of egg for manufacturing vaccine, and the average hen produces only about a hundred and twenty eggs before her contract is canceled and she is sent off to be made into chicken soup. Or chicken with noodles.

For reasons that elude us, scientists are always doing their damnedest to make the chicken into something it isn't. It's not enough that the chicken can walk, fly, work up to sixteen hours a day supplying eggs for the breakfast table, wake you up in the morning from your sound sleep on a pillow stuffed with its feathers, under a comforter filled with more of the same, and finally end its days roasted, fried, or otherwise cooked for dinner. No, they have to change it into something different. Geneticists, for instance, are attempting to breed a four-legged chicken, presumably so there will be enough drumsticks to go around when Bert and Marge stop by for dinner. Someone else is working on a featherless chicken. We thought when we first heard about this that it was to save plucking the feathers, but no, the idea is that the protein that normally goes to produce feathers (feathers being mostly protein) can go into the meat instead, which means that the same amount of feed will produce a meatier bird. (We know exactly how this new breed of bird will feel. We've had the dream dozens of times: there we are, as naked and as cold as a featherless chicken, standing in the middle of Grand Central Station at rush hour. But the difference between us and the chickens is that we always wake up and find that the blanket is on the floor; the chickens will wake up and find that they are really naked and cold.) In Texas, researchers are experimenting with a new method of making eggshells tougher by adding cement to commercial chicken feed. At the University of Georgia, for reasons beyond our comprehension, they're making cookies out of those high-protein feathers.

And now they're going to change the shape of the egg. We always regarded the egg as one of Nature's most successful achievements, but it seems we were wrong as usual. A Danish company has devised a process for forming and freezing what it calls long eggs—the theory being that the normal egg, when hard-boiled and sliced, has two ends that contain no yolk and are therefore unusable in restaurants and sandwich shops. So they've come up with this machine that can take the whites of four to five hundred eggs an hour and form them into eight-inch tubes; these tubes are then filled with liquid yolk and are hard-boiled, cooled, coated with plastic, and frozen. Each long egg, you will be glad to know, is identical in weight, in diameter, and in length and, after being frozen, can be kept for years before it is thawed and eaten. Yummy!

According to its promoters the long egg will be a great boon to catering services and may soon be a "convenience item," available at your local supermarket, ready for the home freezer. As one who equates "convenience foods" with the flavor and nutritional qualities of cardboard, we intend to avoid the long egg as long as we can. We might even change our mind about keeping chickens.

The road from Lexington to Concord is dusty no more, and the smoke in the air is not from muskets but from automobile exhausts. We are at such a remove from our Revolution it is difficult to imagine the impromptu activity in those villages on the crisp morning of April 19, 1775. Accustomed to television and movies, to picture books and magazines, we almost refuse to accept an event as reality unless we see a photograph of it.

The only contemporary visual record of the war's opening engagement are four rather singular engravings Amos Doolittle made from sketches done by his friend Ralph Earl. These two Connecticut militiamen arrived on the scene shortly after the battle, pictured the terrain they saw, recorded the momentous events as eyewitnesses described them, and left for posterity a highly credible, if primitive, representation of what occurred on a fateful April day.

It is not especially surprising that many Americans have difficulty empathizing with their Revolution. It was so long ago, as we reckon time, and it is all so foreign to our mind's eye— Doolittle's curious, sticklike figures in comical costumes, men in powdered periwigs, speaking a language that seems affected and stilted to our ears. On the other hand, none of what happened was strange or amusing to the participants, so in fairness to them we ought to let our minds slide back across the years and try to put ourselves in the places of men and women whose hopes and fears were not so different from our own.

How many of us would willingly risk what rebellion against George III meant—the possible loss of property, friendships, livelihood, or life itself—for the sake of a cause that had never more than the slimmest hope of attainment? How many would have remained loyal to the king—a course that was often safer and—to people of property—saner, for who of them was not made uneasy by the number of have-nots and malcontents in the Boston mobs?

So it behooves us to take stock of our Revolution—to think what it meant to the anonymous New England farmers and tradesmen and artisans and dockworkers, on the one hand, and to the John Hancocks and Joseph Warrens on the other—who had no need to risk their necks or their considerable fortunes on such a dicey venture.

There is another aspect of April 19, 1775, that is worth attention more than two centuries later. We have survived a long time now, for a democracy—longer than any other in modern history—and while there are a number of reasons for this (not least our geographical location and the bounty of an incredibly rich continent), we owe much of our good fortune to the way our ancestors faced up to life. The message of the Revolution goes deeper than the tale of battles lost and won; it tells us of a resolute people, thinking through their problems and the possible courses of action, and then acting in concert.

Considering what has happened to America in the past two decades, one wonders if senility and hardening of the arteries began to set in as we approached and then passed the age of two hundred, manifesting themselves in a slowing down of the thought process. Whatever it is, we don't seem to be thinking as clearly nowadays as we once did. In fact, we are not even asking the questions—questions central to our political institutions, our society, our present and future welfare. It appears to us that the difference between those men of Lexington and Concord and ourselves comes down to a matter of self-confidence and self-reliance—two old-fashioned phrases that have gone out of style lately. Where our ancestors fell back upon their own resources, we have a growing tendency to let George do it—and George, it turns out, is more often than not the government, a dim, unknown surrogate we have anointed to handle the tough problems. Yet the irony is that in relegating to government so many of the challenges confronting us, we are in danger of losing the very thing the men of Lexington and Concord went out to fight for on the morning of April 19, 1775.

Long after the accident at the nuclear plant on Three Mile Island, we continued to wonder how people in that part of Pennsylvania felt about their situation. Considering the talk in 1979 about what might happen if an explosion or a meltdown occurred, the people around Harrisburg—not to mention those living in a great swath downwind from Three Mile Island— had been granted a reprieve, as it were, a new lease on life. And so, in a way, had the rest of us, because it had become clear that "We all live in Pennsylvania," as the antinuclear demonstrators in West Germany had shouted.

Some thoughtful persons to whom we talked realized that it had been a very near thing, that they had looked the unthinkable in the eye. Our friends Nancy and Michael, for example, who live eleven miles from the reactor, first learned about the unexpected release of radiation from friends in New York State, who telephoned to say they would be welcome to stay with them until the crisis was over. Nancy and Michael decided not to accept the offer, but instead packed camping gear and, as soon as their son got out of school, headed west (so as to be upwind from the crippled reactor) and set up a tent some thirty miles from home. What worried them initially was the thought of the traffic jam that would ensue if the situation at the plant worsened and people were told to evacuate the area (as it was, telephone lines were jammed and it was virtually impossible to call in or out of the Harrisburg vicinity). Then what concerned them was the increasingly ominous news from Three Mile Island, right up to the time Governor Richard Thornburgh urged that pregnant women and small children living within five miles of the plant be evacuated. It was estimated later that as many as seventy-five thousand to a hundred thousand others—like Nancy and Michael—who did not fall into those categories, had also left the area.

For six days our friends camped near Chambersburg, returning to the farm each day to milk the goats and check on their home. As Nancy wrote later, all they had with them were a handful of possessions and "a few tools for starting all over again, somewhere. We were not at all sure we'd ever see the farm again."

Much the same thought occurred to a high school senior who had a date for the prom in Middletown on Friday night. Some hours before the dance her mother told her they were leaving—it was too dangerous to stay—and despite the girl's protests and her rising anger the family pulled up stakes and left. As they drove away it dawned on the young woman that she might never see her boyfriend or Middletown again.

Understandably, there has been a good deal of psychological fallout in the wake of the accident; in Middletown, Pennsylvania, the stuff of nightmares is very near at hand. Yet on the strength of conversations we had with people in the area during the months following the incident, we sensed that many of them were unconcerned. A young man whose family lives not far from Three Mile Island and sells the eggs from ninety thousand chickens ("It's a small operation compared to a lot around here," he told us) remarked that he had heard numerous stories about the trouble at the nuclear plant and believed that most of them were exaggerated or untrue. The radiation wasn't that much above normal, was it? Nothing had happened, had it? A Harrisburg businessman related how five hundred people had taken a scanner test that revealed no trace of radiation. "This thing has been blown up out of all proportion by the press," he observed. "I want to tell you there is absolutely no reason for concern." And a shoe salesman in the city remarked to a reporter, "That plant out there is one of the facts of the twentieth century. And most people here have learned to face facts."

One reason more people aren't worried, we concluded, has

to do with the nature of radiation. You can't see it, you can't smell it, you can't taste it. We recalled a survey of people who live near atomic plants, the results of which had been announced just ten days before the Three Mile Island episode. Researchers from Penn State University who studied four areas in the Northeast (Plymouth, Massachusetts; Waterford, Connecticut; Oyster Creek, New Jersey; and Ontario, New York) found that the presence of a nuclear plant had no adverse effect on the price of one-family homes within a radius of twenty miles. On the contrary, in those carefree days before Three Mile Island the existence of such a plant appeared to *encourage* the purchase of homes because it meant lower taxes. As one of the men responsible for the study put it, "Judging from the fact that even the value of houses within view of a nuclear plant did not decline, most people in these areas apparently have little fear about health and safety. If [they] really were worried, they wouldn't choose to live near a nuclear plant, and this would be reflected in the real estate market." The study was prepared for the Nuclear Regulatory Commission, and the researchers recommended that no further studies be made—"unless at some time in the future it becomes apparent that society's perceptions and values regarding nuclear power plants have changed."

The supreme irony may be the situation in which the Amish people of Lancaster County, Pennsylvania, find themselves. They arrived in this country early in the eighteenth century and settled on some of the New World's most fertile land, where they continue to farm industriously and to worship and live after their own fashion. Because they regard so highly the customs and beliefs of their forefathers, they cling tenaciously to the old ways—to the form of worship and the style of dress, to certain traditions. This is not to say they are altogether otherworldly. In order to compete with other dairy farmers, for instance (and they *do* compete very successfully), they have bulk milk tanks and milking machines operated by diesel motors and compressors. But most of them work their fields with horses and travel in horse-drawn buggies instead of auto-mobiles. They have no telephones. They have no electricity. And they have no use for the plant on Three Mile Island, nor the energy it produces.

Although the Amish want no part of the outside world, that world refuses to leave them alone. Promoters have turned the main highways of Amish country into tourists traps, lined with souvenir stands peddling Pennsylvania Dutch kitsch. A society the Amish would just as leave ignore looks upon them as quaint, anachronistic relics of a distant past. And upwind from their wonderfully fertile soil is a nuclear plant they never wanted, whose energy they do not use, which threatens to de-stroy them and the land they have tilled with such dedication for two and a half centuries.

What do the Amish make of Three Mile Island and what happened there? How do they manage without the electricity we take so much for granted? Hoping to obtain answers to such questions, we traveled to Amish country. And we came away having learned something altogether different.

The first thing you are aware of is the clarity of clean, well-kept white buildings in the gently rolling landscape. Every Amish farm appears to have a windmill pumping water, and those farms lie cheek by jowl in a bountiful countryside, largely worked and fertilized by animals, where hardly a square foot of soil is unused. Since each farm is in sight of an-other, they seem as much parts of a community as the families and church districts are. Certainly the Amish have many of the qualities our society once had and now wants again: close family and community ties, a deep respect for religion, for their elders and children, and a kind of "social security" that results when each member of the community helps others. You wonder, when you see what they have, if what makes it all possible is their agrarian society—a community whose roots are planted irrevocably in the soil.

We sat in the big, spotlessly clean kitchen, noticing the gas cookstove, the gas refrigerator, the heating stove that burns coal or wood, and the naphtha lantern that provides the only ..

illumination in the house, and we asked our hosts what they thought of the nuclear plant on Three Mile Island. "We don't like it," the man answered, "but what can we do about it?" And he changed the subject, as though nothing more were to be said. The talk then was of the family and of this year's crops, of the Belgian mare's five beautifully matched daughters and how her three-year-old has the makings of a good lead horse, and of the great problem Amish families face today— how to afford a farm for a son when land around them in Lancaster County sells for $5000 an acre. They said this was one reason the Amish were moving out of the area—an exodus that has been going on since the early 1940s, when most of the Plain Folk lived within a thirty-mile radius of each other. Now there are Amish communities in Ohio and Indiana, in Kentucky, Missouri, Michigan, and Nebraska; some have tried farming in Vermont, and there are churches in Canada and elsewhere.

They showed us a copy of their weekly newspaper that consists almost entirely of letters from Amish men and women all over North America, letters that read like the local columns of rural weeklies everywhere—news of births and deaths, of weather and social events and livestock, of the comings and goings of friends and neighbors. One correspondent wrote of hearing an Amish minister from Pennsylvania speak about the atomic plant near Harrisburg, of how "officials first lied about the accident, trying to minimize it," and of how a meltdown would have released "a deadly radioactive cloud that would fall out all over the countryside and kill every green growing plant and crop and tree and then every animal or person who did not get out of the way." Noting that nuclear reactors are concentrated in the states where Amish have settled most thickly, the letter writer asked, "Wouldn't that be something if some of our large communities would have to suddenly evacuate and leave all their farms and animals and houses behind, to flee for their very lives? That is the kind of world in which we are living."

We came away from the visit knowing we had had a privileged glimpse into another world—one not unlike what most Americans knew a century ago. It is a society that knows no energy crisis because it has so little need for energy, so little desire for what most of us regard as necessities, and because it is a conserving—not a consuming—community. People often speak nowadays of how we will live in the postindustrial age, and we realized that the Amish have been there all along. We wanted to say, "We have seen the past, and it works."

Back on the farm, three hundred miles from Lancaster County and Three Mile Island, we read yet one more opinion that there are no alternatives to nuclear power, that nuclear power plants produce 12 percent of our energy requirements, and the question we must ask ourselves suddenly became very clear.

Why should intelligent people tolerate an energy system that requires an evacuation plan?

Perhaps, with a little luck, the American people will rediscover what the Amish have always practiced—conservation, stewardship of the land and its resources.

On Sunday morning after the accident on Three Mile Island, the minister at the Pine Street United Presbyterian Church in Harrisburg, Reverend Fred Anderson, had put the issue squarely to his congregation. "Check your consciences," he told them, "and decide whether your desire for inexpensive electricity has taken precedence over your reverence for human life."

Some inner voice keeps urging us to be a jolly fat man, and one hot afternoon recently we slipped away from the office and headed to the drugstore for a chocolate ice-cream soda. We watched Mr. Jarvis make it, admiring the deft way he handled this modest assignment. First, plenty of thick chocolate syrup, which he had to pour from the jar, since there wasn't enough left to spoon out; then a little cream and stir, just so; then a dab of vanilla ice cream mixed in, followed with soda water (first the thin, hard jet stream, then the switch to soft and sudsy); and finally a huge scoop of vanilla ice cream that made the foam run over the rim of the glass.

While we watched, it occurred to us that the making of a really good ice-cream soda—like a number of other things we could mention—is becoming a lost art. Then we tasted Mr. Jarvis's confection and decided that everything is still right in our part of the world—or was, until we told him how good it was.

"You better enjoy it," he said, wiping off the ice-cream cooler. "You just had the last one."

"The last ice-cream soda? What do you mean?"

"That's the end of the Nestlé chocolate syrup," he explained. "They're not making it anymore."

"Well, surely you can get some other kind," we assured him (and ourself) as we spooned out a mouthful of ice cream.

"Wouldn't have most of 'em in my store," he observed. "Too thin. I've ordered a new brand, but I don't have any hope it'll be much good. Have to wait and see."

Mr. Jarvis will never know how low a blow this was, and on

the way back to the office we got to thinking about all the other shortages we've encountered lately and wondering what's behind them. At times it appears that our entire industrial complex is having an outage, as the utility business likes to call these lapses.

The other morning we called Austin Rumney to order some steel fenceposts and Austin said, "Yup, I got some, but I wouldn't sell 'em to you. Too thin. They'll bend if you look at 'em. Never stop a cow."

And then there was Charles Gaudette, who told us we'd better buy some blue jeans while he still had some. He can't get any more, he says—there's no cotton.

Not long ago we picked up some two-by-fours at the lumber yard and it struck us that they—like everything else—are awfully thin these days. Out of curiosity we measured them and discovered that they were not two-by-fours at all, but one-and-seven-sixteenth-by-three-and-three-eighthses.

Farmers tell us they can't always get seed or fertilizer—or if they can they can't afford them, and the same is true of barbed wire and woven wire for fencing. A friend of ours went in to an automobile showroom last week to buy a new pickup truck. He wanted to pay cash for it and asked the salesman what was available. Well, they had four new trucks, the salesman said, but he couldn't say what the price was. Or wouldn't. As it turned out, he knew a price increase was coming through and figured he could get $150 more by waiting a week.

We can't find the high, leather walking shoes we like (they've discontinued them, they tell us at Purdy's); our shirttails hang out constantly because there isn't enough material to keep them inside a belt; we can't locate a pair of gray flannel trousers (only double knits now, the salesman says); and we can't buy a pair of cotton socks for love or money.

To put it bluntly, everything nowadays is too thin but us, and we're cynical enough to suppose that the next time we go in to order some sticks of wood and ask for two-by-fours they'll really be one-by-threes. So long, two-by-fours. So long, chocolate syrup. We'll be cutting our own lumber from now on and the next time you see us we'll be dressed in the old patched jeans, driving the '69 pickup, heading for home and a dish of homemade strawberry ice cream.

A group of scientists meeting at the University of Maryland has decided that the likelihood of life existing on other planets is very slim indeed. What led the scientists to their conclusion is that no one they know has received any identifiable messages from outer space. If there are any smart civilizations out there, they reasoned, why haven't we heard from them? "Why hasn't anyone tried to colonize earth?" asked one man, who figures that extraterrestrials are surely governed by the same base motives that characterize human behavior.

Although we have probably missed out on a lot of fun, and have become resigned to being thought something of a fool because we do not know who Darth Vader is, we have little interest in what lies beyond earth's orbit. It has always seemed to us that there are so many wondrous byways on this planet and so little time to explore them that we could never work up much enthusiasm for space. Yet when you consider the interest in books and films dealing with the subject, it's clear that millions of people all over the world must have an eye and an ear cocked in the direction of the skies, and for them the news from the University of Maryland conference surely came as a bitter disappointment. If the scientists are right, there will be no encounters of a third or any other kind. If they are right, what's more, it makes our treatment of the earth all the worse. Suppose we are the only intelligent beings in the entire universe—what will we have to say for ourselves when the great reckoning comes? How will we rationalize or defend what we have done to the magnificent planet we have been privileged to occupy?

Numerous explanations have been offered as to why we

have never received any signals from space. If there are extra-terrestrials at work and at play out there, it has been asked, do they have any means of communicating, and if so, what does it consist of? And how will we be sure that what we are hearing is them, and not the rumbling of our stomachs or static on the evening news? Perhaps their level of intelligence has not advanced beyond the equivalent of Stone Age culture, in which case they will not even realize we were trying to communicate with them or were hoping for a reply. (We can imagine them squatting by the cave entrance, shaping spear points and shaking their heads, trying to get rid of that funny buzzing in their ears.) Or, on the other hand—and this is a notion totally alien to most of us—might they not be so far superior to earthlings that their method of communicating with us could be unintelligible, as if *we* had the scholastic aptitude of Stone Age man? After all, *Homo sapiens* has been at the uphill task of getting civilized for a mere fifty thousand years (and not doing very well at it lately, we might add), which is but the flicker of an eyelash as time goes in the universe. On top of everything else, there is the problem of a common language, once we establish contact. We Americans can barely manage to converse with a Frenchman, let alone with someone who speaks Arabic or Tagalog or Urdu. So how are we going to get along with an Arcturian, or cope with the language of Pluto? As you see, there are plenty of obstacles in the way.

We have no wish to become enmeshed in the argument of whether there are or are not extraterrestrial beings. But if there are, we have a few theories about why they are ignoring us—theories that have nothing to do with possible differences in IQs. If those beings out there have any sense at all, and we suspect they do, they've noticed what has been going on down here in the way of war, pestilence, and famine, and have decided they'd just as soon not make our acquaintance. Or perhaps they are peaceable fellows and worry about the size of the U.S. and the Soviet military budgets. Or maybe they just don't feel neighborly toward the folks on the next planet who persist in littering.

We've been making as much of a junkyard of the atmosphere as we have of our own backyards. You may recall reading that RCA launched a one-ton communications satellite into space in 1980 which hasn't been heard from since. No one seems to know what became of it, but we suppose it's out there somewhere, careening around with all the other hardware that has been rocketed into the blue since *Sputnik I,* affording as much peace of mind to a would-be intergalactic traveler as a runaway freight train. (Not long after the communications satellite vanished, while RCA officials were trying discreetly to learn what had become of it, we heard the authentic voice of America's man in the street: "Does this mean," a friend asked, "that I won't be able to watch *Laverne and Shirley?*")

It is entirely possible, of course, that the watchers in outer space have observed how we humans treat the other inhabitants of our own planet. There was the incident that occurred off the Japanese island of Iki, reported in *The New York Times:* "About 4,000 dolphins massed around this island today," the *Times* account read, "forcing fishing boats back to port, a day after fishermen from the island slashed and stabbed about 200 dolphins to death after trapping them in nets." An American who attempted to stop the slaughter—an environmentalist named Dexter Cate—was taken into court in Japan and charged with obstructing the fishermen's business and cutting their nets. (After a long legal battle, we have learned, the charges against Mr. Cate were dropped.) When we read the final sentence of the *Times* story we thought we could hear the sound of a tolling bell. "There was no explanation for the massing of dolphins around the island," it said, but we imagined that observers on another planet would know at once why those massed dolphins were there.

The more we consider the matter of interplanetary communication, the better we like an idea once proposed by Lewis

Thomas. In his *Lives of a Cell,* Dr. Thomas suggested that the most appropriate thing for us to send into space is music. If there is indeed life in one or another part of remote space, he observed, and if we succeed in getting in touch with it, "what on earth are we going to talk about? If, as seems likely, it is a hundred or more light-years away, there are going to be some very long pauses. The barest amenities, on which we rely for opening conversations—Hello, are you there?, from us, followed by Yes, hello, from them—will take two hundred years at least." So Dr. Thomas urged that we simplify the exercise by sending music. "I would vote for Bach," he said, "all of Bach, streamed out into space, over and over again. We would be bragging, of course, but it is surely excusable for us to put the best possible face on at the beginning of such an acquaintance."

The latest ill wind to blow our way comes from a Boston travel agent. Recently we read excerpts from a talk given by Bernard Garber to a group of hotel and motel managers in this area, and we were transfixed by his message.

New England, he told his listeners, has the potential to be another Miami Beach. But that golden vista, he warns, will be realized only if the hotel people invest sufficient money for what he calls "big-time travel promotion." What it comes down to, Garber suggests, warming to his subject like a coach at a pep rally, is that "New England must be marketed and packaged like any other product before we can sell it. With its history and natural beauty . . . this area is a natural for the tourist business." But until hotel men get off the dime, he observed, "New England remains an enigma in my business."

We wouldn't presume to tell hotel managers how to run their business, but we might remind them of a remark made by George Bernard Shaw when he was a young drama critic. As might be expected, Shaw's reviews tended to be acerb, and one playwright who had suffered several times at his hands finally attacked the critic's competence on grounds that Shaw didn't even know how to write a play. "I don't know how to lay an egg, either," Shaw replied, "but I can tell a good one from a bad one."

Having been to Miami Beach, we can see no conceivable reason for duplicating it here. For more than three and a half centuries New England has been holding its own in a contrary fashion, minding its affairs pretty well, content to remain the enigma of which Mr. Garber despairs. It was our impression that its history and natural beauty had already sunk into the public consciousness, and that there is no need to market and package the old place like a spray deodorant.

We suspect further that people from all over the world will continue to find their way to the tranquil mountains and meadows and small towns with which we are blessed. (All we have to do to realize that a good many folk have somehow gotten the word, even without benefit of big-time travel promotion, is to go into town on a Saturday morning and count the out-of-state license plates.)

By the end of the century, it is said, there may be 190 million *more* Americans than there are at present; about 90 percent of them will choose to live in urban areas; and if things go the way we suppose they will, there will be an average of one automobile to every adult. When even a tiny fraction of those people head for what remains of the New England countryside it should not be difficult for hotelkeepers to fill their beds and dining rooms. It is just possible that they will find themselves wondering how to keep the tourist away from the door.

Tourists are one matter, residents another, and we've been giving some thought lately to the plight of New England's original settlers. It seems that the Golden Hill tribe of Indians is trying to find out what happened to their reservation in Fairfield County, Connecticut. There aren't many Golden Hill people around these days, to be sure—only one hundred of them at last count; but they're attempting to locate a missing nineteen and three-quarter acres. The Golden Hills, known also as the Paugusetts, were minding their own business near present Bridgeport, Connecticut, when the first whites arrived to jolly them out of their tribal hunting grounds, and at the end of the Pequot War they were shoved onto an eighty-acre reservation in what is now downtown Bridgeport. There they lived until their wigwams were burned in 1842, when they were given the sum of $1700 and told to move to Trumbull. All that now remains of the $1700 and the twenty-acre reservation they acquired at that time is one quarter-acre lot and a 150-year-old house with aluminum siding in Trumbull.

Much the same fate befell the other four recognized tribes in Connecticut—the Eastern Pequot, Western Pequot, Schaghticoke, and Mohegan peoples. The Schaghticokes, for instance, are supposed to have two thousand acres in Kent, but according to Irving Harris, who is an engineer with the state Department of Transportation when he is not being chief of the Schaghticokes, "We have only three hundred and forty-eight, and nobody even knows exactly which three hundred and forty-eight acres, either." The Indians' common problem seems to be that their destinies were in the hands of the Connecticut Welfare Department for many years. The state would appoint an overseer of the poor to handle affairs for them, but before the Indians knew it, Mr. Harris says, their land would end up being owned by one of the overseer's relatives. "The overseers used to take ten, fifteen acres to pay a measly bill for a ton of coal, and you never got to see where the money went. Or they'd take the land and leave it to their children."

Things being what they are, we doubt that the Golden Hills will soon see tangible evidence of their reservation other than that one quarter-acre plot, but it would be nice to think that there were twenty unencumbered acres somewhere in Connecticut that one hundred tribesmen could call their own.

If you have been in touch with the American National Metric Council (ANMC), you know that the arrival of the metric system is being awaited in some quarters with only a shade less enthusiasm than the Second Coming. Only a few dinosaurs, it is suggested, will fail to welcome the orderly procession of meters, grams, liters, degrees Celsius, and all those other businesslike terms into our midst. So at the risk of appearing an obstructionist, we mention our suspicion that metric has as yet no host of admirers in rural areas; that we are but one of millions of Americans who feel they are being pushed into unwilling compliance with "metrication"; and that the conversion to metric is about as popular as a massive dose of salts.

The metric system is sometimes referred to as SI—which stands for *Le Système International d'Unités.* And that, if we may say so, is at the root of the problem. SI, in other words, is French.

It commenced, as they say, in 1790, when Louis XVI authorized certain studies that led to a reform of French weights and measures. Now it should be remembered that Louis, at the time, was in a peck (i.e., 7.6 liters) of trouble. The Bastille had fallen the year before; the mob had forced the royal family to move from Versailles to Paris; the government was in a state of upheaval; and Louis—who had this funny feeling in the back of his neck—may have thought that a crazy scheme like metric would distract his critics. It didn't. Two years after Louis had gone to the guillotine France's revolutionary government adopted the system and made it compulsory.

In 1812, Napoleon, who believed in simple solutions, did away with metric and not until 1840 was the scheme inflicted once again on the unhappy citizenry of France. Then, as before, the country was torn by domestic disorder and on the brink of war, and presumably it was thought that the metric system would so bewilder the state's enemies, domestic and foreign, that they would go away. As we all know, France somehow survived the metric system—but only just; and in 1973 the U.S. House of Representatives concluded that this nation ought to have a go at it. That year, you may recall, was the year the OPEC countries decided to give us a hard time; it was also the year that Watergate was being written into the language; and the legislators may have felt, as had France's deputies in moments of similar panic, that confusion piled upon confusion might somehow serve the republic.

Whoever devised the metric system came up with the notion that there would be a unit of length, called a meter, which for reasons known only to its creator was to be one ten-millionth of the distance on the earth's surface between the equator and either pole. And there was to be a unit of mass, called a gram, defined as the mass of pure water that would fill a cube whose edges are each 0.01 m, whatever that may be. From these humble beginnings has come an entirely new language—Celsius for temperature readings, grams and kilograms for mass, hectares for area, joules for energy, meters for length. And this is but a scratch on the surface. If the ANMC has its way, we will henceforth deal daily with pascals and roentgens, teslas and hertz, newtons, henrys, moles, and heaven knows what all else.

What this will mean to the American farmer, who has need of no more problems, may be surmised. Instead of acres, he will be expected to talk in ares and hectares and square meters. His cows will give milk in liters. His animals, munching grain that is weighed in grams or kilograms, will be confined within fences measured in meters (or maybe dekameters, hectometers, or kilometers). The farmer's fields will be spread with fertilizer and lime delivered by the metric ton (or, sometimes, tonne), and the lumber he buys will be described in millimeters and meters. After filling his tractor with a number of liters of fuel, the farmer will travel out to the back forty (to be known from now on, we assume, as the back 16.1878) at a speed reckoned in kilometers per hour. At the farmhouse, his wife will be listening for the latest weather report, delivered in terms of Celsius and pascals and kilometers, while she measures the ingredients for her sponge cake in milliliters and grams, and wonders how many joules this will add to her diet. When she drives into town to shop, she can convert to metric as she purchases clothing, orders wallpaper and carpeting, selects yard goods, and buys groceries.

"The beauty of the metric system is its simplicity," we read in one enthusiastic little pamphlet. Then we happened upon a discussion of liters. We had supposed that with all the money and effort expended on the metric system during the course of two centuries, someone would have thought to eliminate the confusion that exists between liquid and dry measurements— between wet and dry ounces, that is. But no—they have merely changed the name. Instead of ounces, liters will now be used to measure both liquid and dry ingredients. And (a characteristically Gallic fillip) liters will also describe the space within objects—such as the ice compartment of a refrigerator. So when someone mentions liters, you won't know if he is describing a tumbler of gin, a box of oatmeal, or the space in his automobile trunk.

What about football, we wondered? Will the 100-yard gridiron become the 9144-centimeter field? A 42-yard field goal a 3840.48-centimeter boot? Will the game be measured in meters, so that we see Terry Bradshaw drop back and complete a 31.5-meter pass (making it first and 9 for the Steelers)? We can hear Howard Cosell now, alluding to that big, 117-kilogram kid from Grambling, or telling us that Too Tall Jones measures 201 centimeters from head to toe.

Recently we lay in bed, woolgathering, and a vision came to us of what lies ahead in the brave new metric world. It is a February morning. Cold. Dark. We realize we have a sore throat. Damn. Struggling reluctantly from the covers, we shut the window, look at the thermometer, and see that the outside temperature is 10° Fahrenheit. Thanks to a book called *Think Metric Now!* by Paul J. Hartsuch, Ph.D., we know what an easy matter it is to convert Fahrenheit to Celsius. All you have to do is remember the handy formula:

$$°C = \tfrac{5}{9}(°F - 32)$$

Standing there in the dark with your bare feet on an icy floor makes it a challenge to work out the answer as quickly as possible. Ah, there it is—the outside temperature is $-12\tfrac{2}{9}$° C. Wonder what it's like down at Bert's, $-12\tfrac{5}{9}$°?

Then it's into the bathroom, to take our own temperature. Just so—$99\tfrac{3}{5}$°. We *thought* we were a bit feverish. Before telephoning the doctor to see what he suggests, we'd better work out those fractions, though, in case he wants it in Celsius. Let's see: $\tfrac{5}{9}$ ($99\tfrac{3}{5}$ -32) becomes $\tfrac{5}{9}$ ($\tfrac{498}{5}$ -32). Hmmm. Probably the easiest way out of this is to tell the doctor we're running a slight fever: Nothing much, Doc—just five-ninths times four-hundred ninety-eight over five, minus thirty-two. He probably runs into these minor elevations a lot this time of year. Now then, where's that cough syrup? Let's see—one and a half teaspoons every four hours. That would be seven and a half milliliters, right? Or is it centiliters? Maybe better call Doc back and tell him we can't locate the conversion chart. Oh hell, just take a swallow.

What impresses us is how simple it all is. As Paul J. Hartsuch writes, "the metric system [is] the easiest one that was ever devised."

The most charitable thing to be said about November weather is that it is sure to be uncertain. The sere autumn leaves rattle disconcertingly underfoot, each gust of wind brings the taste and smell of winter, and we think of it as a sad, barren month—an interval between seasons. The first snow flurries are not far off, and one day when we least expect them they will slant in unannounced, reminding us of the remoteness of spring. These thoughts called to mind a remark made by an aged Negro friend, a memory that cheered us considerably. The two of us were looking up at the sky, surveying the swift, darkling clouds overhead and speculating on what kind of day it would be, and he observed that no matter what came, "We jest has to stay in it till we gits out of it."

Which is the way we have come to feel about politics and other such matters. We were shoving the leaves around the yard in desultory fashion the other afternoon, piling them where they are virtually certain to be spread like a blanket over the lawn when the first stiff breeze comes up, and it occurred to us that November has come to mean more than election day and Thanksgiving—it is also the time of year when we cannot walk in the woods. Now, it is true that no self-respecting deer would be seen wearing our Day-Glo vest while sauntering along a woods road, but we are not sure the hunters realize this. One thing we have observed is the growing laziness of those who seek deer. The roads are alive with them—cars, jeeps, and pickup trucks bristling with guns and sinister figures in black-and-red-checked jackets, driving slowly along, scanning the fields and hillsides for a sign of movement. (We say "sinister" advisedly, because even our friend at Chase Manhattan looks that way with a two-day growth of beard and a gun in his hand.) Suddenly they see a slight motion, and the barrel of a rifle slides menacingly out the window of the car. Is it a deer they have spotted? Or is it us? And will they recognize the difference? Thoughts such as these prompt us to stay indoors, counting the days until The Season ends, wondering if there is not some way to flush the roadside hunters out of their automobiles to take their chances on foot with the rest of us.

Flushing out was, it happens, a technique favored by New Hampshire's former governor Meldrim Thomson, Jr., to dispose of bureaucrats who happened to hold a point of view with which he disagreed. Fire them, said Governor Thomson. He had no patience with federal employees who oppose the use of nuclear power and urged President Ford to identify these misfits "and be rid of them as soon as possible." It was not unlike the Red Queen's simple remedy—the off-with-their-heads approach—and while we're sure it would be effective, it might cut down a bit on the dialogue we know as democracy. But the hazard of something like this in these anarchic times was that if Governor Thomson's idea had taken hold, there is no telling where it might have stopped. Who knows but what the taxpayers might take it into their heads to try the same sort of thing on a congressman? Maybe even a governor.

We don't presume to know how Governor Thomson felt about ersatz food, but that's what's giving *us* fits these days. We have seen a product the Blue Bonnet people are plugging, and one look at the label was enough to send us in a catatonic state to the checkout counter. *"Imitation Margarine,"* was the message we had read. Nothing, we concluded, is beyond the capacity of American ingenuity. In the land where the dairy cow was once queen, the bread is now spread with an imitation of imitation butter.

Not that this pettifogging is likely to get us very far. We read somewhere that Americans have become so inured to the packaged outpouring of food factories that they actually prefer frozen orange juice, for example, to fresh. And some years ago the Massachusetts Department of Agriculture indicated that the American consumer spent far more for beer, cigarettes, and bottled soft drinks in one year than he did for beef—a total of $8.85 billion on what are called "unnecessary" purchases.

This avidity for beer and soft drinks is merely the tip of the iceberg, it appears. According to Tom McCall, then governor of Oregon—the only state other than Vermont to have a bottle ban—the nation was obliged, in 1972, to dispose of 54 billion nonreturnable beer and soft-drink cans and bottles. In less than a decade, McCall predicted, we would have the distinction of having to get rid of some 400 throwaway containers for every American man, woman, and child alive—80 billion cans and bottles a year.

It might be thought that this gigantic mountain of trash represents only an aesthetic problem—one that Vermont and Oregon are largely spared by reason of their bottle bans, which have reduced roadside litter by 90 percent. But quite another matter is involved. If, as Governor McCall reported, we had a national bottle bill similar to that boasted by these two states, we would save an immense amount of energy presently required to produce these containers. It seems that it takes four times as much energy, or fuel, to produce beer or soft drinks in an aluminum can as it does in a refillable glass bottle, and if we were willing to take our empty containers back to the grocery store and have them reused, we could save two-thirds of the energy that would be conserved by establishing a national speed limit of fifty-five miles an hour.

As it happens, we are all for a national speed limit, having seen how it can reduce highway fatalities, and we see no reason why we shouldn't have a speed limit *and* a bottle ban. And having gone that far, we have another suggestion for the folks who are running things down in Washington.

In the belief that the American people have a lot more tolerance for reality than they are generally given credit for, we say with some assurance that if the government explained the situation frankly and told us that the only way out of the energy bind was to have gasoline rationing, everyone would go along with a minimum of grumbling. The more we think about it, the more we like the notion of that tidy little ration book—a balance sheet, as it were, to tell us graphically and simply how much of the nation's precious capital of oil we have coming to us and how much of it we can spend in a given month.

Just when we thought the human race was getting the worst of everything, we read a report from the Connecticut Agricultural Station in New Haven suggesting that there are difficult times ahead for certain members of the plant world. No names are mentioned, but on the supposition that some of our old friends are under observation in the laboratory, we are watching the matter carefully. It seems that the scientists have caught some plants wasting the sun's energy and are now busy developing new genetic strains that will perform more efficiently.

All this time we have assumed that the plants we see around us had devised an altogether enviable society. Content to occupy their own small plot of ground and to live peaceably with the neighbors, they ask little more than a simple diet of carbon dioxide and water while they bask in the sun, radiating oxygen, and making the world green and fragrant. But now the scientists have come along and accused the slugabeds of inefficiency and waste, telling them to shape up or ship out. We're not even certain a plant has any control over the amount of sunlight it consumes (we are the same way about ice cream), but the scientists aren't standing on any niceties; they're planning new mutations that will convert a higher proportion of the sun's energy into edible tissue. We accept this news sadly, on behalf of those plants that will lose out in a brave new world, but willingly, in the belief that means must be found to feed the world's hungry. Yet we are touchy and nervous about certain larger implications.

What bothers us is the possibility that the scientists, having succeeded with plants, will turn their restless minds to other fields—editors, for example. Now, we have been trying for years to conceal how much energy we are wasting. When visitors to the office catch us with the green eyeshade pulled down and our head nodding, we always explain that we are merely resting our eyes, that we do our best thinking this way. In fact, we take a certain pride in having made woolgathering something of an art (often, it must be said, to the despair of family and friends, who regard this as a device for putting off matters that require attention). But we should hate to have those New Haven biochemists and geneticists put a representative sampling of our cells in their petri dishes for close scrutiny. We are certain there's a more efficient mutation lurking nearby, and the thought of it makes us wrap the scarf a bit tighter around the neck, where we feel the chill on these spring mornings.

These many autumns, we have waited for a particular gold and crystal day when every leaf and tree and blade of grass is outlined with a clarity painful to behold, and walked across the upper pasture and through the gate to enter the secret road. (It is not really a secret road but it seems like one, and that is what matters.) The hidden path leads up through the deep green of Scotch pine, through the yellow and red of second-growth hardwood, and finally approaches a line of fiery and majestic sugar maples standing guard over an ancient stone wall. Beyond is what we have come to see—one of the few surviving mountain meadows in our corner of New England.

The popple is crowding in, weeds are taking over from the timothy and redtop and clover that once grew here in abundance, but the meadow is still open, and will be for a few more years. From here, on such a day, it is possible to observe all we care to see of the world—a hawk's view of the surrounding farms and our village; beyond, to the south, one of the most beautiful valleys in New England, with the thin white point of a steeple in the distance; and off to the northwest, beyond the near range of mountains, the hazy blue peaks of the Adirondacks, as remote and unattainable as the Seven Cities of Cíbola must have been to the Spaniards.

Ordinarily, on this day, we walk unconcerned, content to soak up the dying warmth of summer, permitting no alien thought to intrude on the rustle of dry leaves, the shimmer of sunlight on the grass, the somnolent hum of insects unaware of winter's offing.

Ordinarily, that is. But this year the plight of O. C. Helton, of Oso, Washington, kept nagging at us, refusing to give us a moment's peace. In case you hadn't heard of Mr. Helton, he's the fellow who, in the mid-1970s, decided to build a log cabin in the woods for his family—which includes his wife, four daughters, and a son. As a man who grew up in the Smoky Mountains of North Carolina, O.C. knows his log cabins and figures they're the best house around for the money. But before embarking on his project he checked in with the Snohomish County Building and Plumbing Code Department to see what requirements he might have to meet. They told him to bring in his plans.

Now, plans aren't the first thing a man who has lived in log cabins all his life thinks of when he starts to build; he knows that you just put the right size log here and another one there, until the thing begins to take the shape you had in mind. But O.C. found a big piece of paper and sketched out his idea for the folks on the board.

"They look like centipede tracks," the director said ungraciously, and told O.C. to hire an architect and to consult a structural engineer.

Since O.C. figured that most architects probably know considerably less about log cabins than he does and would charge him about $1400 for the drawings, he and his family decided to go ahead with the cabin before winter set in and to hell with the Snohomish County Building and Plumbing Code Department.

Well, the department discovered what they were up to, slapped a stop-work order on the project, and charged O.C. with building a log house without a permit. And the upshot of this, last we heard, was that O.C. had accumulated $350 in attorneys' fees and faced a potential fine of $300 a day for nonconformance to the SCBPCD's order. For a man who has set aside only $4500 after nineteen years of marriage, that kind of money doesn't come easily.

We don't know how O.C. will make out with the Snohomish County authorities, but we want him to know that we wish him well and applaud his reasons for fighting the case. "I don't think people realize . . . how they're being taken over by all these government officials," he said. "If you don't get this government slowed down and back to the people, by the time my children want to build their home, they'll be surrounded by rules."

Slowing down the government and giving it back to the people happens to be an idea that appeals to us, and this is the theme of a book called *De-Managing America,* by Richard Cornuelle. The author, a former executive vice-president of the National Association of Manufacturers, knows front-office America the way O. C. Helton knows log-cabin America, and he has observed that things just aren't working where they're overmanaged—whether it's politics, the federal government, employment, housing programs, the Postal Service, the educational system, agricultural programs, foreign affairs, race relations—you name it. Somewhere along the line the belief took hold in this country that everything needs managing and that management is what got us where we are today, and the result is that there are now more managers than producers in the United States (as of 1970, 21 million front-office clerks, managers, officials, or proprietors vs. 18 million who were doing real work).

According to Mr. Cornuelle, a revolution is coming—may, in fact, be here—and he describes its watchwords as self-discovery and self-expression. Take the presidential election most people think of as a Nixon landslide. Looked at another way, the results reveal no landslide, but a national disaffection with the way politics are managed. The vote was 22 percent for McGovern, 33 percent for Nixon, and 45 percent for neither man. And Cornuelle sees this as a sign that more and more people sense that the nation is in the sort of trouble that can be rectified only by de-politicizing and de-managing society in order to make it more responsive to the people's will.

Which brings us back to O. C. Helton. All around us we see the O. C. Heltons of America taking matters into their own hands because the managers have botched things. They are starting their own small businesses, forming food cooperatives, generating their own power, operating subsistence farms, starting health clinics, creating schools that function outside the system, joining together to keep the peace. There is a popular tendency to think of these people as dropouts from society, but they are not—they have come to realize that the system is not working and have decided to run their lives their own way and not the way someone else tells them to do it. And it is just possible that in doing so they have stumbled onto the true meaning of free enterprise—a system characterized by conscience and caring, by flexibility, by a willingness to experiment, and by a capacity for personal growth and satisfaction.

If we can believe Alvin Toffler, the author of a book called *The Third Wave,* the impending collapse of industrial society is going to transform man and the way he lives. What Mr. Toffler terms the First Wave of change in human history occurred some ten thousand years ago with the coming of agriculture. The Second Wave took place three hundred years ago with the Industrial Revolution. And with the advent of the Third Wave a "new man" is about to appear on the horizon—a chap characterized by traits quite different from those familiar to us.

For one thing, Mr. Toffler says, parents will be less permissive, and the child of tomorrow will be reared in a society far less child-centered than ours. Education will be less structured, more learning will take place outside the classroom, and the years of compulsory schooling will grow shorter, since the process of education will be interwoven with work and be spread out over a lifetime. Work itself will commence at an earlier age, adolescence will be abbreviated, and the emergent new man will be self-reliant, able to adapt and survive under difficult circumstances, and have a new respect for doing things with his hands. As Mr. Toffler describes life in the Third Wave, there will be "balance between work and play, between production and prosumption [by which he means that in doing things for ourselves, we both produce and consume, or 'prosume'], between headwork and handwork, between the abstract and the concrete, between objectivity and subjectivity."

All of this struck us as very heady stuff indeed, even though we kept wondering whether we had not been there before and have merely strayed from the path. Certainly his notion of less permissive parents, of learning taking place outside, as well as inside, the classroom, of work beginning earlier in life, and of adaptability to trying conditions match precisely the circumstances of our own father's youth. But never mind. What caught our eye particularly in Mr. Toffler's discussion was what he calls the "electronic cottage." There will be a significant shift of workers out of factories and offices back into the home, he says. Two factors will bring this about: the sky-rocketing cost of transportation on the one hand, and the falling cost of communications and minicomputers. As a result, it will be cheaper to put "electronic work stations in the home than to transport vast numbers of workers back and forth every day." In many homes, Mr. Toffler suggests, the family will become a self-contained unit of production, as it was before the Industrial Revolution, with children assuming an important and responsible role in the household's output. (A fleeting glimpse of Fagin's boys passed before our eyes, but we set it aside.)

We have been giving some thought to how this might work in an enterprise such as a rural publishing firm, say, and the only problem we have been unable to solve is the question of who would go to the office. We've an idea that virtually everyone on the staff would be willing to stay at home, sending in the occasional message via electronic device between trips to the vegetable garden or between intervals of what Mr. Toffler calls "flex-time," perhaps even prevailing upon the children to draw pictures or to edit the article that was two weeks overdue. But who, we kept asking ourself, would mind the store? Who would sit in the office, sorting out the disparate communiqués from electronic cottages strung across the countryside, and put things together? We are hung up on this point, and while we waited for an answer, we got to thinking about that long period of human history that preceded Mr. Toffler's First Wave.

And long it was. Man, in a form more or less familiar to us, has been on the scene for approximately 2 million years, and for all but ten thousand of them he was in a preagricultural stage. He was a hunter-gatherer. Scholars believe that the numbers of these nomadic people were small enough, and the bounties of nature so numerous, that they may have spent no more than a few hours each day collecting food. The remainder, we suppose, they regarded as flex-time, and while the women pounded seeds into flour, made clothing, and did the ironing, the men sat around laughing and talking, drawing pictures on the walls of the cave, or perhaps playing a game that involved taking a stick and driving a little, round white stone across a field to see if they could put it into a gopher hole. It is of some significance that no word for "work" has been found in the various languages of hunting-gathering societies, and perhaps even of more interest that their population growth rates were virtually negligible—estimated as between .0007 and .0020 percent per year, in contrast with the rate of 1 to 3 percent in modern times.

According to Walter Ebeling's story of agriculture, *The Fruited Plain*, very little effort was required to gather the abundant wild grass seeds: in an hour, he tells us, a person might harvest more than two pounds of wild wheat in Turkey—wheat that contained 57 percent more protein than its modern counterpart; in three and a half hours, an eleven-day supply of "wild corn" could be collected in what is now Mexico. What altered this Eden-like existence was the slow but inexorable increase in population. Unlike other creatures on earth, man had the capacity to adapt, through technological change, to population pressure—and he did so in the first instance by turning from hunting and gathering to farming. Had he not done so, it has been suggested, the maximum number of people the earth's surface could sustain would have been on the order of 20 or 30 million.

There were several ironies attached to the advent of agriculture. In the first place, even primitive farming required a greater expenditure of energy per unit of food produced than the effort expended by the hunting-gathering peoples. Not only that. The farmer—then as now—had to work from dawn to dusk to raise food for his own family and for those non-farmers who, freed at last from the burden of sustaining themselves, settled in the expanding communities and became merchants, craftsmen, priests, or bureaucrats. The farmer soon came to depend on his children to perform the stoop labor of scratching the soil, planting seeds, and harvesting crops, and eventually to support him in his declining years. So there were more and more children, a growing need for food, and eventually the ultimate irony: most of those people whom the farmer had liberated to perform other tasks found themselves, at last, slaving twelve or fifteen hours a day in the factories and mines of the Industrial Revolution.

The villain of the 2-million-year drama, of course, is man's propensity for procreation. A system that grows by doubling, as the world's population has done, is said to grow exponentially. Starting with A.D. 1, nothing much happened as a consequence of the first few doublings: the numbers involved were too small. Then, around the year 1850, the population curve began to bend upward like the letter *J,* and took off. Just now, with 232 babies being born every minute, the increase in population is nearly two hundred thousand people a day, which is why almost half the world's families are hungry and three-fourths are without adequate housing. Human numbers are growing so rapidly that even if we should suffer a repetition of the greatest catastrophe in history—the Black Death of the fourteenth century, which killed 75 million people—we would replace all those dead in a little more than a year's time. It would take only three days to replace all the Americans killed in all the wars we have fought.

Since every problem we face—the exhaustion of natural resources, hunger, pollution, the paving over of our land, crime, the threat of war—may be traced to overpopulation, we keep coming back to a line of Mr. Toffler's, in which he predicts that the Third Wave's new man will have the "ability to adapt and survive under difficult conditions." He'd better possess that ability. For unless we vestigial Second Wave folk find the handle on population control, the days when the earth could support people at a decent standard of living are running out. The top of that ominous *J*-curve moves faster, hour by hour. And the task of stopping it is the most difficult ever faced by humankind.

During the annual season of goodwill to men we suppose the telephone company will be making its pitch for everyone to keep in touch. The beginnings of Ma Bell's campaign were discernible along about September, at a time when merchants were testing the string of tree lights and straightening out last year's tinsel so as not to be caught short by the imminent coming of Christmas.

If actual experience counts for anything, we are here to tell the telephoning public to forget about completing a long-distance call forty-eight hours either side of Christmas. We don't pretend to any expertise in such matters, but it seems a rather elementary deduction to say that there just aren't enough circuits in existence to accommodate everyone who wants to talk with Grandma on the holiday. And if the phone company wants our advice, they will cancel all those unnecessary television commercials featuring the rotund, white-haired old lady blinking back tears of joy as she converses with the folks back in Springfield. Because all the folks in Springfield are going to get for their trouble is the metallic voice of an operator, saying there are no circuits to Grandma.

As it happens, we are not much in charity with the telephone company these days. The first intimation we had that trouble was afoot came in the form of a printed note attached to our monthly statement. "The enclosed bill," it read, "may reflect a general increase in rates." (As if there were any doubt that it did.) Now, we had been following the newspaper accounts of the company's request for a rate increase and knew that the telephone people had been dealing rather cavalierly with the Public Service Board, refusing to submit detailed information about its actual cost of service, and that sort of thing. So we were in no mood for higher prices.

Then a second note arrived. Before getting into *that* matter, we might just say that we have been minding our own business lately, only bothering the phone company when its Direct Dialing System keeps forgetting the number we have been giving it. We have kept our complaints to a minimum in the belief that New England Tel, like the impersonal giants we used to read about in fairy tales, isn't very bright and is having enough trouble just keeping the cobwebs out of its electronic brain in this cold weather.

The second notice had to do with the unlisted telephone we have in the barn. For years we regarded unlisted numbers as the perquisites of movie actresses and Howard Hughes. Certainly not farmers. So we were slow to realize that such hidden fruits were for us.

At the barn, we find, outgoing calls are essential—Whitman's will have to be told to increase the grain order, a wheezing tractor requires immediate first aid, the veterinarian must be summoned to look in on a sick calf. But incoming calls we don't need. Nothing is more exasperating than a telephone ringing in the farm office when you are milking the goat in the back of the barn or when you are tying up the bull's hind leg in order to trim his hoof. The point is, we like to call out but we don't want anyone calling in. So we got an unlisted number—a number we don't even remember ourselves most of the time. And since we don't give out the number and don't have it listed in the directory, no one calls. It's as simple as that.

Or was, until the phone company wrote us. The notice, couched in the form of a friendly questionnaire, stated that "customers with unpublished service" would be charged $1 extra per month for this "service." We were given three choices: (1) we could surrender our anonymity in exchange for a listed number, in which case no additional charge would be made; (2) we could keep the number out of the telephone directory but have it included in Directory Assistance Records, for a charge of 50 cents a month; or (3) we could retain our unlisted number and pay $1 more a month.

Loosely translated, this means that it will cost us $1 extra each month for the privilege of receiving no service. We make no demands on New England Tel. They do not pay to have our name and number set in type or printed or proofread. We occupy no space in their directory. And since no one knows we can be called, no one asks for our number. (Now that the secret is out, we trust that a legion of friends will badger the company to reveal the mystery number, thereby making them work for their dollar.)

As is so often the case, we find ourselves yearning for days past. When Lloyd McGuffin was manning the switchboard of the small private telephone company in our town, it used to be that a stranger could ring up and ask for directions to Carleton Howe's place, for instance.

"Oh sure," Lloyd would tell the caller, "just take the road to the end of the Hollow, where you see the mill wheel. That's the place—a whole lot of farm buildings." And then he might throw in a bit of extraneous but useful local lore: "Mind you don't take the little road to the right. You might end up in one of the potash kettles." And while the stranger was digesting this piece of information Lloyd would plug in another line and pick up a conversation with someone else.

Nowadays, Directory Assistance is thirty-five miles from home, and as near as we can make out the operators there have never heard of our town, much less the potash kettles. But Lloyd knew everything.

One night our parents called long-distance and after listening to our phone ring half a dozen times concluded that we must be out and told Lloyd to cancel the call.

"Better let it ring a few more times," he told them. "They sleep in that back bedroom over the garage and it takes 'em a while to get to the phone." And sure enough, before long we answered.

It used to be that Lloyd would wish us a Merry Christmas when we picked up the telephone on December twenty-fifth. But this year we have forebodings about the greeting we will get from New England Tel. In the toe of our stocking, where Santa used to put the orange, we will find a computerized request for more money.

We've always pictured Ma Bell as a jolly, grandmotherly soul who looked like Mary Worth—short and plump, white-haired and apple-cheeked, in a fading gingham dress and steel-rimmed glasses. We imagined her as helpful and efficient—something of a busybody, even—and liked to think of her perched at the old wooden switchboard, nimbly plugging and unplugging those long cords, her eyes brightening wickedly when she caught snatches of the juicier neighborhood gossip. Since we never heard a word about Pa Bell, we assumed the old boy probably didn't have all his marbles and sat by the stove, amusing himself by stacking nickels from coin-operated phones.

Our assessment of Ma, we're obliged to admit, has proved wrong. Ma Bell, we've concluded, has more in common with Hetty Green than with Mary Worth.

Unfortunately, the falling out we had with Ma when she began charging us an extra $1 a month for that unlisted telephone at the barn was only the beginning of what she had in store for us. An intimation that trouble was brewing again came in the form of a leaflet we received in the mail, called "A Directory Assistance Charging Plan for VERMONT." With sinking heart, we read "the Five W's of Directory Assistance charging" and learned that henceforth we would be permitted only three free calls a month for information, after which we would be charged 20 cents for each such call. And in case we needed assistance from an operator or, in a burst of nervousness, dialed "0" by mistake, that would cost 40 cents.

Since Ma's new money-making scheme is limited for the time being to information about in-state numbers, it occurred to us that we could avoid these extra charges by obtaining telephone directories for the entire state and looking up the numbers we needed. In a flash, we called the phone company's business office and were connected with someone whose name sounded like "Mrs. Nargasock." Yes, Mrs. Nargasock said, she could send us all the Vermont books; but this was the last time they would be available at no charge. In order to cover the whole state we would need eight directories and she would mail them as soon as they were printed.

"When will that be?" we inquired.

Mrs. Nargasock was not sure. They would be rolling off the press at different times during the year.

"And meantime?"

Meantime, we would be charged for anything more than three Directory Assistance calls, even though we had no directories in which to look up numbers. It seemed an unfair if not highly questionable practice, but we settled for the books that would soon be out of date and asked Mrs. Nargasock to put them in the mail. A week later eight Vermont phone directories arrived.

Our first experience with how things are going to work was the night we decided to call Howard Solomon to see if he or his wife knew someone who might buy our billy goat, Harley Davidson. We remembered that the Solomons live in Lincoln, but Lincoln was not listed in the front of any of the eight directories Mrs. Nargasock had sent us. We thought of dialing Operator and asking which book Lincoln is in, but we figured that would set us back 40 cents so we bundled up, ran through the snowstorm to the garage, and rummaged around in the glove compartment of the truck until we found a Vermont map. Back in the house again, we located Lincoln and concluded that it might be listed in any one of three directories: Rutland, Barre-Montpelier, or Burlington-Middlebury. We looked through the books in that order and finally found the Solomon's number in the Burlington-Middlebury directory. They didn't answer.

Reflecting upon this, we realized that it had taken approximately twenty minutes of our time, a trip out into a snow-storm at night, a detailed state map (which we fortunately had on hand), and three area directories to learn the telephone number of some people who had gone out to dinner.

It used to be that nearly every town had an operator who was willing to reveal someone's telephone number when you asked for it, but one day when no one was paying attention the telephone company did away with all those local operators and replaced them with something called "Directory Assistance" centers. Now they're doing away with *those*—in Vermont, reducing the number from nine to one, putting a lot more operators out of work. And the Public Service Board's response to this streamlining is almost gleeful: as one of its spokesmen remarked recently, "People are expensive."

Another reason we'd like to put Ma Bell permanently on "hold" has to do with long-distance rates. A recent study in our local newspaper shows that someone in Rutland, Vermont, can dial Los Angeles cheaper than he can call Burlington, sixty miles up the road. And a call from Rutland to Bennington, which is about the same distance in the opposite direction, costs more than a call from Rutland to Plains, Georgia. In fact, it turns out that the first minute of a conversation that covers one hundred miles in Vermont costs 69 cents. But if you are talking to someone in another state, that same first minute for a hundred-mile call will cost you only 43 cents. At the root of this crazy system lies the whole matter of corporate profits, and what it comes down to is that Vermonters simply aren't doing enough long-distance talking. Since they're not meeting their quota of out-of-state calls, Ma Bell is raising the rates for intrastate calls.

Still another episode in our running gunfight with Ma Bell and her crew is the Great Base Rate Dispute. A few weeks ago we received the latest decree from the telephone company—this one stating that they had completed a survey and analysis of "subscribers . . . located beyond the base rate boundary of the serving exchange." Though numbed by this singular selection of words, we read on, knowing full well that some-where in the murky depths of the communiqué we would find yet another justification for yet another extra charge, and sure enough, there it was: "When basic telephone service is located outside the base rate area, but within the exchange area, an additional monthly charge applies, based on the airline dis-tance between your location and the nearest point on the boundary of the base rate area."

(Guess who is located "outside the base rate area"? Right.) The message continued.

> The effect of this survey on your monthly bill for basic
> telephone service is reflected below:
> Present Basic Monthly Charge $13.65
> New Basic Monthly Charge $14.46

Our Service Representative, Mrs. Harris, had made the mistake in her letter of inviting us to call if we had any ques-tions. We dialed immediately.

"Where and what is a base rate boundary?" we asked. "And what airline are you flying to determine the distances?"

Well, no one had actually been doing any flying, Mrs. Harris admitted. These things were really determined by com-pany engineers who had made a field study "to find exactly where people were located."

"Do you mean to tell us, Mrs. Harris, that telephone com-pany engineers made a special study to see where we live?" we asked. "*We* know where we live. We could have told you in a minute. And *someone* at the phone company knows, since they installed a telephone here. If the engineers want to know, why don't they just pick up the phone and call? You tell them to turn right at the Barrows House, go half a mile to the first bridge and—"

Mrs. Harris interrupted. We didn't understand, she said. Our telephone pole is number 12-4-2, and the engineers had had to make the study to see just how far pole number 12-4-2 is from the base rate boundary. Perhaps if she sent us a map we would understand about the base rate area. We sensed that the conversation was beginning to tell on Mrs. Harris's nerves.

A few days later a topographical map arrived. Someone had lettered on it "SUBSCRIBER LOCATION" and drawn an arrow pointing to a swampy area in the general vicinity of our house. Sure enough, there we are, about a quarter-mile beyond a curious-looking, obviously gerrymandered district delineated by a dotted line, which we took to be the base boundary. And we suddenly found ourself infinitely depressed at the thought of Ma Bell's engineers and their field study. What right had they to impose their base rate boundary on this valley, turning its intimate, embracing mountains, its streams, its sweep of meadowland and woods into mere reference points on a grid?

What we also found depressing, in view of our generous contribution to it, was AT&T's earnings statement. One year the Vermont Public Service Board granted the telephone company a 14 percent increase in rates and evidently this has been a great help to Ma Bell. Net earnings of the parent company increased 28 percent; profits for the quarter were $1.03 billion. As the chairman of the board observed happily, this was "good news because [the results] reflect the Bell companies' continuing efforts to improve revenues and control costs." People, we recalled, are expensive.

All this put us in mind of how folks out in Hickory Corners, Michigan, have dealt with *their* telephone company. A few years ago the Hickory Telephone Company received permission from the state Public Service Commission to raise the monthly residential base rate from $10.60 to $16.35, thereby starting a rhubarb that's still going on. As Buster Shook, a carpenter's helper, said, "We're tired of being kicked in the teeth. We're not going to stand for it." And they haven't. The citizens of Hickory Corners held mass meetings, marched on telephone company headquarters to demand that their service be shut off, hired attorneys, printed bumper stickers, publicly burned telephone company questionnaires, and raised $20,000 to carry their fight to court.

As our friend Doreen Bristol told us, it isn't that most telephone customers in Hickory Corners can't pay the rate increase: what they object to is the high-handed attitude of the company, which spent $1.7 million modernizing equipment and making technical improvements without asking their customers if they'd be willing to pay for it. We also talked with Mrs. Jackie Regis, who had her phone disconnected in protest some years ago and says it hasn't been any hardship at all. "It's very different," she admits, "but you get messages to people all sorts of ways." For one, there's a phone at the gas station in Hickory. "The owner knows what everyone in town's doing," Mrs. Regis told us, "and he can tell you where they are."

There are only about 250 people in Hickory Corners and Jackie Regis says "you can yell across town," but she believes the fight with the phone company has brought the people closer together. "You *saw* people before," she told us, "now you *know* 'em." A lot of visiting goes on in Hickory Corners these days, and when folks aren't at each other's houses they're likely to be talking on the CB radio.

We don't know how the people in Hickory are going to make out in their dispute with the phone company, but we admire their grit. And there are times—more and more, lately—when we envy them their phoneless existence. We think often of what one fellow in Hickory Corners said: "It's so damn peaceful without one I don't know if I'll ever go back to it."

A statistician in the U.S. Department of Agriculture has concluded that the forty-year decline in the number of American farms has "bottomed out." Checking the records, he noticed that fewer farms vanished in 1974 than in the previous year, and this convinced him that things are looking up.

It may be uncharitable of us to be skeptical about this hopeful news, but we are. For one thing, when you have only half as many farms today as you had four decades ago, it seems reasonable to expect that fewer of them will go on the auction block. But for another—and it pains us to say this—we no longer take much stock in official pronouncements. We don't know whether to rejoice or to mourn when we hear one, on the theory that it may be denied or declared inoperative the next morning.

Ours is the reverse of the fable about the boy who cried wolf. Having been gulled by so many big statements during the past decade, we no longer believe the little ones. Probably it is inevitable in this disposable society that government officials—like the rest of us—should come to think that nothing is durable or worth hanging on to. Like plastic drinking cups and the packaging for Big Mac hamburgers, their pronouncements are thought of as throwaways, to be trashed in case of a change of heart.

An example of how things work occurred one May, when the government began spreading the word that an upturn in the economy was imminent. After so many dreary months of bad news and gloomy predictions, someone in Washington decided it was time for a change. So they announced that there were "serious flaws in the old composite index," and conjured up a new index that would prove how rosy the picture is—unemployment, inflation, business failures, and the like notwithstanding.

We don't mean to pick on the USDA, which is having enough problems without us, God knows, but we have observed little to suggest that the farm decline is really "bottoming out," as they put it. On the contrary, the signs point to the fact that there is little in store for most small farmers but continued hard work and prices that don't begin to provide a decent return for their efforts. We see tired men and women unable to continue on the homestead in which they have invested a lifetime of backbreaking drudgery, unable to find new hands willing to take on the kind of work farming means, unable to comprehend a society that gives its farmers the short end of the stick.

Look at it this way: fifteen years ago the dairy farmer received $4.60 per hundredweight for milk (a figure that translates to 10 cents a quart). Ten years later nearly everything the farmer has to pay for—grain, fertilizer, machinery, labor—has doubled in price, and some items have tripled; yet he receives only 17 cents a quart for his milk. Which means that he gets 30 percent less for what he has to sell than for what he has to buy.

Go to the butcher shop and buy a porterhouse steak. Then ask the beef producer what he got for that steer he sent to auction.

Somehow, somewhere, a lot of cream is being skimmed off the middle—the difference between what the farmer gets for his produce and what the customer has to pay. We know the farmer isn't getting it, and neither is the retailer: that fellow in the white apron at the butcher shop is making a net profit of about 4 cents a pound on the steak he sells you, and surely you won't begrudge him that.

It's customary to blame all this on the mysterious "middleman." Now, we have never met a middleperson, but we suspect that all this middlemoney we are fussing about is going not to any one person but to an army of them—buyers, wholesalers, processors, packagers, truckers, commission men, and what have you.

So, rather than try to pin the onus on anyone in particular, maybe we should view this problem as an argument for more locally produced food. Why should the Vermont dairy farmer send milk to Boston at 17 cents a quart, only to have to buy it back for 42 cents a quart? And when the Maine potato farmer may receive as little as $2.40 a hundredweight for his crop, why should his neighbors have to pay five times that for potatoes in the supermarket?

In Vermont a number of people are taking matters into their own hands. In 1850, 75 percent of the land in the state was cultivated or pastured; and it has been estimated that only 18 percent was being farmed by 1979. But some interesting changes are afoot. Almost overnight, it seems, thirty thousand Vermonters have become members of food cooperatives; there are now twelve thousand community gardens in the state (not counting the backyard variety); and suddenly seventeen farmers' markets are flourishing, providing the local farmer with an outlet and the community with fresh produce at lower prices.

In Massachusetts, Frederic Winthrop, Jr., the commissioner of agriculture, made increased food production the number one priority for his state. Alarmed by the relentless erosion of agricultural acreage, Winthrop told anyone who would listen that "the time is coming when we will need every bit of farming land we have." A similar message comes from Connecticut, where the Governor's Task Force for the Preservation of Agricultural Land recommended that the state take steps to preserve enough farmland to produce one-third of the food its citizens require.

Connecticut, incidentally, is also the state whose senate voted to designate *Homo sapiens* as the state animal. We don't know how Connecticut struggled along without a state animal all these years, but the notion advanced by David H. Neidetz, a West Hartford Democrat, appeals to us. As he put it, a species that is so threatened by taxes, unpaid bills, and a deteriorating environment deserves recognition for its plight, and a majority of his fellow senators agreed. But it was a short-lived moment of glory for old *Homo sapiens;* outraged animal lovers complained so vociferously that the bill was sent back to committee to die.

The idea got us to thinking, though. Perhaps, if Connecticut's voters aren't willing to give this plum to man in general, they would consider bestowing it on a subspecies—the farmer—who appears to be low man on everyone's totem.

Modern society abounds in oddities, and one that crossed our ken in recent months is the institution known as the Gross National Product. Normally not one to trouble ourself with economic matters if they can be avoided, we have turned our attention reluctantly toward the GNP after discovering that its movement, down or up, is thought to determine whether we are in or out of a recession. There is a rule of thumb, apparently, formulated by an economic theorist (all economists are theorists, we have learned) which says that we are in a recession when the GNP declines or does not rise for two consecutive quarters. In other words, we are not growing. And not growing is considered bad news.

Lately it has been bruited about by people who ought to know—including the chairman of the Federal Reserve Board—that we are in, or approaching, a recession, but as an economist at the Department of Commerce admitted to us, predicting a recession is "a very inexact science." The more we thought about this the more certain we became that nothing could be less exact or less scientific, since the factors that inspire or shatter confidence or that create or remedy an economic downturn are virtually without number. Who could have predicted that the president of the United States would first announce and then suddenly cancel—with no explanation—a major address to the nation on the subject of its most pressing problem, a cancellation that sent tremors throughout the financial world? Who could have foreseen that he would call for the resignations of his entire cabinet and staff? Who is bold enough to forecast the next revolution in a country like

Iran, the success or failure of the Russian wheat crop, the price of OPEC oil? Talk about your inexact sciences.

Even so, we suppose that tabulating or computing or whatever they do to determine the Gross National Product must be a good thing, because it obviously provides employment for a legion of analysts and economists who might otherwise have nothing useful to occupy their time. But we have an uncomfortable feeling that since the Gross National Product includes *all* the goods and services produced by the nation's economy, it is a measurement of certain items that have no discernible value or use to us, as well as those that do. That is, it comprises—along with such practical items as vegetable seeds and shoes and hoe handles—an infinite variety of junk. Into the reckoning of the GNP go such frills as plastic wrappers for winter squash—a no-nonsense vegetable that manages to grow its own protective, almost unbreakable shell. The GNP embraces Mickey Mouse telephones and Pop Rocks, Horoscope Toilet Paper, Rolls-Royce grilles for Volkswagens, and the Lord knows what all else.

As a consequence, the question that nags at us is this: is there a direct relationship between GNP and happiness? Between GNP and genuine achievement? It is by no means certain to us that just because the GNP goes up in a given quarter we are necessarily any better off, because for all we know the difference between no growth and growth may have been made up of rolls of toilet tissue on which you can read your horoscope. Looking at it another way, if you bake a loaf of bread at home, you may be contented with your lot, but the GNP goes nowhere. On the other hand, if you walk to the store and buy a loaf of Wonder Bread, you have helped the GNP to climb, but do you experience the same sense of satisfaction and well-being?

As long as we were pondering the Gross National Product, we decided we might as well consider some of the other economic indicators that are going sour, and that led us to Representative James Weaver of Oregon, who introduced a bill in

Congress built around the slogan "a bushel for a barrel." Mr. Weaver says he doesn't really expect to see the price of a bushel of wheat equal to that of a barrel of oil, but the idea, of course, is that what OPEC has done with the latter, we can do with the former. In 1970—which is not so long ago, after all—a bushel of American wheat sold on the international market for the same price as a barrel of Arab oil—$2. In the years since, Arab oil has soared to $18 a barrel, while American wheat—until midsummer of 1979, when the price rose substantially—has been hovering around $3. What troubled Representative Weaver was this: although more than half the grain in the international marketplace comes from U.S. farms, and although the demand for food is steadily increasing, neither the American farmer nor the U.S. economy are benefiting as they might from the sale of grain. In fact, if we were *trying* to thwart the farmer and the economy, it is hard to see how we could do a better job of it.

Our balance of payments deficit with Japan alone exceeds $11 billion, but consider what happens when we sell wheat to Japan. In 1978 the Japanese government was buying U.S. wheat at the going price (about $3 a bushel) and then adding an import tax that was double the original purchase price before selling the grain to Japanese millers for $9 to $11 a bushel. In other words, the Japanese government was making a profit of $6 to $8 a bushel on wheat for which the American farmer received only $3. Nor is this an uncommon situation. According to Representative Weaver, more than 80 percent of all American grain exports go to countries with central purchasing commissions that make a profit on grain they resell to their own citizens.

And what of the American farmer? How is he faring? Well, since the average cost of producing a bushel of wheat was estimated to be $4.04 in 1979, and since the price of wheat was $3.73 in June, it doesn't take much of an economist to appreciate that the farmer was losing money on each bushel of grain he sold for $3.73, while the Japanese government was making a profit of $6 to $8.

Representative Weaver argued that we can no longer afford to ignore what may be our greatest asset in world trade—grain. And he suggested that instead of permitting the international sale of grain to be controlled by a handful of large multinational corporations, we establish a National Grain Board that will ensure the American farmer an equitable price for his product and a voice in our agricultural export policy, while obtaining the highest possible international price for American grain.

He saw this as a means of improving our balance of payments (a $1 increase per bushel would yield more than $3 billion to the U.S. treasury) and strengthening the dollar, and he believed it would mean an end to paying the American farmer not to produce. It was high time, the congressman suggested, for the American farmer and the American taxpayer to receive a just return for supplying Russia with wheat, Japan with soybeans, Europe with corn, and Saudi Arabia with rice.

Grain, you might say, could be as important to the United States as oil is to the Arabs, but one hopes that we will use our strength wisely and humanely. While we subscribed to the goals Mr. Weaver outlined, we had some reservations about the means that may be taken to attain them. For one, we are heartily opposed to the nationalization of any industry, and we believe it essential that the people who produce grain be represented on the National Grain Board. And surely no American wishes to penalize the poor and hungry of the world, nor should we handicap the producers of milk and meat in this country by raising grain prices beyond their reach. These and other difficulties deserve examination.

Nevertheless, if a way can be found to deal with these problems, we think that something along the lines of the congressman's proposal would benefit the GNP more than the production of bumper stickers and plastic spoons, while having a salutary effect on the dollar, the balance of payments, and—not incidentally—the American farmer.

"We are all helpless," the letter said, "and we should not be."
Our friend was speaking of the decline and fall of the U.S.
postal system and of how that demise affects everyone living in
the country. He mentioned the mounting cost of mailing a
letter, the deteriorating service, the closing of small rural post
offices, and the nondelivery and mutilation of mail without explanation or apology, and as we read on we wondered how
many more times we would receive a letter from him, since
the post office in his little town in California and ours in Vermont are probably high on Washington's list for extinction.

Some visionary in the capital has calculated that twelve
thousand of our thirty-one thousand post offices could be
closed at an annual saving of $100 million. In case you have
missed it, the message coming through from Washington is
that small-town America—the section of the country most dependent upon mail—is being phased out by the Postal Service.
The nation that brought you a piece of the moon can no
longer afford to deliver a picture postcard to Cousin Fern in
Shreve, Ohio.

We are not exactly certain how the mail will arrive in our
town once our post office has been abandoned or demolished,
but in our mind's eye we construct a scene something like
this. Every ten days or so (always, as we see it, on stormy
mornings) a large truck bearing the familiar red-white-and-
blue emblem of the U.S. Postal Service will roar through town
and someone in the truck will heave out a canvas bag, which
will slide to a stop in the general vicinity of the village green.
Then, presumably, if the sack has not fallen open of its own
accord, the first passerby will untie it, pour the contents onto

the ground, and begin rummaging through the pile for his or her letters and packages. Other neighbors will join the search, and before long forty or fifty townspeople will be crawling around the ground on all fours, throwing envelopes over their shoulders while they look for one that belongs to them. Collaboration of this kind might conceivably lead to a heightened sense of community, but we doubt it; we tend to think it will produce some sharp exchanges of views when Calvin Skinner plants his knee by mistake on Malcolm Cooper's hand, or when old Mrs. Arbuthnot finds someone standing on her Social Security check. The sorting process is bound to take quite a while, especially in a high wind, and some mail will be undeliverable, since addresses written in ink will wash off after prolonged exposure to rain or snow. But we hope everyone will be philosophical about the inconvenience; after all, it isn't every day we can play a part in saving the Postal Service money. And when you consider how many good things our taxes buy—grain for the Russians, aid for dictators, bombers for Arabs and Jews, bribes for foreign businessmen—we surely can't begrudge the Postal Service its economy measures.

Apparently, the mistake we made all along was in thinking that the Postal Service would be what its name implies—a service. It turns out that an argument has been going on since the earliest days of the Republic—dating back to Hamilton and Jefferson—as to whether the post office should be profitable. George Washington saw the postal system's function as drawing the nation together—"with a chain that can never be broken"—and later the Jeffersonians argued successfully that any profit the system might produce should be used to improve service generally.

In the old days, when it cost 3 cents to mail a first-class letter and 1 cent for a postcard, the Post Office Department used to devote most of its efforts to delivering the mail with dispatch. True to a tradition dating back to Xerxes, neither snow nor heat nor gloom of night nor much of anything else stayed its couriers from the swift completion of their appointed rounds, and we can remember a time when a letter posted to us from New York City in the morning arrived in Vermont that afternoon.

That happy situation prevailed until the late 1960s, when a commission headed by Frederick R. Kappel recommended that the Post Office Department be recognized as an independent branch of government and become self-sufficient, or free of subsidy from Congress, by 1984. In endorsing reform of the Post Office Department in 1969, President Nixon said that what Americans wanted was "fast, dependable, and low-cost mail service. They want an end to the continuing cycle of higher deficits and increasing costs." And certainly no one would argue with that.

In 1971 the Nixon administration took the bold, imaginative step of changing the department's name to United States Postal Service, and noised it about that the new agency would operate with the vaunted efficiency of other American businesses, but we could not help wondering whether the word "Service" was merely public-relations talk to make us believe that we were actually receiving it. The passage of time has only confirmed this dark foreboding: what has increased is not the service but the price of getting our letters from here to there. Recently we grudgingly paid 18 cents to mail a letter to Rochester, Vermont—a matter of forty-eight miles as the crow flies—and it took eleven days to reach its destination. What has befallen us, as a result of the reorganization, is slower, more erratic deliveries, greatly increased postal charges, and staggering deficits.

At times, in fact, our postal system appears to be about as badly off as Italy's was a few years ago. Mountains of mail accumulated there and the Italians, ever pragmatic, finally decided that since there was no straightening out the mess, they would begin again from scratch—and threw the entire stack of mail into the river.

Of all branches of government, the Postal Service is the one that touches the lives of most Americans on every day but

Sunday. For two centuries it has been their principal channel of communication with the world outside their homes. Without the mails, American business would have collapsed. Through the mails, knowledge and information and ideas are disseminated, largely through a diverse range of magazines and newspapers. And in many communities, the mails are the only channel through which books may be obtained.

Yet for some reason or other the folks down in Washington decided that the Postal Service—unlike any other federal agency—should make money. No one has seen fit to ask the secretaries of Agriculture, State, or Labor to turn a profit. Nor are the Joint Chiefs of Staff being urged to put Defense in the black. Closer to home, we are not asking our firemen, teachers, policemen, hospital employees, sanitation workers, or any others involved in vital services, to make a profit.

Unfortunately, like so many other aspects of life in this country, the Postal Service has simply gotten out of hand. It just isn't working anymore. You see this when your copy of a magazine arrives, looking as though it's been through a cabbage shredder. We see it when we walk into our local post office and read the sign on the stamp machine in the lobby— "Out of Order." Somehow you would suppose that a nation that spends billions of dollars every year on its postal system ought to have stamps that will stick to an envelope. But we can't even seem to manage that anymore.

Our new, streamlined Postal Service has spent millions developing what is called a "bulk mail system," and we think some of the results are worth reporting. Not so long ago it was found that the system expends more than eight days, on the average, getting a parcel from Washington, D.C., to Los Angeles. (That is slightly less than the Pony Express required to carry the mail from St. Louis, Missouri, to Sacramento in 1861, but the Pony Express was a lot more reliable than the U.S. Postal Service—in its brief heyday it covered 650,000 miles and lost only one mail.) Another test revealed that almost half of the fragile items sent by parcel post arrive broken. (Sorting bins are usually located from five to twenty-five feet away from the clerks who sort parcels—just far enough to encourage the throwing of packages. And in certain post offices, automatic sorters drop packages anywhere from one to four feet.)

But the difficulties are not restricted to parcel post. Take first-class mail. During one six-month period, 13 million letters were missorted in a New York post office. In Washington, the Postal Service has a letter-sorting machine it describes as "the equipment of the future." And alas for all of us, it may be. This 91-foot-long sorting device, which is manned by twenty employees, has an error factor that has run as high as 17 percent. That is, there are times when one letter out of every six is going to the wrong destination. And every time a letter is missent, it may be delayed as long as five days. They will tell you that this sorting machine—which, with others like it, was supposed to save taxpayers $1 billion a year—can correctly sort 1100 letters per man hour. And that sounds impressive until you learn that in the old, presorting-machine days *1700* letters per man hour were being sorted. How, you ask? By a method devised by Benjamin Franklin when he was running the postal system, in which letters are placed, one by one, into the proper pigeon holes.

For those who are not swayed by claims for the sorting machine, we call attention to the Postal Service's canceling machines, which print postmarks on letters faster than the eye can see. The trouble seems to be that these labor-saving gadgets jam as often as every ten or fifteen minutes, and when they do, they rip up large quantities of letters, which then have to be taken away and mended painstakingly by hand in another part of the post office.

We had assumed, somehow, that the almost universal use of zip codes would speed the delivery of mail and, indeed, that is the impression the Postal Service likes to give you. But in truth, zip codes don't achieve much positive effect. They merely stave off disaster. For if a substantial segment of the population quit using them, the entire postal system would collapse.

The Postal Service's machines were designed to replace people, but since the machines don't work properly, the Postal Service continues to rely on people. And since there are some 700,000 postal employees, it is no wonder that 85 percent of the Postal Service budget is for labor and benefits. For the sake of comparison, the average basic wage of postal employees is about $2000 a year more than the national average salary for policemen, firemen, and teachers. It is the same salary, in fact, that is received by the average assistant professor at a four-year college.

As if all that were not enough to worry about, we were also told that the Postal Service planned to do away with the old rural post-office buildings and replace them with new, factory-produced structures. If we are to believe Robert E. Isaacs, the assistant postmaster general for Real Estate and Buildings, the new models will be "economical, flexible, and attractive." Now there is certainly nothing wrong with economy, flexibility, and attractiveness in a post office or a postal service, but as Mr. Isaacs expanded on his notion our misgivings grew.

Communities, he explained, will be offered a choice of four different architectural styles—"Southern, Colonial, contemporary, and Northwest," but as it turns out, the only difference between these simulated regional variations will be the façade. Southern, it appears, will wear red-tile roof and stucco walls; Colonial, plain old brick; contemporary will have "stone-like slabs" (stone-*like*, we have learned, means that it is not stone); and Northwest is to have veneered walls and timbered fascia. (Mr. Isaacs did not state what might happen if the village of East Haddam, Connecticut, were to opt for Northwest instead of Colonial.) Other than these surface differences, the buildings will be as like as McDonald hamburger stands.

Oblivious as ever to the real crises of the nation, the government has decided that none of these buildings will have windows that open. They will be air conditioned. And in the spirit of the times, they will be clothed in anonymity: the "new, efficient, mansard-roofed" edifices will not even proclaim the name of a town to the passerby. Only the stark numerals of a local zip code will be emblazoned on the wall. (We can just see the couple from New Jersey, tired and cross after the long drive, arriving in town and wondering if they have reached their destination, only to stare at the brick-veneered post office and read that they are in a community called 05255.)

All we ask of the Postal Service is that they deliver our mail promptly and relatively intact, and we wish they would concentrate on that instead of fooling around with phony façades on their real estate. Some good friends of ours toil diligently in outmoded rural post offices nearby, and we have a hunch that what concerns them is not so much the surroundings in which they work but the lack of qualified hands to help with the task. Maybe, instead of putting $3 billion into stone-like slabs and timbered fascia, the Postal Service could hire some additional people to get the mail through on schedule.

We seldom contemplate a national election nowadays without thinking wistfully of Will Rogers, and we're sorry he wasn't around to enjoy the recent ones. Will had a way of cutting public figures down to manageable size, and he was sure to be at his best around election time.

"Every time we have an election," he once said, "we get in worse men and the country keeps right on going. Times have proven only one thing and that is you can't ruin this country ever, with politics."

Thinking about the many congressmen he had seen in his day, Will remarked, "You know, they are the nicest fellows in the world to meet. I sometimes wonder if they realize the harm they do." And speaking of the way the country is run, he observed, "Lord, the money we do spend on government and it's not one bit better than the government we got for one-third the money twenty years ago." As Will saw it, there wasn't much choice between Democrats and Republicans: "You can't make the Republican Party pure by more contributions," he said, "because contributions are what got it where it is today." And when he looked at the other party, what did he see? "The Democrats . . . having a lot of fun exposing the Republican campaign corruptions, but they would have a lot more fun if they knew where they could lay their hands on some of it themselves for next November."

Will didn't spare a man just because he happened to be president, and the one he most liked to talk about was Calvin Coolidge. It was a long way from Indian Territory, where Will grew up, to Vermont, where Coolidge—as someone suggested—had been weaned on a pickle; but the two had more in common than you might suspect. Both came from rural backgrounds. Both had a touch of Indian blood of which they were proud. (Will once teased a group of New Englanders with the remark, "My ancestors didn't come on the *Mayflower*—but they met the boat.") Both had a simple way of saying things and a subtle, dry wit. But that was about as far as the similarities went.

Will was taken to the White House by Nicholas Longworth to meet Coolidge, and on the way Longworth bet him that he couldn't make the president laugh. Will won. When he was introduced to Coolidge his opening comment was, "Pardon me—I didn't catch the name."

Coolidge, Will realized, "was the first president to discover that what the American people want is to be let alone." The Vermonter had a theory that the best government was the least government; as Will put it, he knew that "over half the things just needed leaving alone." And Coolidge, he went on to say, "either does one of two things: he does what nobody thinks he will do, or he don't do nothing. Generally the latter." Will once asked Coolidge how he coped with the job that had broken the health of Woodrow Wilson, and the president answered, "By avoidin' the big problems."

The trouble with Coolidge, Will decided, was that "nobody ever knew when he was acting and when he wasn't. He was like a ukelele. You can't tell when somebody is playing one or just monkeying with it."

Americans of that generation admired Will Rogers as much for his horse sense as his humor. We often think we have a corner on the world's problems, so it's worth recalling that Will was troubled by many of the same things that bother us. What it all came down to, he concluded, was this: "It's just got so that 90 percent of the people in this country don't give a damn. Politics ain't worrying this country one-tenth as much as parking space."

He had a facility for putting his finger on the quirky American character, and doing so in a way people didn't forget. In the depth of the Depression he remarked that "We are the first nation in the history of the world to go to the poorhouse in an automobile." He knew our propensity for meddling in other nations' affairs: "When you get into trouble five thousand miles from home," he said, "you've got to have been looking for it." Perhaps because of his no-nonsense rural upbringing he had no patience with diplomats: "A diplomat's job," he observed, "is to make something appear what it ain't." And he saw us warts and all: "The income tax has made more liars out of the American people than golf has." And again, "We have more toothpaste on the market and more misery in our courts than at any time in our existence."

When Will Rogers was killed in a plane crash in 1935, one of his friends said, "A smile has disappeared from the lips of America." Sure enough, it had, and the smile has been missing for a long time. Will was the most beloved figure of his day, a man whom millions of his countrymen—even though they never met him—regarded as their friend, and Will himself once came close to explaining why. "I am just an old country boy in a big town trying to get along," he had said. "I have been eating pretty regular and the reason I have is—I have stayed an old country boy."

Today, it would appear, the country has gone out of a great deal of America—above all, the old sense of community, the neighborliness, the feeling of belonging, of helping out, of trusting in others. Will Rogers once declared that "A politician is not as narrow-minded as he forces himself to be," but they seem to have forgotten, down there in Washington, the way we do things in the countryside. When a neighbor's house or barn burns, you help him out, whether or not he has been balancing his checkbook. When there is a death in the family, the women in the neighborhood cook and bake and see to it that everyone is fed and that the children are looked after. When the farmer next door breaks an axle on his tractor, everyone in the valley comes round to get in his hay.

More than two centuries ago, when America declared its independence from Great Britain, one of those present in Philadelphia was a man with the same kind of horse sense Will Rogers possessed, and we recall the words attributed to him at the time the historic document was signed, at such grave risk to all who did so. "We must indeed all hang together," Benjamin Franklin is said to have told his colleagues, "or most assuredly we shall all hang separately."

Not that anyone has inquired, but if these fellows who are running for president would like to know what they can do for us, we have a simple request. They could take a small piece of paper (a three-by-five card would do nicely), tack it beside the shaving mirror, where they will see it every morning, and on it print in large block letters the following words from Henry David Thoreau:

THAT GOVERNMENT IS BEST
WHICH GOVERNS LEAST

At last count, there were 2,900,000 employees of the federal government—a bureaucrat for every seventy-six men, women, and children in the United States—and each passing day brings evidence that a good many of them are underemployed. Or perhaps it is more charitable to say that they are employed at doing the wrong things.

To give you an example, last fall our friend John Kristensen, an attorney, told us about a form letter he had received from the Internal Revenue Service. The IRS, in a state of some dudgeon, was informing law offices that the envelopes it had provided to taxpayers for filing their Form 1040ES payments—the quarterly estimates—were being returned to the senders by the post office "because the envelopes do not meet their specifications." Whether the Postal Service had not informed the IRS of its regulations, or whether the IRS regards itself as above such matters we do not know, but the result was that one branch of the government—the Postal Service—was refusing to process return envelopes furnished by another branch of the same government. We decided to look into the cause of this interdepartmental rhubarb.

If you are in the habit of sending first-class mail (and some people, despite efforts of the Postal Service to make this process as painful as possible, continue to do so), you will find that weight is no longer the only consideration. You must also reckon with the height, length, and thickness of the letter you are sending to loved ones or business associates, far and near. The way to learn whether or not your first-class envelope meets Postal Service requirements is to obtain what the service lyrically calls a "Letter Size Mail Dimensional Standards Template." Onto this outsize plasticized card (which, incidentally, will fit into none of the cubbyholes in our desk) you lay the envelope or card to be mailed. If it is smaller than the "Minimum Standards" dimensions indicated on the left-hand side of the card, you are out of luck and out of options. It "cannot be accepted for mailing." So much for the little informal notes decorated with cheerful birds that Aunt Agnes sent us for Christmas. So much also for hundreds of postcards we had on hand at the office, and so much for the giant view of Saint Petersburg, Florida, we had planned to mail to a friend in Nome.

Since the *maximum*-size envelope accepted by the Postal Service is now 6⅛ by 11½ inches (a size we have never encountered), no longer can we mail at regular first-class rates an unfolded sheet of standard-size typing paper on which we have inscribed, say, a poem. Unless, that is, it weighs more than one ounce. If it weighs *less* than an ounce, for some reason or other we have to pay a 7-cent penalty, and all our poems weigh less than an ounce and are not worth an extra 7 cents.

There are other stipulations. One is that even an envelope that is suitable as to height and length must, with its contents, be no more than ¼ inch in thickness (a handy slot has been cut in the template for determining maximum thickness) nor *less* than .007 inches thick. And so, as we laboriously addressed our valentines this year, we were obliged to place each one on the Letter Size Mail Dimensional Standards Template to see if it conformed as to size, then to insert it into the Maximum Thickness slot, and finally to measure each with the micrometer we had borrowed from a machinist friend to see if it was more than .007 inches thick. It made for a tedious evening and an end to the mood appropriate to valentine sending. (We never did find out if the elaborate heart with paper lacework surrounding the pop-up bride and groom, which we sent anonymously and without a return address to our best friend, passed muster. The outer edges exceeded .007 inches and were less than ¼ inch in thickness all right, but the packet was rather lumpy in the middle—rather more than ¼ inch, we supposed.)

In our case, all that was at stake was our disposition, but we couldn't help wondering how these postal regulations have affected the makers of greeting cards and the owners of a thousand stationery stores and bookshops across the land, whose inventory of cards and letter paper has been declared obsolete. Is it at their expense—by outlawing the cards and envelopes that don't conform to the electronic sorter—that the Postal Service could make its triumphant announcement of operating in the black for the first time in thirty years?

One trouble with our society is that we are designing everything for the convenience of machines instead of the convenience of people, and the thought of this reminded us of something Thomas Jefferson once said. "The care of life and happiness," he observed, "and not their destruction, is the first and only legitimate object of good government." The sentence is a bit long to be printed in block letters on a three-by-five card, and not as terse as Thoreau's message, but we recommend the thought to all presidential hopefuls.

And while we are on the topic of unnecessary rules and red tape, we might mention the regulations Underwriters Laboratory has inflicted on the manufacturers of woodstoves. To comply with standards devised by the UL consumer-protection service, every new stove must carry a permanent label, large enough to be readable at a distance of five feet, which bears the following warning:

CAUTION: HOT WHILE IN
OPERATION—DO NOT TOUCH. KEEP
CHILDREN, CLOTHING, AND
FURNITURE AWAY—CONTACT MAY
CAUSE SKIN BURNS

Now for approximately four hundred years we have managed to get along in this country without providing people with printed notices that a fire, when burning, is hot, but clearly the end of the frontier is at hand. Steven Morris of Vermont Castings, a company that makes a line of stoves acclaimed for their beauty as well as their efficiency, commented ruefully, "I have an eleven-month-old daughter who might need to be told that a stove is hot, but unfortunately she can't read." Perhaps that will be the next challenge for the lads at UL's consumer-protection service—a stove that talks in a metallic voice, like a Barbie Doll, saying "Hot! Mustn't touch!" when the fire is burning.

What these regulators need to know is the scandalous amount of wasted time and energy they're causing. According to economists at the Chase Manhattan Bank, the cost of complying with government regulations comes to more than $100 billion a year. The steel industry, for example, must conform to a staggering 5600 regulations administered by twenty-six different federal agencies. (And people wonder how Japanese and German steelmakers can undersell us.) General Motors alone spends more than $1 billion a year—an amount equal to 2 percent of its sales and to one-third of its net profits—to comply with government regulations.

Not long ago we read some remarks by Howard M. Temin, who is a professor of oncology—the study of tumors—at the University of Wisconsin and the winner of a Nobel Prize. Speaking of the work that goes on in his laboratory, Professor

Temin said that he is obliged, every month, to attest—in trip-licate—"that all of the people on my grant have worked at one-hundred percent effort that month and . . . I have to send [copies to the other people on my grant] so that they can sign that their people have and so I can sign that they have signed. . . . Every month I must sign a yellow piece of paper that says seventy percent of my support comes from non-federal money . . . when I have no way of knowing that in fact that has happened." Instead of concentrating on cancer re-search, Professor Temin says he is obliged to concentrate on the increasingly frustrating governmental regulations, which consume his time in the laboratory and his effectiveness in a vital endeavor.

Not surprisingly, Thoreau's friend Emerson had a pre-scription for problems like Professor Temin's: "The less gov-ernment we have the better."

To give the devil his due, not all bureaucratic foolishness is confined to Washington, D.C. A committee up in Burlington, Vermont, is suggesting that Vermont farmers "improve the visual quality of agriculture." In the manner of committees everywhere, this one has prepared a checklist—in this case, of various steps farmers should take to upgrade the state's agricultural image. These are "little things," the committee says, "like keeping fences in repair, machinery stored properly, fresh paint jobs on houses, barns, outbuildings, and even mailboxes." With tourism on the increase, the committee adds brightly, "a heavier than usual number of outsiders will be getting a first-hand look at our farms." And to give farmers something else to occupy their idle hours, they are urged "to take the viewpoint of consumers, and rate their product's acceptability on the basis of the general neatness of their operation."

These helpful suggestions come at a time when the gross revenues of Vermont's dairy farms are $163 million, with gross, pre-tax profits of $390,000. In other words, the man who is working seven days a week in order to make a profit of two-tenths of one percent before taxes is being asked to spend some extra time and money sprucing up the barnyard for the tourists. And when he is not busy milking the cows, he can poll his visitors on "product acceptability."

We wish the committee members well with their program, but as they forge ahead toward their sanitized vision of the countryside, we hope they will stumble onto a few inducements for the farmer to keep the home place going.

"Why, it's almost as if they'd rather have you draw welfare than work," she said. We were sitting in Nellie's house, talking about how the federal government had suddenly entered her life. It was summer and unusually hot for Vermont—hot and humid, with no air stirring. She had just given Lanson his lunch and while he ate she showed us some of her handiwork. "I used to make quilts, too," she was saying, "but now, unless I have a special order, I mostly stick to crocheting—that and the knitting." The crocheting was beautiful: white coverlets for babies' cribs, with thousands of tiny rings forming the shapes of animals; gaily colored potholders; several types of doilies. And in one corner of the room there were neat stacks of knitted ski hats in various stages of completion—some waiting to be stitched up the back, some finished except for the pompoms, some ready to be sold. On a table by the window was a curious, long device, bristling with spikes, that was evidently some sort of knitting machine, and beside it were three big spools of yarn—red, blue, and white.

"It takes me forty or forty-five minutes to knit a hat," Nellie observed. "In the summer I generally make six in the forenoon. That leaves me free to be out in the garden the rest of the day. Last winter I finished forty-eight hats a week, but when the good weather came I told them I wouldn't make so many for a while. That's all right with them—as long as they know how many to count on. The money helps out a lot, don't you know. It's not easy to get by on the Social Security."

The "they" to which Nellie referred is a Bennington, Vermont, company called CB Sports, which buys ski hats from her. The concern is being sued by the Department of Labor for alleged violations of the Fair Labor Standards Act of 1938—the so-called sweatshop law. Intended to rectify the sometimes inhuman conditions prevailing in the garment and other industries, that law established a standard workweek, determined minimum age requirements, and set a minimum wage (25 cents an hour in 1938; $3.35 an hour after December 31, 1980, in case you were wondering). The particular provision of the act that the Department of Labor is trying to enforce here is the one forbidding the employment of people in their homes to produce certain items: women's apparel, jewelry, knitted outerwear, gloves and mittens, buttons and buckles, handkerchiefs, and embroidery.

During the nineteenth and early twentieth centuries, it was common in industries that required little or no sophisticated machinery for employers to supply their employees with the materials they needed and then to pay them by the piece for work done in their homes or in crowded workrooms known as sweatshops. Women, children, and the elderly were often victimized by a system in which fifteen-hour days, an appallingly low wage scale, and unsanitary conditions were all too frequent.

That is hardly the situation here. According to one newspaper account, the fifty women who knit hats for CB Sports are content. They don't want the government meddling in their affairs. But Herbert Cohen, assistant administrator of the Labor Department's wage-and-hour division, is quoted as saying it doesn't *matter* if the knitters are content. "It's our experience," he states, "that it doesn't work to let workers decide if they need protecting."

Now that's an attitude that doesn't have a whole lot of appeal for your average Vermonter. The trouble with the government is that it's always getting these big ideas about how things should be run, without asking the people who are most affected if the ideas make any sense. If Mr. Cohen had taken the trouble to get Nellie's opinion, he would have learned that she doesn't feel exploited, that she doesn't need or want the protection the government is trying to force on her. What's more, she enjoys what she's doing, she's satisfied with the money she makes, and all Mr. Cohen would have had to do to see why she likes working at home is to look at the view from her doorstep—rolling meadows and hedgerows, a few houses and barns, a little brook that runs behind the house—all surrounded by a bowl of mountains, dark green and cool-looking even on a sultry summer's day.

Nellie and Lanson have a place that's not much bigger than an average city lot, but it's one of the most productive pieces of ground you can imagine. They raise all the vegetables they need for eating, canning, and freezing, and have a surplus to sell. (Whenever anyone in the neighborhood discusses garden peas, Lanson's are the standard of comparison, because he always seems to have the tallest, fullest, best-looking vines around.) They have a berry patch, keep a few chickens, and, being independent and resourceful, turn their hands to a variety of projects to supplement their Social Security payments. They used to drive to a farm about fifty miles from here and pick strawberries to sell. At the end of a day's picking they'd head for home with a hundred and twenty-five quarts in the truck and have them all sold before they got back to their place. But with the price of gasoline so high they decided not to go for the berries this year, which meant that the work Nellie does at home is even more important to them.

Well, what do Mr. Cohen and the Department of Labor have to offer Nellie in place of what she has? They insist that she is an employee of CB Sports (not an individual entrepreneur, as the company maintains), and as such, she has to work in the company factory. Although that means that she would have to drive sixty-six miles to and from Bennington every day, they don't seem concerned about the gasoline that would be wasted in order to do things their way, nor to care about the time and effort and money it would cost Nellie to do all that traveling. Nor have they bothered to ask Nellie what *she* would like to do.

Implicit in the Department of Labor's suit, if the department has its way in court as it has in similar cases in the past, is
that there is an option open to Nellie and the other knitters if
they do not choose to work in the factory. They can go on
welfare. They can cease being productive, useful members of
society, who take pride in their work and in paying their own
way, and become instead wards of the state.

This summer the signs of economic slowdown were all
around us: logs lying unwanted and unsawed in lumberyards, a
local factory laying off employees, a farm machinery dealer
cutting his workers' weekly hours from forty to twenty. With
problems like these, we don't need the Labor Department
making up new ones for us. So while we salute the signs of official concern for the welfare of workers, we hope the department will consider what effect its zeal to enforce the letter of a
forty-three-year-old statute may have on those very workers.
There is a message for the department in Thomas Jefferson's
first inaugural address: ". . . a wise and frugal government,"
the president said, "which shall restrain men from injuring one
another, shall leave them otherwise free to regulate their own
pursuits of industry and improvement, and shall not take from
the mouth of labor the bread it has earned."

Once every four years, we notice, the candidates for office
tell us what we already know—that the size of the government has to be reduced and that spending must be cut. We
would be willing to humor them and let them think they've
discovered something important if only they would do something about it. But we send them to Washington and that's the
last we hear about the problem until four years later, when
they tell us how much worse things are.

Recently a Washingtonian informed us there's real danger
that the federal government will collapse—not for any of the
reasons you might suspect, but because it has become nearly
impossible to find people in the capital who are willing, or
able, to work as secretaries. Maybe this will prove the solution
to the mess we're in—a better one even than the old spoils

system, where the winners cleaned house from top to bottom, threw the rascals out, and started fresh. How can you be a bureaucrat if you have no way to write or duplicate or transmit memoranda, directives, position papers, and new legislation? You might have to find useful employment.

 *July 1976*

When we were very young two dates loomed as immense mileposts off there in the dim, uncharted future. One was the year 2000, and the other was 1976. It seemed somehow terribly important to be present on both of those occasions, but now that one is at hand we find ourself wondering uneasily if the celebrations that are planned are appropriate, considering the significance of the anniversary. Two hundred years, you may say, is not such a great age as nations reckon the passage of time. But two centuries happens to be the longest that any democracy has survived, and that precious and fragile achievement is reason for profound gratitude as well as fireworks and rejoicing.

There have been signs, especially in the recent past, that our democratic society was suffering the twinges of age—shortness of breath and slightly impaired vision, the creaking of joints and a fatty buildup around the middle—and having experienced all these symptoms ourself, we had no trouble deciding what our birthday present to the nation should be. No frills, simple, frugal, it's the perfect gift for the land that has everything—advice. A wish, if you will, before the candles on the cake are blown out.

Our wish has to do with those young Americans who will be around in the year 2000 even if we are not, the men and women whose adulthood will be spent in America's third century. What we hope for them, and from them, is commitment—commitment to ideals, to their fellow man, to their native land and their local community, commitment to all they believe in. And if they should require a model, we can think of none better than Thomas Jefferson.

Jefferson is in our thoughts for many reasons these days, not only because of those majestic, moving lines that form the Declaration of Independence but because he, of all the figures from our revolutionary beginnings, is the one who has endured, who comes down to us as a man of our time as much as he was of the eighteenth century.

We like to think that Jefferson, who was only thirty-three when he wrote the document that was to bring the promise of liberty to all mankind, has more in common with the young men and women of 1976 than any of his contemporaries. As the historian James Parton observed, when Jefferson entered Congress he could "calculate an eclipse, survey an estate, tie an artery, plan an edifice, try a cause, break a horse, dance a minuet, and play a violin." These talents—which would have been so unusual among the acquaintances of our own youth—are by no means uncommon among those we see around us in the countryside today, among those who would subscribe to Jefferson's belief "that every honest employment is deemed honorable." Those same young people would understand Jefferson's reverence for the land—his belief that even though the landowner might hold title to it, "actually it belongs to all the people because civilization itself rests upon the soil."

There was nothing that did not interest Jefferson—architecture, science, politics, philosophy, farming, horticulture, music, mechanics—and if ever there was an inquiring, insatiably curious mind, it was his. Seemingly there was no field of human endeavor on which he failed to keep informed.

As our first great democrat and champion of the people, his only real intolerance was in defense of the rights of the individual. Freedom, he believed, "is the most sacred cause that ever man was engaged in," and he never ceased fighting for it. After our Revolution, as with so many other uprisings that followed it, a high percentage of the revolutionaries became the new ruling class, as firmly entrenched and as conservative as the Tories they had unseated. But not Jefferson. A revolutionary he remained, his life dedicated to reform and to opposing the system where the system was wanting or corrupt. When the news of Shays's Rebellion, which terrorized Massachusetts in 1786 and 1787, reached him he took the word calmly, saying, "I hold it that a little rebellion now and then is a good thing, and as necessary in the political world as storms in the physical." The leaders of an unsuccessful rebellion, he suggested, should be punished mildly, so as "not to discourage them too much."

Jefferson was also a superb practical politician—involved, committed, willing to serve when he was needed. By the time he left the presidency he had given forty of his sixty-six years to the public service.

It was one of the supreme coincidences of history that Jefferson and John Adams, who had served together on the committee to draft the Declaration of Independence, should both die on the fiftieth anniversary of America's day of freedom. Off in Quincy, Massachusetts, John Adams's life was slipping away as July 4 approached. Long years before, he had urged that the day of independence be "solemnized with pomp and parade, with shows, games, sports, guns, bells, bonfires and illuminations, from one end of this continent to the other, from this time forward, forevermore." And had he not been too feeble to see it, in 1826 he would have gotten his wish.

Jefferson's health had been failing throughout the spring of 1826; he knew he was dying, and on July 2 he bid farewell to the members of his family. Although he grew progressively weaker it was evident that he was fighting with all his remaining strength to live until the day of jubilee. As the hours wore on he became delirious and spoke of sending a warning to the Committee of Safety; then he lost consciousness, and at ten minutes before one in the afternoon of July 4, 1826—fifty years to the day after signing the Declaration of Independence—Thomas Jefferson went peacefully to join his Maker. About five hours later, at sunset of the same day, John Adams died. The Virginian had been in his mind until the end. Adams's last words were, "Thomas Jefferson still survives." And so he does.